How Sanctions Work

How Sanctions Work

Iran and the Impact of Economic Warfare

**NARGES BAJOGHLI,
VALI NASR,
DJAVAD SALEHI-ISFAHANI,**
and
ALI VAEZ

STANFORD UNIVERSITY PRESS
Stanford, California

Stanford University Press
Stanford, California

Printed in the United States of America on acid-free, archival-quality paper

Library of Congress Cataloging-in-Publication Data
Names: Bajoghli, Narges, 1982- author. | Nasr, Seyyed Vali Reza, 1960-
    author. | Salehi-Isfahani, Djavad, author. | Vaez, Ali, author.
Title: How sanctions work : Iran and the impact of economic warfare /
    Narges Bajoghli, Vali Nasr, Djavad Salehi-Isfahani, and Ali Vaez.
Description: Stanford, California : Stanford University Press, 2024. |
    Includes bibliographical references and index.
Identifiers: LCCN 2023017223 (print) | LCCN 2023017224 (ebook) |
    ISBN 9781503637313 (cloth) | ISBN 9781503637801 (paperback) |
    ISBN 9781503637818 (ebook)
Subjects: LCSH: Economic sanctions--Iran. | Economic sanctions,
    American--Iran. | Iran--Economic conditions. | Iran--Politics and
    government. | United States--Foreign relations--Iran. | Iran--Foreign
    relations--United States.
Classification: LCC HF1586.4 .B36 2024 (print) | LCC HF1586.4 (ebook) |
    DDC 327.1/17--dc23/eng/20230717
LC record available at https://lccn.loc.gov/2023017223
LC ebook record available at https://lccn.loc.gov/2023017224

Cover design: Will Brown
Cover photograph: Hosein Charbaghi / Unsplash

To the people of Iran who have suffered under decades of sanctions.

CONTENTS

CONTENTS

PREFACE

WHEN SANCTIONS WORK

One of the most important developments in international affairs is the growing primacy of economic sanctions as a tool of foreign policy. Increasingly, the US response to international crises is first and foremost the application of sanctions. But do sanctions work? If so, when and how, and at what cost? The case of US sanctions on Iran is particularly instructive in this regard. For over four decades Iran has been a foreign policy concern for the United States: a country that refuses to deal directly with the US, and that maintains anti-Americanism at the core of its foreign policy and even its identity. The United States has addressed its Iran problem primarily through sanctions. Since their first imposition in 1979, sanctions have become more far-reaching and sophisticated; so much so that, at the time of this writing, Iran is the most sanctioned country in the world. In the process, the US has come to consider sanctions as a nearly unassailable necessity; to the point, we will argue, of a counterproductive overreliance on them.

Additional sanctions, and more punishing sanctions, have failed to realize US policy objectives. The experience of Iran shows how ineffective this seemingly effective foreign policy tool can be. Waged by warriors in dark suits in the US Department of the Treasury, the sanctions are assumed to be more efficient and less costly alternatives to what warriors in the Pentagon and diplomats at the State Department are capable of. The decades of sanctions exacted on Iran, and the application of "maximum pressure" sanctions under the Trump and Biden administrations, challenge this assumption. The extended period also allows us to gain a better understanding of the humanitarian, social, and political costs of sanctions, as well as the less noticed costs that sanctions inflict on the US. The case of Iran also shows that sanctions are far from being an efficient tool; while they are more easily applied than direct military or diplomatic measures, that very facility is also at the root of their failure because they become so difficult to lift, regardless of whether they are accomplishing their goals.

———

The forty-plus years of US and international sanctions, and recently the maximal use of sanctions, have been levied on Iran not only to punish its behavior but also to force the Islamic Republic to change course: desist from supporting terrorist activities, refrain from aggressive regional policies, and abandon its nuclear ambitions. President Trump in particular believed in the promise of sanctions to achieve this course change, but his administration failed on each of these three counts, and in fact the threat of Iran has appeared to become increasingly grave on every front of concern to the US.

Iran has shown greater defiance and more willingness to directly and dangerously confront the US and its allies in the Middle East. The application of maximal sanctions, beginning in 2018, provoked an aggressive response from Tehran. A year after the imposition of maximum pressure, Iran attacked four tankers off the coast of the United Arab Emirates (UAE) port of Fujairah on the Gulf of Oman; downed a high-flying US surveillance drone; and launched a sophisticated attack with drones and missiles on oil facilities in Abqaiq and Khurais in eastern Saudi Arabia. The audacity of this latter attack, and Iran's ability to evade Saudi and American radar and air defense systems, caught Washington by surprise. But all of the aggressive actions were cause for alarm, given that Iran carried them out while subject to the worst sanctions it had ever faced. In 2022, the world was shocked when Russia deployed lethal drones that Iran had developed under sanctions.

Throughout 2019–20, the US response to Iranian provocations only invited escalation. After US missiles attacked an Iraqi militia base in response to the killing of an American contractor, Iran and its Iraqi allies laid siege to the US Embassy in Baghdad. In turn, the United States used

an attack drone to kill Iranian general Qasem Soleimani, who played a
key role in Iran's regional policies. Iran was neither chastened nor de-
terred, and in January 2020 it launched nearly two dozen Iranian-built
ballistic missiles at a military base in Iraq, which hosted US forces. This
attack on the Ain al-Asad base in Iraq—in retaliation for the assassination of Soleimani—was not only a precise strike, but the largest missile
attack US troops have ever faced.

Through such actions, Iran showed that Trump's maximum pressure
sanctions had not bent the nation's will to accept Western demands. Instead, the sanctions had achieved the opposite effect: making Iran more
aggressive, risk-taking, and dangerous. Indeed, this was a *consequence*
of sanctions. Instead of sanctions offering an "alternative to war," maximum pressure sanctions on Iran have shown that they could be a cause
of war.[1]

"Do sanctions work?" is often asked by policymakers and pundits.
Perhaps that is the wrong question. When a country with the size and
economic power of the United States imposes harsh sanctions on a country, of course they "work": sanctions create massive disruptions in the
everyday lives of citizens, impact the political culture of the targeted
state, and induce shocks in the economy. But do sanctions—as some
claim—bring about the behavioral changes in targeted states as intended
by Western foreign policy? Do sanctions work the way they "should"?

Consider Iran, the most sanctioned country in the world. Comprehensive sanctions are meant to induce uprisings or instigate pressure
that leads to a change in the behavior of the ruling establishment, or a
lessening of its hold on power. But after four decades, Iran has shown
the opposite to be true. In fact, despite periodic protests, sanctions have
strengthened the Islamic Republic, weakened and impoverished its population, and increased Iran's military posture vis-á-vis the US and its
allies in the region. It is not only that the Islamic Republic is still around
despite harsh sanctions; most importantly, Iran has become a more bel-
ligerent state *as a result of* increased American sanctions.

As this book shows, then, sanctions *do* work. But not in the way most
think.

ACKNOWLEDGMENTS

To our many interlocutors inside Iran who opened up their lives and worlds to us over the years in hours of interviews and conversations, our heartfelt gratitude. We hope that we have done justice in these pages to your life stories.

We would like to thank the scholars who have participated in the Iran Under Sanctions project at Johns Hopkins University, and whose invaluable insights contributed greatly to this book: Esfandyar Batmanghelidj, Orkideh Behrouzan, Shahrokh Fardoust, Kevan Harris, Kaveh Madani, Adnan Mazaeri, Arzoo Osanloo, Hadi Salehi Esfahani, Tara Sepehri Far, Nazanin Shahrokni, Alexander Soderholm, Leili Sreberny-Mohammadi, and Sara Vakhshouri.

Thank you to Ghadir Asadi, Brendan Keating, and Arin Shahbazian for their research assistance.

We are extremely grateful to Ben Platt not only for his expert editing skills but also for his many conversations and prompts that helped expand this manuscript in fruitful ways. Thank you for believing in the importance of this project and for being an incredible intellectual interlocutor along the way.

Thank you to Kate Wahl at Stanford University Press for her support of the book and to our editor at Stanford, Daniel LoPreto, for his enthusiasm for our work and helping to so expertly bring it into the world. Many thanks to Marie-Catherine Pavel and the rest of the team at SUP for all their hard work. A special thanks to the anonymous reviewers, whose recommendations strengthened the book.

INTRODUCTION

The Invisible War

"I am a forty-four-year-old woman who has lived forty-one years of her life under varying degrees of economic sanctions," said Habibe Jafarian, a writer and editor, writing nearly two years into the US "maximum pressure" sanctions on Iran. "I grew up with the sanctions; I went to school with them; I learned to read and write with them hovering over my head; I fell in love, and began my career as a journalist, and have stayed alive, all under sanctions from the United States of America. Sanctions have been a part of my life like the weather."[1]

A century before Jafarian's lament, US president Woodrow Wilson described sanctions differently. Sanctions, he explained in 1919, are "an absolute isolation . . . that brings a nation to its senses just as suffocation removes from the individual all inclinations to fight . . . Apply this economic, peaceful, silent, deadly remedy and there will be no need for force. It is a terrible remedy. It does not cost a life outside of the nation boycotted, but it brings a pressure upon that nation which, in my judgement, no modern nation could resist."[2]

Yet the Islamic Republic has demonstrated that a nation can, in fact, resist attempted economic suffocation. The pressures of sanctions have not reduced tensions in the region nor have they turned Iran into a ruined shell of a nation ready to abide by Western dictates. The pressures of maximal sanctions have contributed to vast social uprisings, but each

1

time the state has responded with violent repression and the further suppression and securitization of civic spaces.

That sanctions have failed to match their intended goal is damning
enough. But, as Jafarian makes clear, even worse is that sanctions don't
decisively end conflicts. Instead, sanctions can linger on for decades, an-
tagonizing the state even as they impoverish and harm ordinary people.
Most of all, sanctions, once started, are seemingly impossible to stop.
After all, how does one stop the weather?

Revealing the truth about sanctions is the goal of *How Sanctions Work*.
How, for example, do prolonged comprehensive sanctions affect a targeted country's society, politics, and economy? Are they, in fact, a costless
tool for the United States and the Western-led international system—
something that can be done easily "over there" with no impact "over here"?
What does it mean for a country to experience four decades of economic
sanctions? And what are the ricochet effects of sanctions in international
politics, if any?

Iran is the perfect case study for understanding sanctions broadly.
It is also a worthy site of examination in its own right. Despite the fact
that Iran has been under decades of Western sanctions, little systematic
knowledge exists on the short-, medium-, and long-term impacts of sanctions on the growth patterns of the Iranian economy, or on the general
welfare of its people in the cities and rural areas, or on societal dynamics,
or on civic space, or on the country's environment. Instead, the focus has
often been on a few metrics that flare up with the tightening of sanctions:
currency depreciation, inflation, and recession, which are then followed
by increases in unemployment and poverty. Yet the more comprehensive
picture remains lost in political cacophony.

We aim to correct that lacuna. In this book, we analyze what prolonged comprehensive sanctions have *done* to Iran's society, politics, and
economy; moreover, we show what these decades of sanctions have *cost*
Iran, the United States, and the broader international economic and political order.

We take readers inside Iran, to hear from Iranians from different
walks of life and from across the political spectrum about their experiences living under decades of economic sanctions. We examine the be-

havior of state and military actors, as well as opposition activists inside the country. We take a critical look at the economic data to understand how the Iranian state has attempted to resist sanctions and what their impacts have been on the lives of citizens. As we analyze the impacts of comprehensive sanctions on Iran's society, economy, and domestic and regional politics, we also consider the blowback costs of sanctions to the international community—a point, we argue, that needs to be considered more seriously as Washington levies additional sanctions on larger states, such as Russia.

Ultimately, our aim is to show how sanctions have impacted the political calculus of those in power in Iran: who sanctions have empowered and who they have disempowered. What we found inside Iran is alarming. As the use of this "economic weapon" has proliferated against Iran, the Iranian state, in response, has become more militaristic. Prolonged, comprehensive sanctions on Iran have created shocks within society: leading to new social classes, changing social bonds, and a hardening of the political sphere. These trends have only accelerated since the imposition of maximum pressure sanctions in 2018.

Why would Iran react in these specific ways? Because the Trump administration's maximum pressure campaign—which the Biden administration has continued unabated—is in effect a "shadow war," fought on multiple fronts and across the region, against Iran and its allied forces. Shadow wars are intelligence wars first and foremost. And so, in response, Iran has relied on the Revolutionary Guard's extraterritorial forces, the Quds Force, and the intelligence services of the Revolutionary Guard. Indeed, Iran has infused this shadow war worldview into all realms of decision-making within the Islamic Republic. Sanctions have caused the Iranian government to increasingly view the world as waging external *and* internal war on Iran, outside in the international community and inside its own borders.

Such a sanctions-derived worldview has had an outsized impact on Iranian political culture, anchoring it in security and repression. Iran has responded to sanctions by intensifying the "securitization" of the domestic sphere: meaning that civil liberties are even more repressed, and importantly, activists have been lethally targeted, imprisoned in larger numbers, or have withdrawn from their activities. Although Iran, due to the size and makeup of its economy, has not faced the humanitarian crises that have resulted from comprehensive sanctions in Cuba, Venezuela, and Iraq in the 1990s, its medical, educational, and agricultural sectors are showing cracks under the economic pressure.

Ultimately, sanctions have enriched—by orders of magnitude—enterprises tied to the Revolutionary Guard and the supreme leader's office. While it is nearly impossible to provide exact numbers, given how sanctions-busting requires trade on the black and gray markets, with attendant bribes and kickbacks, it is crucial to acknowledge that sanctions have lowered economic transparency, weakened the independent private sector, and strengthened business owners with ties to the regime, and especially the Revolutionary Guard. All of which has led to major shifts in who comprises the capitalist class in society, with long-term consequences. As later chapters show, Iran's middle class—the sector of society from which much of the resistance against the Islamic Republic has stemmed, and the sector that therefore should be supported by Western policy—has been impoverished in tandem with the escalation of sanctions pressure, and markedly since 2018. These trends are not promoting a more peaceful Iran, but, instead—both internally and externally—a more violent one.

Bombs may not be dropped under long-term comprehensive sanctions. Even so, such sanctions create social realities and generational impacts akin to war.

———

This understanding—of sanctions *as* war—contradicts commonly held views on sanctions. Throughout most of their history, economic sanctions have been imposed without much regard for their impacts: the humanitarian costs have been dismissed as necessary, and the political costs as marginal.[3] By and large, policymakers and scholars in the West presume that sanctions (eventually) work; that if the tools of sanctions are tweaked *just right*, the targeted actors suffer and eventually change their bad behavior.

Why did this belief take hold? In the aftermath of the horrors of World War I, Western leaders and policymakers sought to create peaceful tools as an alternative to war. The idea of economic sanctions was born.[4] Their appeal was in what they portended: the application of pressure on a "bad actor" to induce change, not by military exertion and dead soldiers, but by policymakers, lawyers, and bankers sitting behind desks. The notion that economic sanctions could leverage a certain kind of power that would help avoid conflicts and diminish the need for troops has appealed to many in the West since the early twentieth century. Now, with Americans becoming warier of troop deployments, economic sanctions come across as a desirable alternative: reinforcing the belief that "we are doing something," but without the costs associated with armed conflict. Today, economic sanctions are among the most salient tools in US foreign policy, "one of liberal internationalism's most enduring innovations of the twentieth century."[5]

Yet the research and literature on the impacts of sanctions, especially over time, remains unfortunately thin.[6] Sanctions have become a favored foreign policy tool in Washington and the European Union, but they have held that favored position even though their impacts remain largely understudied, and therefore mostly unknown. Worst of all, despite their unknown impact, US sanctions have increased by more than 900 percent since the start of the twenty-first century.[7] It is this increase of an unexamined tool that makes it especially vital to reveal how sanctions really work.

———

For revealing the truth about sanctions, Iran is the perfect case study. Moreover, given that Iran is the most sanctioned nation in the world, it is worthwhile to illuminate the unique struggle of Iran and its people.

In the early 1950s, Iran experienced Western economic blockades and sanctions for the first time in response to its prime minister, Mohammad Mosaddegh, nationalizing his country's resources, the first third world leader to do so. When Mosaddegh's government ended the unjust agreement that gave the Anglo-Iranian Oil Company complete control of the country's oil, Great Britain not only imposed sanctions on Iran but also supported the coup in 1953 that removed Mosaddegh. Great Britain's aim was twofold: to protect its oil interests in Iran and to make an example of Mosaddegh in order to deter other newly independent countries from nationalizing their own assets. While the purpose of those sanctions was to force Iran to yield to British demands, it is important to note that a military coup, not sanctions, ended the crisis in the 1950s. Nor did sanctions on Iran dissuade Egyptian president Gamal Abd al-Nasser from nationalizing the Suez Canal shortly after in 1956. The sanctions on Iran in the 1950s were lifted once there was a new government in place willing to arrive at a new oil agreement with Western oil companies.

The belief that Iran had experienced a serious blow to its sovereignty when Mosaddegh was removed from power in 1953 festered internally over the following decades, eventually manifesting as a main driver of the 1979 Iranian Revolution, and has fueled resentment toward the West ever since. The coup and revolution set Iran on a collision course with the West, and sanctions were its first manifestation.

Sanctions returned in 1979. Since then, Iran has been repeatedly sanctioned over the ensuing decades for a variety of reasons. In fact— even though in this book we focus mainly on the experience of Iranians under the nuclear sanctions—the sentiment exists in Iran that the country will *never* free itself from sanctions, as long as it refuses to abide by US hegemony in the Middle East.

"If the nuclear sanctions get removed," explains an Iranian university professor interviewed for this book, "then the West will sanction us for our ballistic missiles. Then it'll be human rights sanctions. Then it'll be another reason for sanctions. Just look at any country that has challenged Western power—whether political or economic—what do you see? They get sanctioned in order to break their will and make them succumb to Western power."

In a sense, this professor is right. Sanctions originated in the aftermath of World War I. Western sanctions were soon used on states that defied Western norms: the Soviet republics of Russia and Hungry in 1919. Blockades of these states were enacted because, from the beginning, sanctions "were considered suitable for use mainly against peripheral European states and 'semi-civilized' countries."[8]

"Just look at any country that has challenged Western power." In the case of Iran, then, the history of sanctions—who is sanctioned, and what that means about the underlying principles of the international community—cannot be overlooked, neither by Iranians nor by those studying how sanctions really work.

Some might argue that, despite this troubled history, sanctions *have* worked in Iran. After all, wasn't it sanctions that compelled Iran to agree to negotiations in 2013 and then sign on to the 2015 "nuclear deal"?

Iran did show more flexibility in 2013, after President Obama increased sanctions. Thus, many in Washington touted this as proof that the Obama-era comprehensive sanctions against Iran worked, setting the stage for the 2015 nuclear deal (technically, the Joint Comprehensive Plan of Action or JCPOA). Trump tore up that deal in 2018 and increased sanctions on Iran from 750 to over 1,500, with the stated logic that he could get a "better deal" with more pressure.

But, as we see in later chapters, Trump's action failed; 2018 would not be 2013. Simply applying more sanctions, it seems, does not achieve policy goals. Why?

As this book will show, there is a flaw in the logic of sanctions. As painful as the experience of sanctions has been, it has also forced Iran's leaders to create infrastructure to resist sanctions. In fact, Iran's current supreme leader, Ayatollah Ali Khamenei, has called for the creation of a "resistance economy" (discussed in chapters 2 and 4) and has tasked policymakers to search for ways to increase the resilience of Iran's economy in the face of sanctions in order to build long-term economic stability. Indeed, such an outcome was the goal of many Iranian leaders, *regardless* of what political regime they served.[9] It is plausible to argue that, as bad as sanctions have been for Iran's economy, these external restraints have forced the country to rely more on its non-oil resources for economic growth.

Sanctions, then, have not forced Iran to stagnate. Instead, sanctions have actually forced Iran to innovate; just not in ways that are amenable to the West. The result is that Iran has evolved along a path that has been dictated by sanctions. Its economic and social institutions, politics, and more broadly the nature of its state, reflect that path dependency, one which we know from the history of states around the world is not easily corrected and likely irreversible.

———

Sanctions offer incentives for certain kinds of development, and present obstacles to others. After four decades, it is clear that those incentives have not pushed Iran toward a more just society and a more peaceful role in the world. Instead, sanctions have created an economy both resilient and resistant, one capable of—and ready to—shower missiles on US military bases or Ukraine's civilian infrastructure. And, within Iran's borders, sanctions have impoverished nearly all elements of society except, perhaps, the Revolutionary Guard and the businesses and social strata allied with them, the very institutions and classes that sanctions have targeted.

When economic sanctions were first envisioned after World War I, it was assumed that they would not be used.[10] The devastating impact of sanctions would be worse than war, which would deter countries from engaging in adventurous foreign policy behavior that would disturb the international order. Russia's invasion of Ukraine, begun during the US's maximal sanctions assault on Iran, shows that the deterrence value of sanctions is not what it is made out to be.

If more countries risk sanctions to challenge the international order, then sanctions will become purely punitive. They will no longer deter. Instead, they will simply shrink global economic relations, which would, in turn, make defying sanctions easier.

Despite their intention, sanctions are not diplomacy nor are they instruments of peace. As the case of Iran shows, sanctions wage war on societies within their own borders, and at the same time loosen war on the wider world.

Methods

As anthropologists, political scientists, economists, and policymakers, we engaged a variety of research methods for this book. We did so with the aim of providing a fuller picture of how prolonged comprehensive sanctions both impact the targeted society and reverberate outward into international politics and economics.

We first began to untangle the multifaceted impacts of sanctions in 2019 at Johns Hopkins University, gathering dozens of leading scholars from international institutions: a multidisciplinary group that included economists, climate and energy scientists, and social scientists to explore the multifaceted impacts of sanctions on Iran. The scholars all conducted original research and were able to place their observations within the wider context of their long-term engagement with and scholarship on Iran.[11] We continue to engage different researchers to produce new scholarship on the impacts of sanctions in order to better, and more deeply, understand how sanctions work on a targeted society.

In addition to that body of work, this book also draws on multiyear, long-form oral history interviews with eighty Iranians inside Iran, including political and social activists; political actors; university professors and researchers, especially those conducting their own research on the impacts of sanctions on Iranian society; psychiatrists and social workers; workers (white collar and blue collar); large independent business owners; and former members of the Revolutionary Guard who are now business owners. Furthermore, multiyear discourse analysis of Persian-language media and social media was conducted.

The economic analysis in this book relies primarily on survey data and official global and Iranian statistics. Iran produces more survey data than most developing countries—about fifty surveys of income and expenditures and labor force surveys are publicly available in unit record. These surveys have been used and tested by researchers across the globe, and are generally considered reliable and of high quality. In addition, they are consistent with 2 percent samples of census data that are also available. Other official economic data (GDP, inflation, etc.) are also publicly available and are generally accepted by international institutions.

The analysis of all these aspects of sanctions is broken into thirds. Chapters 1 and 2 examine the impact of sanctions on the internal society and politics of Iran. Chapters 3 and 4 explore the economic history of sanctions alongside their escalation over the decades. Chapters 5 and 6 reveal the true costs of sanctions, not just for Iran but for the world at large. The Conclusion raises moral concerns about economic sanctions that predominantly target noncombatant civilians, and shows that the efficacy of sanctions as a foreign policy tool is open to question.

ONE

When Society Is Sanctioned

Fariba—a recently retired teacher, who once led a solidly middle-class life in Tehran with her husband, an electrical engineer—struggles to get by today.[1] "Every day I leave the house, the prices at the fruit sellers go higher and higher. We've reduced what we buy quite heavily." Her daughter and son live abroad. "When my daughter suggested that she send money to us on a monthly basis to help out, I died inside. As parents we're the ones who are supposed to ensure the stability of our children, not the other way around, not when both my husband and I are still relatively young and have worked our whole lives."

Fariba keeps herself busy by joining her former colleagues in organizing teachers' protests for higher pay. "I gather with them a few times a week to talk and strategize and join them on the streets in protests. At least we're doing something. Being around others like me as we agitate for some changes gives me an avenue to take out my anger and frustrations about the hard times we're living through."

To make ends meet, Fariba sold a small plot of land that she had inherited from her father in their provincial town over two hundred kilometers outside of Tehran. "Before these sanctions, that money could have lasted us for many years. But now we're budgeting our daily expenses in order for this money to stretch as far as possible. At least my children are already out of the country and I don't have to think about their future or how to provide a good life for them here," she says with resignation in her voice.

In interview after interview, Iranians across the country recount how the rise in prices has been "utterly insane." And this rise is the direct result of the increase of comprehensive US sanctions under President Trump; sanctions that, as of this writing, President Biden has continued unabated. From 2019 to 2022, Iranians explain in interviews just what happens to society when such extreme sanctions are imposed.

They recount how the increased prices force them to cut back on purchases or pawn their prized possessions. Or they express exasperation, uncertain of how to move forward. Middle-class families bemoan the loss of their life savings and are anxious about their futures and those of their children. Those in the working classes have found themselves in even more precarious situations, as they hustle to make rent, feed families, and survive. Families in rural areas have descended rapidly into poverty.

In comparison to other countries under comprehensive sanctions (such as Venezuela, Cuba, and Zimbabwe), Iran has an education and health system that has developed on par with middle-income countries.[2] Moreover, the country is relatively food-sufficient. Thus, while the steep rise in food prices due to sanctions has shrunk food pantries and calorie intakes, there are no food shortages in Iran from sanctions.

Nonetheless, maximum pressure sanctions have plunged many Iranians, in both rural and urban areas, into poverty. It is true that the black and gray markets, which are endemic to sanctions-busting, have created enormous wealth for those at the top strata of society. Yet such markets, simultaneously, have greatly increased economic inequality. Over eight million individuals have fallen from the middle class to the lower middle class. And the ranks of the poor have swelled by more than four million.[3]

These shocks to Iran's economy have forced changes in Iran's society. In response, new social classes are emerging, social bonds are changing, and domestic politics has swung toward the hardliners. Meanwhile, attacks on civil and political liberties have become even more severe. Bombs may not be dropped under long-term comprehensive sanctions. Even so, such sanctions create social realities and generational impacts akin to war.

Sanctions target the economic lifelines of a society. In so doing, prolonged comprehensive sanctions induce an environment of siege, shortage, and intense pressure, bearing down in the form of collective punishment. Richard Nephew, a key architect of US sanctions on Iran in the Bush and Obama administrations, writes:

> Because of the different practical effects of sanctions and military force, policymakers treat these two tools differently. Military conflict creates causalities and damage for each side, and the results are visible for all to see. The impacts of sanctions can be less visible and may seem less destructive, certainly on a visceral level. This no doubt explains part of the attractiveness of sanctions as a tool of force. . . . *But on a strategic level, the imposition of pain via sanctions is intended to register the same impulses in an adversary as those imposed via military force.* . . . And just because the damage wrought by sanctions may be less visible (at least, with some sanctions regimes), it need not be less destructive, particularly for economically vulnerable populations that may be affected [emphasis added].[4]

If society is like a sea, then prolonged sanctions regimes create waves: leading to the rise of new social classes, new economies (especially in black and gray markets), new coping mechanisms, a heavy brain drain, the breakdown of infrastructure, and the further militarization of politics in impacted countries.

In this chapter we ask: What do economic siege and comprehensive sanctions "do" to a country's society? What happens when members of the middle class confront the (often sudden) loss of value of their income and savings? Has Iran's society changed in the way that those who sanctioned it intended? And what can all this tell us about sanctions in the abstract?

Since sanctions—especially prolonged comprehensive ones—impact multiple sectors and domains of life simultaneously, it is nearly impossible to isolate only the ways sanctions impact social life. Yet scholars in different countries have observed similar direct consequences, especially over time. Humanitarian catastrophes resulting from comprehensive sanctions—such as food shortages,[5] the breakdown of medical systems,[6] and the unavailability of critical medicines—have led to thousands of deaths around the world.[7] The United Nations special rapporteur on unilateral coercive measures said, after a May 2022 visit to Iran, that sanctions were especially affecting those suffering from "severe diseases, disabled people, Afghan refugees, women-led households and children."[8]

Comprehensive sanctions regimes also target critical infrastructure and the opportunities available for knowledge producers, professionals, and students. Over time, this leads to compounded crises that span generations: distressed hospital systems, brain drain, and a decline in the quality of education. It can have a difficult-to-quantify but clearly destabilizing effect on social life: a pervasive hopelessness at the demoralizing prospect of vanishing dreams and aspirations.

Maximum pressure sanctions have indeed increased outward expressions of anger and frustration toward the ruling establishment in Iran and generated discourses of state failure. It may appear as if this evidence suggests that sanctions are working. Yet, as this book demonstrates, despite palpable and growing popular discontent, maximum pressure sanctions have actually *weakened* the Iranian population and made it *more* dependent on the state.[9] Simultaneously, these sanctions have further securitized and militarized the domestic sphere. Hamid, a disaster management specialist in the civil society sector, responds angrily when I ask him about the sanctions. "Don't ask me about the sanctions. Don't write about the sanctions. All they've done is make the Revolutionary Guard more powerful. Those of us in civil society are suffocating—we're constantly worried about saying something that may come across as a 'security threat' by those in charge."

This chapter argues that comprehensive sanctions have produced four key social changes in Iran. First, comprehensive sanctions have created conditions of mass suffering. Second, comprehensive sanctions induce the world to view—and invent—Iranians as enemies. With no clear path to sanctions removal, all facets of Iranian society and the movement of Iranian peoples are regarded as either outright illegal or subject to constant legal scrutiny. This contributes to the creation of what we term an "everyday life of resignation."

In this atmosphere of resignation, sanctions prompt the third and fourth key social changes: the growth of independent autarkic institutions and businesses, and the general exit from arenas of civic engagement with a corresponding retreat into private life. Such an inward turn is especially notable in the lives of activists and artists, in contrast to the effervescence of civil society activity that was ubiquitously credited with the collapse of the Berlin Wall and democratization of Eastern Europe in the 1990s.

Ultimately, then, comprehensive sanctions impact the everyday lives of the vast majority of the population: impoverishing them, making them more reliant on the state for help, and driving exponential inequality. And in the face of this multipronged war, moreover, the state and its military apparatus become wealthier and more militaristic, both externally and internally, while society increasingly weakens.

Mass Suffering: Disaster Swarms and Discourses of State Failure

Iran now faces what Yarimar Bonilla (writing about Puerto Rico and its neighbors) conceptualizes as "disaster swarms."[10] Disaster swarms characterize places facing "economic crisis, imperial violence . . . earthquakes . . . climate change, privatization, profiteering, and other forms of structural and systemic violence all acting as a disordered jumble upon a collective body that cannot discern a main event or a discrete set of impacts, only repetitive and enduring trauma."[11] In the case of Iran, US maximum pressure sanctions (ongoing since 2018) have coincided with seemingly endless waves of COVID-19 (the pandemic has impacted Iran more than any other country in the Middle East), increased tensions between Iran and its regional adversaries, chronic state mismanagement, severe droughts, natural disasters, profiteering and increased privatization, political upheaval, and threats of chaos and even war. The resulting trauma and stress have entered into the everyday lives of Iranians, alarming Iranian psychiatrists, psychologists, and social workers.

Nazanin is a 63-year-old mother and wife who has run a small catering business from her home in Tehran for fifteen years. The main breadwinner of her family, she has worried about their future since the price of food sharply increased after the maximum pressure sanctions imposed by US president Trump in 2018. "On top of sanctions, when COVID-19 hit Iran in February 2020 and we eventually started lockdowns, I thought that's it for me and my family. My whole business relies on people getting together for gatherings and on businesses having in-person functions."

Nazanin had gotten her family through tough years before. Her husband was a technocrat at a state ministry. It was steady income, but it barely allowed them a middle-class life. When her two children were in their teens, her husband began battling alcoholism. "We lost the small apartment we had and became renters. That's when I decided to start my own business. I couldn't allow my kids to face such an uncertain future as their father dealt with his addiction." Nazanin's business eventually flourished and allowed her family to reclaim a middle-class perch, albeit one without home ownership in Tehran's hot real estate market. And so, when her business took a heavy hit with the onset of Trump-era sanctions and COVID, Nazanin's family found themselves dealing with the heavy stress of insecure housing. "Making monthly rent is hard enough under normal circumstances when you run your own business and it all depends on how many clients you have per month. But add to that the looming feeling that my business might be gone for good because of sky-high food prices and then the pandemic, and in the middle of all of that my daughter was getting a divorce . . . I was having nervous breakdowns. My daughter took me to see a therapist."

Leeda, a psychiatrist and professor at a leading university in Tehran, has been overwhelmed with patients. "The combination of the sanctions making life harder for people and later the pandemic," she explains, "has caused a mental health crisis in the country." Along with her colleagues, Leeda organizes monthly meetings to discuss what they are hearing from their patients and how they can better support those who come to see them. Taboos around mental health have steadily decreased over the years; now, Iran boasts large communities of people tuned into new-age self-help books, group sessions, conversations around mental health on state television, and pop psychology Instagram pages. Such a turn has made talking about mental health and seeking therapy and counseling more of a norm, especially in large urban centers. For her part, Leeda has created both public and private seminars to engage more people and has started to toy with podcasting as another potential avenue to engage a wider community. "The sheer numbers of patients we're seeing is incredible," Leeda admits. And so, along with her colleagues in sociology and social work, Leeda helps to initiate research studies to trace longer-term impacts of the sanctions.

"Some of the most dire things we heard from people were in our interviews in late 2019 and early 2020," explains Hamed, a leading sociologist involved in the research. "The shock of the sanctions had entered society and people were extremely worried. It was unclear what Trump would do next. There were huge nationwide protests in November 2019 against the sudden hike in fuel prices, with reports of state forces killing hundreds of protestors. And then less than two months later, the US assassinated General Qasem Soleimani, and a few days after that, Iran shot down a passenger airliner on the same night it sent missiles to an American military base in Iraq. It was a time of extreme loss, anger, mourning, fear, and uncertainty. Were we going to head into another war? Would we turn into the next Iraq? And anger at the regime was palpable everywhere you turned for the way they lied about downing the Ukrainian airliner and the rage at the deaths themselves. And then a few weeks after all of that, COVID-19 hit the country hard, second only to China, and people felt the authorities were lying to them and not protecting them from this pandemic. There were daily news articles around the world about how badly Iran was handling COVID and that the authorities were digging mass graves and lying about the numbers of those dying from the virus. Every day the news got worse and worse, and in the quest to find information and not trusting the authorities, there was also this barrage of bad, and at times exaggerated, news from Iranian diaspora television networks. We picked up on that collective anger in our interviews."

Especially illuminating is how Iranians' understanding of this global crisis was, necessarily, filtered through the way in which the sanctions regime designated their country as an outlier. By this time in the pandemic, Leeda adds, "I distinctly remember how angry and helpless my patients felt and how many new calls we had from people looking to come in for the first time for counseling. It wasn't until Europe and the US began to be overwhelmed by COVID and their numbers peaked that people here began to calibrate what they were saying to us about the dire situation in Iran with what was going on in the world."

Hamed nods along to Leeda's recounting of the period, then leans in toward the screen, adding, "One of the things we're finding is that as wealthy countries were unable to deal with COVID and later the global economic situation started to get worse, within Iran the sense of 'we're the only ones suffering like this' decreased, at least in our interviews and what we're hearing from psychiatrists and psychologists."[12]

Leeda, with her characteristically alert eyes, remembers "the level of despair that we heard across the board in winter 2019/2020 was so high, and we heard a lot from people about how they had become addicted to following the news from abroad, especially the Persian-language diaspora media stations."

The battle over the narrative and affective domain is an element of the maximum pressure campaign and other comprehensive Western sanctions regimes. Writing about Iraq under sanctions during the 1990s, Omar Dewachi notes how sanctions created a discourse of "state failure," whereby citizens repeatedly bemoaned the state's inability to meet the needs of its population.[13] In the maximum pressure sanctions against Iran, discussions of state failure were even part of the sanctioners' toolbox. For example, the Trump administration approved an extensive Pentagon campaign to conduct sabotage, propaganda, and psychological and information operations in Iran. The campaign, led by the military's Special Operations forces, "was designed to undermine the Iranian people's faith in their government as well as shake the regime's sense of competence and stability."[14] This campaign involves "things that would cause the Iranians to doubt their control over the country, or doubt their ability to fight a war," as a former senior defense official recounts.[15]

Over two dozen satellite television channels broadcast these messages into Iran on a daily basis, despite the state's attempts at blocking the coverage. In addition to the US-funded Voice of America and the British-funded BBC Persian service, there are new channels such as Manoto (broadcast from the UK with programming that leans toward support of the former monarchy) and Iran International (a multi-million-dollar television station, launched in mid-2017). All of these channels broadcast cutting-edge productions and news programs into the country, often with the express aim of countering Iranian state narratives and promoting discourses of regime change.

In addition to these channels, social media campaigns and troll armies increasingly entered the digital fray with the launch of the maximum pressure campaign. And, as might be imagined, this social media realm became increasingly polarized: there were troll farms run by armed Iranian opposition groups;[16] there was US State Department funding that, while ostensibly meant to counter the Iranian state's disinformation campaigns on social media, targeted and smeared American scholars, journalists, and analysts who publicly questioned the Trump administration's policies on Iran;[17] and there was disinformation campaigns run by "digital warriors" loyal to the Islamic Republic.

The same sort of scorched-earth tactics ("you're either with us or against us") that, in the United States, created stark divisions in the social media environment during the Trump presidency, now began to appear in Persian-language social media, especially Twitter. Social media apps such as Twitter already amplify content that drives anger, in order to create engagement and capitalize on ad revenues. So, within the context of sanctions, the algorithms added fuel to the fire with the foreign funding of Persian-language troll armies that drove the discourse on social media toward conflict. The Trump administration and other anti-Iran states poured resources into furthering resentment and anger among Iranians at this time.[18] The Islamic Republic is also an active player in this terrain: with hacker groups that target adversary nations, troll and bot armies that sow discord in the opposition, news websites and YouTube channels loyal to the Iranian regime and its allies, and multifaceted disinformation and smear campaigns.

All of this social media polarization and near-constant warring discourses—between anti-regime activist groups, diaspora satellite television outlets and news organizations such as Iran International and BBC Persian, and the vast media and social media world tied to the Islamic Republic—contributed to the distress experienced by Leeda's patients, which reached another climax in fall 2022 with the #MahsaAmini uprisings in Iran. The severe repression of the uprisings, and the ensuing heated battleground of social media, have only deepened rage and polarization. These have all contributed to a widening discontent toward the political establishment.

Of course, it is not the result of the sanctions alone. The Islamic Republic itself creates the conditions whereby the affective strategies of sanctions are impactful. Years of policies and actions have created deep frustrations, resentments, and anger among increasing swaths of the population against the ruling establishment. Among the most common phrases repeated throughout interviews for this research were "they [the Islamic Republic] have ruined us," "things are destroyed," "they can't run the country's affairs," "nothing works." We repeatedly heard among those who had lived through the revolution some version of "we're worse off than we were prior to the revolution. The revolution was a mistake."

These discourses may seem to confirm US desires for sanctions. But, in fact, such sentiments in other countries under comprehensive sanctions have not led to social change. Instead, as witnessed in cases such as Cuba, Venezuela, and Iraq—as well as in Iran—widespread disillusionment or even uprisings in conditions of prolonged comprehensive sanctions are met with strong repression from security forces. Those who join uprisings are often treated as enemies of the state. We have yet to see an instance in which prolonged comprehensive sanctions have led to popular uprisings that force either behavioral changes in the ruling establishment, or regime change altogether. More often, the discourses of state failure lead to a prevailing resignation, a consuming struggle to make ends meet from one day to the next, and in the case of Iran, an onslaught against activists and civil society actors to the extent that those who are not imprisoned, killed, executed, or driven to exile withdraw from the securitized public sphere (discussed in chapter 2).

In Iran, the combination of decades of neoliberal governance, economic mismanagement, sanctions, corruption, and media wars has led to both conditions of disaster swarm and discourses of state failure. Such a state does not further US policy goals. Instead, it further entrenches anti-Americanism not only within the ruling establishment in Iran but also among ordinary Iranians who did not express such sentiments before maximum pressure sanctions.[19] But worst of all, living under disaster swarm and state failure simply wrecks the daily lives of ordinary people.

Defining a Society as the Enemy

Comprehensive sanctions regimes are literally tools of economic pressure. Perhaps more importantly, sanctions are, both by design and by implementation, *a strategy to define an enemy*.

For years, the United States actively worked to make any contact or trade with Iran toxic, even and especially for those—like the European countries, South Korea, and Japan—that relied on energy trade with Iran.[20] Thus, the United States turned trade partners and potential allies of Iran into enemies.

At the same time, Iran was depicted as a "pariah" state: through direct economic sanctions and via media, there has been an attempt to present Iran as an enemy not only of the US but also of the global world order.[21] In this multidecade process, Iran has gone from a state that challenges US (and by extension, Israeli) hegemony in the Middle East, to an official global threat. This transformation is manifested in the 1984 US designation of the country as a "state sponsor of terrorism" (in more recent years, US officials have amplified that designation by adding that Iran is a "leading state sponsor of terrorism").

Consequently, a logic of enmity paralyzes both the US and Iran, making it now nearly impossible to lift sanctions. Embedded in this enemy-making dynamic are affective logics, whereby Iran (for the West) and the West (for Iran) become opponents committed to a zero-sum game of destruction. It is crucial to note that this logic applies to other comprehensively sanctioned countries as well, with a similar reality: a multilayered web of sanctions, with no real path toward removal. Comprehensive sanctions designate a country—and its targeted population—as an enemy *perpetually.*

What happens in the everyday lives of people when their society is defined as an "enemy" to the international system, outside of a formal declaration of war? How does this impact the conduct of everyday life, internal domestic developments, the international movement of citizens, and the wider sociopolitical context of a people?

By coupling sanctions with a "terrorist state" designation, the US further hinders international travel, student visas, and the movement of professionals for academic and medical conferences and artistic exchanges. During the Trump years, for example, the US "Muslim Ban"—which disproportionately targeted Iranians—worked in tandem with the sanctions not only to "punish" the Islamic Republic as a state but to criminalize the movement of Iranians across borders. Added to this ban were multiple cases where Iranian students in the US, on valid student visas, were denied reentry into the US or deported.[22] This targeting of student and professional classes—oftentimes, the very people who on-the-ground have led the most sustained efforts to challenge state power—has become a key component of the comprehensive sanctions regime, with effects that seem to contradict the US's own policy goals.

Again, the sanctions turn friends and allies into enemies and accomplices. Take literary and scientific publishing houses. The vagueness of language in the sanctions regulations themselves have led to publishers *overcomplying,* so as to avoid censure: this has taken the form of issuing directives not to publish work from *any* Iranian writers or researchers.[23] Scientific and academic conferences often cannot accept the work of Iranian researchers. Collaborative academic work between Iranian universities and those outside Iran constantly runs into roadblocks imposed by the sanctions. This, over time, effectively sidelines Iran's researchers and industries of knowledge production.

The vague language of sanctions regulations has also led US universities to curtail the academic freedom of social science researchers to conduct research in places such as Iran.[24] This, in turn, has led to university lawyers forbidding the invitation of Iranian scholars, artists, and journalists to virtual conferences and invited talks, even when no money is being transacted. It has only been through extensive—and expensive—legal fights that the US Treasury Department admitted that these entities are overinterpreting the sanctions and offered a (often only slight) corrective.

Despite some clarifications, most sanctions directives continue to be vague in language and, therefore, ripe for overinterpretation and overcompliance. This ensnarls Iranians in a Kafkaesque web of legalese that spans the globe. Yet the US government insists on maintaining the vague language in sanctions directives, even in the face of calls for clarifications and clearer regulations. Clearly, then, vagueness is a tool in the enemy-defining strategy. By making interactions with Iran sanctionable and depicting the country as "special and not in a good way" (as Richard Nephew, an architect of the US sanctions against Iran, has proclaimed), US policymakers have *made* Iran and its people into pariahs, in every realm of business, exchange, and engagement.

Even worse, there is no off-ramp to the comprehensive sanctions. As such, this enemy status—which attempts to economically strangulate Iran—has a stubborn, sticky quality to it, one that reverberates in the everyday lives of Iranians.

Coping Mechanisms: Mutual Aid and Autarky

"Sure, the situation is tough," Zahra, a lower-middle-class homemaker from Isfahan in her late sixties, explains about life under comprehensive sanctions. "But, at least for those from my generation and my kids' generation, we remember what it was like to live through eight years of war. There was food rationing then. There were bombs flying over our heads. I didn't buy cherries this summer because they were so expensive. We're eating less red meat. But in comparison, we're making do. There aren't long lines for food like during the war. The shelves in all the markets are full. It's frustrating that we can't buy what we used to, and its maddening that we're at this stage after all of these years, but at least for me and those I'm surrounded by, we're getting by. When we don't have enough of something, my cousin's family sends it over. When my friends need something, I drive it over. We know how to take care of each other. The other month a girl from our family was getting married.

Everyone chipped in what they could and we all bought her everything she needed to start her new life. Sure, before this situation her parents could have done it on their own, but now we all help out. We make sure no one stays without."

In her free time, Zahra has picked up knitting and sewing again. She and her friends started a clothes-making circle, for children whose families may not be able to afford new clothes. Every month they send bags full of new clothes to lower-income neighborhoods of the city and have expanded to surrounding small towns and villages.

The latest round of sanctions, the parallel psychological and information wars, the social and political pressures from the Iranian state on society, and the ongoing nature of the sanctions with no end in sight, have led to an "everyday life of resignation" as well as ways to cope with the new and ever-changing realities. One coping mechanism that has become widespread and been pushed to the forefront, both on small and large scales, is mutual aid networks (like that of Zahra's clothing circle).

After all, Iran is a society that, less than fifty years ago, toppled millennia of monarchy through a popular revolutionary movement. The kind of sustained movement necessary to topple an autocratic leader backed by the United States demanded that society forge deep bonds of solidarity. The ensuing four decades, for a variety of reasons, deeply fractured these bonds. Even so, Iranians have responded to disasters since the revolution—both human-made and natural—with continued social solidarity that, in times of crisis, crosses class lines. These efforts, led by both citizens and state/semi-state organizations, play an important role in coping with sanctions.

Sara, an upper-middle-class homemaker in Shiraz, helps lead an informal charity with other women who have disposable income. Every three weeks, they collect everything from computers to cell phones to shoes for those in need. "We coordinate with women who are from neighborhoods with less resources. They tell us what families need—from actual material goods to cash in order to get their sons or daughters set up in a home after marriage. We go around and collect the goods from families with means in Shiraz and every month so far we've met the demands in our network. There are at least seven other networks I know of like this personally."

In southern Tehran, Leyli, a single mother of two, rushes to pick up her brother's car after six hours threading eyebrows at a salon in central

Tehran. Since the imposition of maximum pressure sanctions and the exponential rise in the cost of food, Leyli began to drive "Snap," Iran's version of ride-share apps like Uber and Lyft. She rotates her kids from her brother's house to her aunt's house during the week when she works late driving. "If it weren't for my brother's car, I'm not sure what I would do. I've sold all the jewelry I have, I've run out of everything possible to pawn. I don't want to think about what I would be forced to do . . . how I would need to work the streets, to provide for my children with the prices the way they are. I just thank god every day for my brother," she says with relief in her voice, a mere few seconds before tears well up in her eyes and she drops her head. The suppressed sob and her attempts at wiping her tears muffles her voice. After gaining her composure, she repeats, "I hardly ever see my children anymore. My daughter has started acting out and her school called me to say they were worried about her behavior. I know she wants me around more. I only see them when I get them ready in the mornings and on Fridays. It kills me to be this absent, but with my husband gone and prices the way they are now, what choice do I have?" Leyli is among the legions of new households headed by women who have been plunged into poverty due to the sanctions.[25]

Prior to the death of her husband in a road accident, Leyli had a job threading women's hair at a family-owned beauty salon in central Tehran, and had been there for ten years when the pandemic started. "For over one year when the pandemic began, people were too afraid to come in and get their faces threaded," Leyli explains. At the same time, her children needed laptops to participate in virtual school, given the lockdowns. Without even needing to ask, the owner of the salon called some of her clients; they gathered secondhand laptops and tablets to give to Leyli and the other employees of the salon for their children. Other clients sent her money regularly during the lockdowns, saying they would be paying her regularly if the lockdowns weren't in place.

Throughout the country, these women-led charity networks—at times formal and registered, but often informal—help create a wider network of mutual aid and care. It is hard to measure how extensive these networks are and how much they cover, as far as needs are concerned. Nevertheless, what they do reveal are the deep connections that zigzag through the country, and have done so for decades. These networks of mutual aid and charity have proven key during large natural disasters like earthquakes and floods and during the Iran-Iraq War. Sanctions, then, are just another obstacle for the embattled Iranian people to overcome, rather than a unique pressure that might lead them toward US policy goals.

In addition to these informal networks, formal charities are also very active, as are mosques, religious centers, and wealthy foundations, especially for the dissemination of food, money, furniture, appliances, and personal technology. Although no substitute for the dwindling state-led social safety nets under the pressure of sanctions and years of privatization and neoliberalization, these sustained networks help in dealing with everyday shortages.

While women-led circles and mutual aid networks attempt to alleviate some of the harsh impact of sanctions, opportunities born of isolation and a desire for autarky have arisen for others, especially some young men and women. With the import of goods diminished and increasingly out of reach for everyday consumers, the market has opened up to domestic producers and smaller businesses. With the help of apps such as Instagram, Telegram, Whatsapp, and Iran's growing e-commerce and tech sector, small businesses have popped up in homes and shared office spaces throughout the country. A homegrown fashion industry is booming in urban centers, increasing the demand for manufacturing domestic textiles, while similar booms are apparent in home décor, businesses pertaining to children, and the entire ecology of creatives involved in the production of digital content for social media outreach and brand development for these small businesses and influencers. Here again, despite the great hardships of the sanctions, Iranians are adapting.

Vida, a 32-year-old entrepreneur who had spent four years studying in Malaysia, has no intention of leaving Iran again and "starting from zero. I'll make do with the situation here, as difficult as it gets." She had grown up in a middle-class family in central Tehran. After earning her civil engineering degree and working for a few years in a private company doing what she had studied at university, she finally quit her job and decided to try what had always been her dream: to become a pastry chef and run a catering company. She runs her pastry and catering business mainly through Instagram, WhatsApp, and Telegram, and, prior to the pandemic, had gathered a steady and increasing clientele. When she divorced her husband one year into the pandemic, she knew she had to find her own place to live and try to pick up extra work to be financially stable on her own. She sought investors from the network she had created through her pastry business and opened a small grocery market that sells domestically made artisanal food products. She advertises both of her businesses on Instagram through Iranian social media influencers and in pop-up food events throughout Tehran. "Things have gotten very expensive, but there's also this odd opening for those of us who are running small businesses here. People still want a good time, they want good food and experiences, and we can now offer that to them and reach them through social media as our business platform. And we're not competing with foreign products as much anymore. Of course, the government slows down the internet during protests and it's unsure if we'll have access to Instagram in the future—it has all of us who work through that platform worried. But, we'll find our ways," she adds with a brief laugh. "Every day is a hustle to find ways around government restrictions and sanctions and somehow make things work."

For small and micro business owners, such as Vida and Nazanin, the caterer who is the main breadwinner in her family, they describe being extremely busy and having lots of orders, despite inflation and growing concerns over the economy. "The restaurants all over the city are full virtually every night of the week," Vida recounts. "I'm in motion every day throughout Tehran, going from east to west and south to north to buy what I need for my businesses, and scoping out new opportunities. I'm telling you, after the lockdowns, the restaurants and cafes all over the city are full and for those of us who cater, we're back at full capacity, at times even more." Nazanin agrees. "Don't ask me to explain it to you how despite high prices people are still spending money to enjoy themselves," she laughs. "I guess there's a lot of money circulating. All I can tell you is I have so many orders and not just from homes in wealthy parts of the city. There's usually a lull of a few weeks after the currency depreciates, but then orders start up again once people adapt to the new prices."

Interviews with Iranians in other cities around the country also echo the same sentiments: despite soaring prices and a decrease in buying power, the entertainment, food, fashion, and leisure industries are vibrant.

Dashed Aspirations

Prior to the Obama-era sanctions and Trump's maximum pressure campaign, Iran experienced years of economic growth, as will be discussed in chapter 4. Not only were standards of living increasing in urban areas, but rural areas saw an exponential rise in living standards and developed aspirations for middle-class life. Since 2010, however, poverty rates have doubled in rural areas and increased by 60 percent in urban areas.[26]

A common theme in interviews was how bleak the future seems. Many parents search for ways to get their children abroad, and increasingly more so since the violent repression of the #MahsaAmini uprisings. This potential new wave of brain drain has caused further narratives of dismay and anxiety to course through Persian-language social commentary in online spaces and offline conversations. Diminished opportunities, skyrocketing costs of living, and an uncertain future have created the conditions for "migration fever," as journalist Ferial mentions. Covering the social beat for a leading Iranian newspaper, she comments, "Everyone around me is either in the process of leaving or wanting to leave."

Yet for those who stay, the most repeated sentiments in interviews for this research included dismay, resignation, rage, despair, and hope. Ali, a chemist in his mid-thirties, unplugged from the news and current events in 2019–20, and began to find refuge in the mountains on the outskirts of Tehran. Hiking and mountain climbing are regular pastimes in the areas of Iran with mountain ranges. On Thursdays and Fridays, the weekends in Iran, hiking paths are often crowded, as people seek an escape from the urban sprawl or healthy exercise. For Ali, it became a refuge away from what he describes as an all-enveloping negativity. "All of the negative news, all of the talk of impending doom and people being angry and depressed around me . . . it was really impacting my own mental health. The problems seem so much bigger than what we can solve. Everything seems absurd. So one day I just said, I'm done. I'm done with all of it. I wanted to spend time in nature. My friends and I started going on weekly hikes in the mountains. Then we started to camp. We all work for companies where we can work remotely, and some of my friends eventually even quit their jobs because they weren't making enough to live. They downsized their lives and we all hit the road. We drive to different areas of the country. Camp throughout. Make our own food at campsites. We've met so many young people doing the same. We're just disconnecting from all of this," he waves around, "and reconnecting with nature and with other people.

Kaveh, an architect in his late thirties from Karaj, a city just west of Tehran, recounts a similar journey: "I started hating going to work. They couldn't pay me well anymore. I was frustrated watching my peers who had gone abroad shine on social media with their careers. I remembered how my mother created what felt like a cone of light and creativity for me and my siblings during the [Iran-Iraq] war. We'd always have music on in the house. We went on picnics every week, we went hiking. She would scrape together money and put us in music and art classes. We knew the war was going on outside, but inside our cone, it was light and full of love and music and art. So I looked around myself and really started to question why I had forgotten that. I was striving so hard to be a success-ful architect and make money and live a certain lifestyle. Just like the war interrupted my parents' lives, this economic war of sanctions was interrupting mine. So I decided to do like my mother had done: I created my internal world and turned away from the darkness and frustration of what was going on outside that felt too big for me to impact anyway. I quit my job, I began to play music again. I hike and cook and document it all on my Instagram. I've found so many others my age who are doing the same thing on Instagram. We've been meeting up, some of us are now traveling around the country together. None of us come from wealthy backgrounds. We've literally downsized our lives to two backpacks. We've given up the race of being 'successful' and instead have decided to connect with nature and music and art and each other."

Golnaz, a painter and illustrator in her mid-thirties, has a similar story: "Before the sanctions and COVID, it felt like we had to live our lives BIG. Keep up with exhibitions here and there. Plan how to get on the radar of art collectors. The sanctions limited all of that for us. It hurt a lot at first. But then with COVID, the whole world had to downsize and turn inwards. All of a sudden I saw all of my friends who had moved abroad struggle very deeply. They had to take on whatever jobs they could to pay rent and afford to live abroad. They were isolated from ev-eryone they loved. At least here I am surrounded by family and friends. I could unplug from the life I had built and do small-scale projects that I didn't care if they 'succeeded' or not.

"And with the 'Woman, Life, Freedom' uprisings, I have work to do here. The repression has been so hard to witness, and about ten of my friends were arrested. But as an artist, my gaze has shifted from getting into the latest exhibitions to creating visions for the future here in Iran. In some ways, my world has gotten smaller. In other ways, it's become fuller and I'm present in this struggle."

These consequences to society of young people retreating from their involvement in formal public spheres are clear in the stories of Ali, Kaveh, and Golnaz, but perhaps none more so than Ava. Ava, an environmental activist who used to be involved in political organizing during the reformist years, has turned inward: "I just shut off all of my social media. It was too depressing. The state arrested my friends and colleagues in the environmentalist sphere. For a while I knew my activities were being monitored. I'd talk to my friends in prison on a weekly basis. They kept encouraging me to do what I needed to do to stay alive and free and healthy. I started to read more, to play some music again. To slow down . . . instead of rushing like I used to, I now take my days slow, enjoy my friends and family. I've learned to cook new things and have started to learn how to paint from some Instagram painters. What does that mean for my future? I don't know. But I don't care, because at this rate, none of us may actually have a future given how the climate crisis is going and how conflict-driven the world is. We lived limited lives during the Iran-Iraq War, we can do it again now. And perhaps most freeing of all is that I've given up the urge to organize for change in formal ways in this system. The atmosphere is so tense and securitized. We need to create new visions. So, we'll do like our parents taught us in the 1980s: we cultivate . . . we plant seeds of beauty and culture, we push the confines of this state every day with our presence, and when the situation gets better and it's not as dangerous to organize again, then we'll reemerge, and hopefully healthy again and with newer ideas for how to build and grow."

TWO

When Politics Is Sanctioned

It was the week before the 2021 presidential elections in Iran. Traditionally, voter turnout mattered to the state, which, after all, had been founded by a popular revolution. But, over the preceding three years, since 2018—when the Trump administration pulled out of JCPOA (the 2015 nuclear deal) and initiated its maximum pressure sanctions campaign against Iran—the atmosphere had drastically changed.

Up until maximum pressure, the postrevolutionary state had differentiated itself from the shah's dictatorial rule by claiming a particular kind of legitimacy: that the Islamic Republic of Iran originated in the mass movement that gave birth to the 1979 Iranian Revolution. In March 1979, reportedly 99 percent of the electorate voted for the Islamic Republic and its constitution. Since then, the presidential elections every four years in Iran had touted relatively large voter turnouts, both legitimizing the Islamic Republic to its own supporters and serving as a buffer against its myriad opponents. It was true that the electorate had suffered a big blow after the violent suppression of the 2009 Green Movement uprisings, which protested what many saw as voter fraud in President Ahmadinejad's reelection. But that was nothing compared to just over a decade later. In June 2021, the disappointment, defeat, and anger of the electorate resulted in the lowest voter turnout in postrevolutionary Iranian history: less than 50 percent of the electorate cast ballots.

"The past two presidential elections [2013 and 2017] we told people, 'Go vote so we don't get sanctioned anymore and we can solve our issues with the West,'" says Shadee—a former student activist tied to the Green Movement of 2009—rolling her eyes at how absurd that argument sounds to her today. Letting out a big sigh, she adds, "My generation is the generation that believed in the power of the ballot box to push the system to reform and moderate itself," her voice sounding increasingly resigned, as she considers the high hopes and deep losses her generation of civic and political activists have endured in Iran. "But after everything we've been through because of Trump pulling out of the deal and reimposing sanctions . . . I cannot go back out on the streets and try to convince people to vote. What am I going to say? We have no arguments left. We've been rendered speechless." She raises her hands in resignation and looks down and away in exasperation for what feels like a long minute.

A pregnant silence fills with a mixture of resignation and anger. "People voted in 2013 and 2017 to make relations better with the West, to ease the economic situation, and we're worst off today than we were before JCPOA," she finally says. She excuses herself for a break from the conversation to regroup.

Alireza is another activist from the Green Movement, who spent time in prison in 2010, and again landed in prison during the 2022 #MahsaAmini uprisings. He stayed in Iran upon his release in 2011 and says he plans to do so again now that he has been released from prison after the 2022 uprisings, in order to continue working to preserve space for civic engagement. He explains the years since the imposition of maximum pressure sanctions: "It's like we're in a boxing ring fighting against two opponents at the same time: the US and our own hardliners. Trump's reimposition of sanctions knocked the air out of us and opened the field for our hardliners to pounce on top of us and just keep punching so we don't have the space or ability to get back up. Even when we rise up again . . . the 'Woman, Life, Freedom' protests, which have been so crucial in reclaiming the language of revolution and uprising from the state . . . but the state responds with such breathtaking violence. It feels like a total knockout and I don't know when we will be able to find our footing again . . ." His voice trails off, the last sentence lingering uncertainly.

Fatemeh, meanwhile, is on the other side of the political spectrum, but no less shaken by recent events. An active member of the young generation of self-described "revolutionaries" (enqilabiyun)—those who helped organize campaigns for young hardline candidates in Tehran's city council elections in 2021—Fatemeh describes the harsh experience of the Trump era: "The reformists and moderates who believed that the US would keep its word in JCPOA were naïve. The US government rescinded every treaty it's had with Native Americans in its history. It's a regime that has gone back on its word time and again with its own Black citizens. If that's how it treats its own people, we're fools to believe it will honor its word in its foreign policy. The reformists and moderates have the same problem Iranian leftists and liberals had at the beginning of the 1979 revolution: they believe in an inherent goodness of the West. They're brainwashed by the West and they put our people in this economic situation because of it. Hopefully this bitter lesson of Trump teaches our people once and for all that the US and the West cannot be trusted."

It is an understatement to say that Iran had a bitter experience with JCPOA, particularly the ease with which President Trump pulled out of the accord and reimposed harsh sanctions (everything from overt sanctions to covert operations to propaganda wars). As this chapter demonstrates, the recent US maximum pressure campaign will have long-lasting impacts on Iranian politics and political culture. In just a few years, the US actions severely contracted political space in Iran; as shown in chapter 1, the results were not a flourishing of liberal opposition but a strengthening of the hardline right with its attendant penchant for violent suppression. Moreover, the sanctions militarized political culture and discourse, which has contributed to an atmosphere of polarization and resignation even as it further strengthens hardliners. In fact, the most direct result of maximum pressure has been an almost total consolidation of political power by Supreme Leader Khamenei loyalists, and a hastening of the increase of economic power by the Revolutionary Guard by orders of magnitude.

Maximum pressure, and comprehensive US sanctions in general, have resulted in political hardening and increased military control over political culture. And, worst of all, they have done so while suffocating the voices for engagement and change.

Yet the discussion in the following pages also shows that none of this—not the securitization of Iran's political sphere, nor the contracting of the political arena, nor even the near complete takeover of political and military decision-making by the more conservative camps of the Is-

lamic Republic that occurred after Trump imposed maximum pressure—
was a foregone conclusion. Indeed, this chapter shows how, without US
sanctions and pressure, Iran might truly have charted a different path,
even in this last decade.

Lessons from Iran's Political History

"For Americans, pulling out of the Iran deal and reimposing sanctions—I
doubt it's impacted their daily lives at all," says Hasan. "Many may not
even remember it or care to know much about it. But for Iranians, not
only did it make day-to-day life more expensive, more tense, and bring
about a sense of cynicism . . . which is a true tragedy in my opinion, when
hope dissipates and deep cynicism and resignation set in . . . but it also
undid almost two decades of many of us pushing for an opening and
easing of tensions with the West."

A 60-year-old intellectual who volunteered to fight during all eight
years of the Iran-Iraq War, Hasan had written, lobbied, and traveled
across the country implementing programs and activities to increase
dialogue and promote what he often described as "a culture of peace."
His desire to reduce tensions did not come from his fear of battle, he is
always quick to point out, but precisely because he had spent so many
years of his youth on battlefields. "There is nothing like experiencing
war up close to make you hate it and never wish for its specter to be anywhere near you, your family, your country. That's precisely why so many
of us who had experienced that war and all that our tensions with the US
have tried for so long to bring about a discourse of gradual trust building
and reducing tensions."

Hasan was a supporter of the revolution and the postrevolutionary
system but believed that deep cultural changes were necessary. Hailing
from a pious middle-class family in the southern city of Bushehr, he had
lived in Tehran since the early 1990s and seen many of his friends from
the war gain high political and economic positions. To him, their "blind
pursuit of money and power" was creating an out-of-touch political elite
like those of the shah's regime, causing a deep disconnect between those
in decision-making positions in the system and ordinary people. Hasan
adamantly maintained his independence from both the reformist and
conservative camps within the political establishment. Although his
ideas are more in line with those on the reform end of the spectrum, he

often criticizes reformists just as harshly as he does his more conservative colleagues.

"The other side calls us naïve, and maybe we are . . . ," Hasan trails off for some time, his eyes looking outside the virtual frame of his camera, "but we need to keep creating space for peace and engagement. It's just too bad that this experience with JCPOA was so sour. It's been a major earthquake in our political and social history."

Although Iran was never directly colonized, experiences with colonial powers in its modern history—not to mention the myriad intellectual, political, and activist reactions toward foreign powers that have tried to wield control over the country's vast natural resources and its geostrategic position—have helped define Iran's political culture over the past century. In 1953, the CIA and MI6 helped orchestrate a coup to depose Mohammad Mosaddegh—the first third world leader to nationalize his country's resources and take them out of the hands of the British, for which the West imposed sanctions and an embargo—and replace him with a despotic monarch, the shah. Since then, the widespread belief that Iran had experienced a serious blow to its sovereignty in 1953 festered. Indeed, a main kernel of the 1979 Iranian Revolution was its struggle against the shah, who was widely believed to be doing the bidding of the United States.

The experience of the 1953 coup loomed large over the early events of the 1979 revolution, as the population demanded national sovereignty in the face of powerful outside forces. "Every morning we woke up and wondered if the US embassy had staged another coup to return the shah to Iran," a leftist activist recalls from those early months after the shah had fled the country. It was these fears that first led leftist guerillas to attempt a takeover of the US embassy in Tehran in February 1979. Seven months later, in November 1979, Islamist student revolutionaries loyal to Ayatollah Khomeini did succeed in overrunning the US embassy, after President Carter had acquiesced to allowing the shah to enter the US. The students eventually held fifty-two Americans hostages for 444 days.

Over the four decades since the hostage taking, relations between the two countries experienced far more ebbs than flows. The US supported a war of attrition between Iran and Iraq in the 1980s, turning a blind eye to more than five years of chemical attacks on Iran during that war; Iran was involved in the creation of Hezbollah in Lebanon and a deadly attack on US Marine barracks, showing its willingness to hit back at the

US outside of Iran's national borders. President George W. Bush included Iran in the "axis of evil," despite US and Iran cooperation in toppling the Taliban in the aftermath of 9/11, and US-led sanctions against Iran spanned decades; Iran in turn sponsored and trained Iraqi militias to battle US forces in their country. Meanwhile, there were the multiple fronts of proxy wars in the region between Iran and the US and its allies, Israel and Saudi Arabia. But the signing of JCPOA in 2015, which included direct negotiations between Iranians and Americans, appeared to signal a departure from the previous four decades.

For JCPOA to become even a possibility, however, entailed a battle of ideas and discourses. The two countries had shared a bitter history. Moreover, there was debate concerning the legacy of the Iranian Revolution: after all, one of the revolution's desires and promises was to establish sovereignty vis-á-vis the imperial powers of the US and the Soviet Union at the time. And there was debate over how Iran could or should relate to the world's superpower, which, since the 1979 revolution, took concrete steps to build a military presence in the Middle East, and since 9/11 formally occupied two of Iran's neighboring countries.

A crucial role in this battle of ideas was played by Iran's majority young population. Born after the revolution, Iran's youth pushed—politically at the voting booth, and socioculturally in their everyday practices—against the myriad social and political restrictions of the post-revolutionary state.

Why did activists like Shadee and Alireza, quoted earlier, feel so resigned in the 2021 elections and the aftermath of the violent suppression of the 2022 uprisings? To answer this question, it is important to understand first the role their generational cohort played in the political realm since 1997. At that time, young Iranians who did not remember the revolution, and who were children during the Iran-Iraq War, came out in droves to vote in the presidential race for Mohammad Khatami: a reformist cleric who spoke of the power of dialogue for both internal and external relations.

Khatami's election was experienced as a rupture of Iran's revolutionary experience to that point. Key to understanding postrevolutionary Iran is to appreciate the deep sociopolitical changes that occurred, both individually and collectively, through the very processes of mass mobilizations that led to a revolution as "unthinkable" as the one in Iran.[1]

The 1979 Iranian Revolution came about through massive social movements, which included people and groups from all walks of life. The postrevolutionary political project, which issued from the fierce power plays endemic to revolutions, was an Islamic Republic led by Ayatollah Khomeini. So the subsequent 1980s were marked by two concurrent political battles. The first was a domestic battle against other revolutionaries who disagreed with Ayatollah Khomeini. They were heavily repressed, imprisoned, executed, or pushed into exile. The other was external, an eight-year war with Iraq. In the same decade, Iran underwent a massive demographic change, with the arrival of the baby boom generation in the 1980s.

The postrevolutionary period has been marked by cycles of continued popular mobilization. These have taken place in the form of protests, movements, and struggles for change in political discourse, and have used everyday actions and practices to push against sociocultural redlines. Also taking place were the controlled mobilization of the state at the warfront in the 1980s, enforced by religio-political organizations, and the sustained mobilization of paramilitary and other forces.

In such a fluid situation, it is foolhardy to attempt to project with certainty who or what "wins out" in such struggles. What does become clear in these pages, however, is that comprehensive sanctions tend to strengthen one side of this dynamic and weaken the other, the latter contributing to the feeling of "suffocation" voiced by Shadee, Alireza, and other activists.

Battle over Discourse: Newspapers and Protests (1997–2009)

The domestic struggle to change Iran's relationship with the West and to reform the revolutionary state played out publicly in the pages of Iran's newspapers and on the streets in protests. But the change itself was fueled by massive demographic changes in the 1980s. These, in turn, led to public support for a different approach in the mid-1990s.

Twenty million people voted Mohammad Khatami into office in 1997, representing almost 80 percent of the electorate. This presented a fierce challenge to the conservative factions within the Islamic Republic. This was primarily experienced as a shocking defiance of the supreme leader, Ali Khamenei, who did not enjoy the popularity, charisma, or legitimacy of his predecessor, Ayatollah Khomeini (1902–1989), and had been supreme leader for less than eight years. Remarkably, Khatami even drew support from within the ranks of military and security forces, notably among the Revolutionary Guard, including people like Hasan (the 60-year-old veteran who believed in peace, introduced earlier).

This reformist wave challenged the grip of the conservative clerical establishment on Iranian politics. Perhaps most importantly, it attempted to move the country toward domestic democratization—which would inherently reduce the power of the supreme leader—and international integration vis-á-vis the West.

"We kept writing and giving speeches about the necessity to ease tensions with the West and to ease tensions internally," Hasan recalls of all the dynamic energy of the Khatami presidency. "There was a palpable current in society at the time for change on all fronts. But it was a battle of words and ideas. We had to fight to carve out a different discourse than what had become the norm in Iran due to the eight years of war and the revolutionary fervor."

The primary arena in which all of this played out was the media, especially newspapers. Prior to Khatami's election, the newsstands were mostly dominated by the conservative dailies such as *Kayhan*, *Resalat*, and *Jomhouri-e Eslami*. In less than two years after Khatami's election, numerous newspapers began publication, each representing a specific political and social viewpoint. And this was largely thanks to a push from young journalists and editors.

As the number of newspapers exploded, the press itself was in a simultaneous process of transformation and radicalization. The press became increasingly bold and aggressive in its criticism, echoing people's opposition to the conservative domination of the Islamic Republic, the conservative turn in postrevolutionary politics, and the interpretation of Islamic law prevailing in the Islamic Republic. Even older newspapers were full of critical editorials against the conservative factions of the Islamic Republic; some even openly called for a reform of the entire system and a reevaluation of its foreign policy. At times, newspapers even echoed people's broader discontent, questioning the right of the religious establishment to exist in its present form.

Due to the absence of legal opposition parties, the various newspapers acted as surrogate political parties, with each newspaper publishing a specific political perspective. Most, however, were united in calling for reforms within the framework of the Islamic Republic and a reconsideration of Iran's foreign policy stances. Thus, the press increasingly functioned as a platform for political debate among various factions in Iran. This, in turn, led to a "war of editorials," which raged over the details of the liberalization of Iranian society.

The reformist media attempted to hold the regime accountable for its actions, directly threatening conservative forces headed by the supreme leader. For example, the daily *Jame'e* (Society) newspaper published reports about threats its staff received from the Revolutionary Guard. It even ran interviews with well-known figures who were incarcerated and faced torture in prisons, especially in the unit run by the Revolutionary Guard, which is under the supervision of the supreme leader.

Alireza, the reformist student activist who was imprisoned in 2010 and 2022, remembers the Khatami years as a time where nothing was fixed and things were in motion: "You had the reformist intellectuals writing things that hadn't been published before. . . . It was so exciting. We'd rush out to buy the newspapers and magazines. The newsstands were always crowded with people taking part in the 'war of editorials' that dominated this time. At the time I was sixteen and would follow my sister around to all her university student meetings where they'd discuss how to push for change on the streets and in the schools. It felt like everyone in our social circles were involved, but especially the younger generations. We felt that we had a say finally in the direction our country could take and what our politics could look like."

To stop the reformist wave—spearheaded by students, women, teachers, artists, and youth—conservative elements of the state, backed by the supreme leader, launched a multipronged attack. Reformists and their allies were labeled as puppets of the United States, enemies of the revolution, and superficial admirers of the "Western" way of life. As the new press challenged the state—which had survived since 1979 by heavily censoring all channels of information—conservatives denounced the press itself as an "enemy" of the state. The conservative factions began to take relentless actions against the various reformist newspapers: shutting them down one by one, imprisoning journalists, student activists, and others.

Just a few years into Khatami's presidency, then, protests against the conservative forces mounted, especially after the student uprisings in July 1999. But, by then, senior Revolutionary Guard officers began attacking the reformists. "There were big splits within the Revolutionary Guard at the time," Hasan recalls, who had just retired from his position in the powerful military institution prior to Khatami taking the presidency. "Many of my colleagues desired change and were not in line with how the country was developing politically after the death of Imam Khomeini. But the supreme leader did not appreciate this momentum for change and did not agree with the demands being made. He felt it threatened his power, so he and his allies in the Revolutionary Guard and within the political establishment of the system began to retaliate." In a letter addressed to Khatami in the conservative newspaper *Jomhuri-e Eslami* that same summer of 1999, twenty-four senior Revolutionary Guard officers stated that they "cannot tolerate the situation anymore," and would take action if Khatami did not change his policies.

Alireza remembers that summer of 1999 as defined by the university protests in which his older sister took part. At the time, these university protests were the biggest public demonstration challenging the conservative establishment since the revolution. "After that massive demonstration at the University of Tehran, Sara could never take me with her to campus meetings. Everything became heavily securitized. They checked all student IDs cards at the entrance to the universities and their paramilitary Basij forces and plainclothes security forces were spread out throughout campus, and they jailed many students who had partaken in that uprising."

In the realm of foreign policy, the situation deteriorated. In the first years of his presidency, Khatami had attempted rhetorical overtures with the West and especially the United States, and even aided the US in its initial fight against the Taliban. But none of this diplomatic work—which was supported by the reformists and condemned by the conservatives—stopped George W. Bush from labeling Iran as part of the "axis of evil" in 2002, and invading Iraq (which, of course, bordered Iran) in 2003. In fact, members of the Bush administration openly talked about invading Iran next—even going so far as to stage military games with Iran as the target.[2] "With the US now on both of our borders and with talks that Iran would be next," recalls Hasan, "it helped harden views even among my colleagues in the Revolutionary Guard who sympathized with the reformists. For them, it turned everything into a national security issue."

After all, Iran's popular reform government that sought détente with the West had been met with derision and even threats of war. So, it should come as little surprise that Iran responded in kind. Consequently, as Khatami's presidency drew to an end in 2005, reformist Revolution-

ary Guard members were sidelined. This left their conservative counterparts well positioned within the political and economic realms to
increase their power. The supreme leader took it one step further. To decisively counter the remaining reformists, he began actively appointing
more conservative Revolutionary Guard members to political positions;
meanwhile, he continued to provide vast resources to training younger
members of the conservative paramilitary organization Basij, making
sure they would be loyal to his worldview and leadership.

For the most part, those who came into political power under the
Ahmadinejad presidency (2005–13) had been kept on the economic sidelines within the ruling elite during the previous presidencies of Hashemi
Rafsanjani (1989–97) and Mohammad Khatami (1997–2005). Those two
administrations had been driven by political figures with long-standing
ties to the West and a desire to slowly expand Iran's relationship with
the West. The economic policies at the heart of both administrations had
been neoliberal, with a strong push to further privatize the country's
economy.

When the conservative populist Mahmoud Ahmadinejad ran for
office in 2005, the narrative of his campaign focused on giving a voice
and opportunities to those who had been left behind by the neoliberal
flank of the Islamic Republic, which had been in power since the end
of the war in 1989. (Although Hassan Rouhani, elected in 2013, would
return to the same neoliberal, Western-oriented policies of Rafsanjani
and Khatami.) During his 2005 campaign, Ahmadinejad's populist message and slickly produced campaign videos and rallies resonated with
those upset over growing wealth inequities and the undelivered promises of the revolution. For them, the demands of the reformist movement
were seen as out-of-touch with the economic reality of those "left behind"
by the state's neoliberal economic policies.

Vahid was a student leader in the Basij at Sharif University during
the Ahmadinejad years; today, he is a leading member from his generational cohort in a prominent technology company affiliated with the
Revolutionary Guard. Vahid recalls what he saw as the reasons for the
disconnect he felt with other students at his university who supported
reformism: "They were making all of this noise about political and social
freedoms while they were completely blind to and had nothing to say
about the growing economic inequality in the country. The reformist
student leaders on the university campuses in Tehran mostly lived in

the middle- and upper-middle-class neighborhoods of the city and constantly wanted to act and be Western. They seemed to us to care more
about having their parties in peace than in thinking about the lived realities of those of us in the southern [working class and poor] parts of
the city." It certainly helped Ahmadinejad's cause when, in the runoff
presidential elections, he went head-to-head with Rafsanjani, the former
two-term president of Iran (1989–97), who had become the symbol of un-
bridled postrevolutionary wealth creation.

The neoliberal economic policies of the Rafsanjani and Khatami
administrations, with their emphasis on privatization, had taken small
steps away from the revolutionary rhetoric of serving the oppressed (*mo-
stazefin*) promoted during the first decade of the revolution. In the process, socioeconomic divisions within supporters of the Islamic Republic
began to widen in visible ways. When Ahmadinejad surprised observers
by sweeping into the presidency with a populist message aimed at those
who felt left behind by the revolution, he ushered new political actors
into the centers of political and economic power.

Eventually, Ahmadinejad's presidency became known for threading
the needle politically: taking an aggressive stance against the clergy,
while, at the same time, adhering to a more hardline politics in both
domestic and international affairs. Driving power away from the clergy
was a popular move among the general population. Even so, given Ahmadinejad's other actions and their consequences—restrictive social,
cultural, and civic policies; the suppression of the Green Movement;
harsh sanctions by the West and United Nations; and rising inflation
and economic isolation—he was a highly polarizing figure. During his
two terms, a number of his declarations, starting with "wiping Israel off
the map" and denying the Holocaust, set the stage for the rapid deterioration of relations between Iran and Western powers. Ahmadinejad soon
became a lightning rod internationally. It was a 180-degree turn from his
predecessor, Khatami.

Shadee, a prominent student leader at the University of Tehran during
the Ahmadinejad years, including the 2009 Green Movement, describes
Ahmadinejad's first term: "The domestic sphere during those first four
years was suffocating for those of us who wanted the system to reform
and to open the space for civic engagement and better relations with the
West. The conservative forces at the university began to act bolder and
would intimidate us on a weekly basis. Especially for all of us female

students, they made life more difficult during those years, but we didn't back down. During his two terms, he and his allies couldn't succeed in changing much socially as far as pushing women to veil more or policing interactions between the sexes . . . they were dealing with a generation who was done taking their commands and who knew how to push for social changes with our everyday actions. Yet they did succeed in shutting down spaces for civic society and in changing the tenor of discussion on politics and foreign relations."

Fatemeh, quoted earlier, hailed from a pious family with humble means. She was a student in Amir Kabir University in Tehran during the Ahmadinejad years. Today, she organizes political campaigns for conservative "revolutionary" (enqelabiyun) political hopefuls from her generation. "I was never personally against what the reformist students asked for at the university. But for those of us who didn't come from their neighborhoods or backgrounds, and who didn't have their style of dress or didn't act like they did, we were barely even acknowledged by them. We were nobodies for many of them . . . at least that's how their interactions with us made us feel."

It is not necessarily true that the reform movement, and the Green Movement specifically, were solely middle- and upper-middle-class movements. Even so, they were often depicted as such, both by the foreign press and those opposed to these movements inside Iran. Nonetheless, ethnographic research and interviews with politically active Iranians from the same generational cohorts who led the Green Movement indicate that those who did not belong to the middle and upper-middle classes of society often felt excluded from these spaces. These class and subcultural divides have continued to have wide-reaching reverberations in Iranian politics and social movement alliances to the present day.

Arash, now a veteran of the NGO world in Iran, started as a student activist during the Khatami years. He continued his work despite the repression that followed in the Ahmadinejad period, witnessing many of his colleagues being called in for regular interrogation sessions with security officials or sent to prison. "Everything became more securitized," he recalls of the eight years Ahmadinejad was in power. "Especially after the crackdown on the Green Movement."

In the lead-up to the 2009 presidential elections in Iran, the population was galvanized once again by the newest wave of reformism, and the push for a domestic and foreign opening. Attempting to regain power—and pushing for civic spaces to stay open and engage with the world—a coalition of students, women, teachers, workers, and veterans allied behind Ahmadinejad's two main contenders, Mir Hossein Mousavi and Mehdi Karrubi. Yet Ahmadinejad was reelected, although under accusations of widespread fraud. When the 2009 Green Movement erupted in protest, it evolved into the largest public challenge to formal politics in Iran since the 1979 revolution.[3] With millions of protestors on the streets chanting "Down with the Dictator," Supreme Leader Khamenei faced the most publicly widespread challenge to his legitimacy. Predictably, he ordered his security forces to clamp down in support of Ahmadinejad. Consequently, throughout the course of less than a year, the Green Movement was suppressed and eventually its leaders placed under house arrest. They remain so to this day.

Securitizing Political Culture (2009–20)

Unbeknownst to protestors pouring into the streets in the first week of the Green Movement, the United States and Israel had launched the Stuxnet cyberattack on Iran's nuclear facilities, in what became the first large-scale cyberwar in history. But the security establishment of Iran blamed the Green Movement, not foreign adversaries, for the attacks on the country's centrifuges. More importantly, perhaps, they claimed the movement was not homegrown but orchestrated from abroad. For example, then–US secretary of state Hillary Clinton personally requested that Twitter put off updating its software (which would take the service down for some time) in order to ensure Green Movement protestors had access to the online sphere to continue reporting on protests and their battles with security forces.[4] The Islamic Republic perceived Clinton's actions, coupled with the Stuxnet cyberattack, as similar to how the West backed the recent "color revolutions" of eastern Europe.

But the widespread suppression of the Green Movement and the concurrent contraction of the sociopolitical sphere did not end domestic support for change. Just a few years later, in 2013, Iran's under-40 population, women, and reformists again attempted to bring about an opening, both domestically and with the West, at the ballot box. A new and important coalition emerged. Hasan Rouhani was a moderate without a popular base, who held top security positions in the regime and was a supporter of former president Rafsanjani, yet he courted the reformist vote in 2013. In the last few days leading up to the 2013 vote, supporters of the Green Movement rallied for Rouhani. They backed his rhetoric to engage with the West, in order to ease the pressure of Western sanctions imposed during the Ahmadinejad presidency and to de-securitize the domestic sphere.

Despite their support leading him to victory, Rouhani was unable—or perhaps unwilling—to spend much political capital to free the leaders of the Green Movement from house arrest. Instead, he went all in on making a deal with the West, in exchange for sanctions relief, which led to the "Iranian nuclear deal" (the Joint Comprehensive Plan of Action, or JCPOA) negotiated with the Obama administration. When JCPOA was signed in July 2015, jubilant citizens poured out onto the streets to cele-brate, much as when the Iranian national soccer team won big matches. There seemed to be a collective sigh of relief and a desire to no longer be isolated and punished economically by the US and the West.

Even after Trump won the presidency in the US a year later—he had campaigned to rip up the Iranian nuclear deal—Iranians still turned out in large numbers to reelect Rouhani in 2017. They hoped that he and his foreign minister, Javad Zarif, could keep the deal alive, maintain good relations with the West, and stave off further sanctions.

Instead, Trump pulled out of JCPOA and implemented the maximum pressure campaign, which included not only comprehensive economic sanctions but also covert operations, cyberwar, propaganda wars, overt actions, and assassinations. In so doing, Trump dealt a heavy blow to the political actors and constituencies that, allegedly, the West most sought to cultivate: those who had struggled for over two decades to maintain an open domestic sphere and engage with the West.

Trump's maximum pressure campaign—which Biden has continued unabated as of this writing—is a shadow war, fought on multiple fronts and across the region, against Iran and its allied forces. Shadow wars are intelligence wars first and foremost. It is not surprising that, in response, Iran extended the reach of the Revolutionary Guard's extraterritorial forces, the Quds Force, and the intelligence services of the Revolution-ary Guard into all realms of decision-making within the Islamic Repub-lic. This, in essence, is the main factor causing the exponential increase in the securitization of Iranian political culture.

During Rouhani's second term (2017–21), for example, there was a sustained and loud debate inside Iran between his administration and opponents regarding the extent to which the "battlefield" (*meydaan*) mentality informed by the Quds Force—indeed, the head of the force, General Qasem Soleimani, was openly assassinated by the United States in January 2020—should determine Iranian political decision-making. For example, in an audio interview leaked in the last months of the Rouhani administration, Javad Zarif, Iran's foreign minister who had negotiated JCPOA, speaks at length about the battlefield mentality and the struggle between himself and the by-then-assassinated Soleimani.[5]

The conservative-led media sphere had slammed Zarif and Rouhani throughout their administration for not implementing a battlefield mentality in the face of maximum pressure. Yet by 2020, the assassination of Soleimani in January, coupled with public threats by Trump to bomb Iran's cultural sites, made it nearly impossible for those against a *meydaan* outlook to retain control of political discourse. Further cyberattacks on critical infrastructure, military sites, and manufacturing facilities in Iran, some of which resulted in physical explosions, only increased the battlefield mentality. And all this strengthened the hand of the Revolutionary Guard security apparatus.

In the leaked tapes from the 2020 interview, Zarif claimed that a security outlook came to dominate the Ministry of Foreign Affairs from the beginning of the revolution. Not only was it informed by widespread belief that the US could undertake espionage to weaken the new revolutionary state—especially given the revolutionary anti-imperialist rhetoric and the importance of Iranian oil to Euro-American strategic interests—but also by the real internal battles between different revolutionary groups in the power plays surrounding the postrevolutionary political project.[6] Even so, Zarif explained, the security outlook did not turn into a battlefield mentality spearheaded by the Revolutionary Guard until later.

In fact, the origins of the battlefield mentality (though not articulated as such until decades later) can be traced back to the 1980–88 Iran-Iraq War, where many of the current commanders of the Revolutionary Guard and those within high echelons of the Islamic Republic served. The war was not only a terrain where the nascent Revolutionary Guard gained experience in how to fight a war. Instead, the war became the very way through which they began to develop their understandings of international relations. It was how they learned to see the world, and Iran's place in it.

For many of these men, the war was where they experienced first-hand what it meant to fight a multipronged war where the enemy was not only the forces in front of them but also outside powers who sought to arm both sides in a war of attrition. Thus, through their experiences on the battlefields of Iran and Iraq, Iran's new leaders began to understand how the US and the West fight proxy wars. To fight this type of war, the Revolutionary Guard developed asymmetrical strategies, which have since come to define a core strategy of the organization. They also developed allied armed groups throughout the region, which are similarly opposed to US meddling and Israeli expansion.

Decades after the Iran-Iraq War was the US "war on terror," when the United States invaded two of Iran's neighbors, Iraq and Afghanistan, accompanied by loud proclamations and finger-wagging that Iran would be next. In response, the Quds Force took what they had learned from the Iran-Iraq War—their strategies of asymmetrical warfare, their ability to build alliances, and their development and manufacturing of indigenous weaponry—and deployed it to fight against the US, and eventually, the wider axis of US allies in the region in the war in Syria.

For the Quds Force and their allied groups, the *meydaan* is not only physical battlefields throughout the region. They understand the conflict as a hybrid war that also includes the intelligence, cyber, propaganda, and financial wars that span the region, with the US and its regional allies on one side, and Iran and its regional allies, or what they call the "axis of resistance," on the other. In this formulation, the domestic sphere, especially protests and criticism, also entails a critical part of the *meydaan*.

A veteran of the Iran-Iraq War, Reza was a professor in some of Iran's most prestigious universities after the war, including Imam Jafar Sadegh University, which grooms students who are intended to eventually comprise the political elite of the Islamic Republic. A popular professor, Reza has trained countless students who have acted as regime loyalists throughout the years. He was appointed to political positions during the presidency of Ahmadinejad (2005–13) as well as under Ebrahim Raisi (2021–). He is outspoken against the writings and speeches of people like Hasan. "What my friends from the other side have constantly miscalculated is how the US operates as an empire," Reza says. "They actually believe the liberal discourse of the West, its talk of an 'international order,' and operating as supposed equals. They think it's a genuine discourse. They constantly turn a blind eye to all the examples throughout history of when the US and the West in general do not extend their rhetoric to non-Western nations, not to mention their own nonwhite populations."

For Reza and others who train the younger generation of conservative elites in Iran, there is no need for conspiracy theories about the United States or even, in their view, to have a pessimistic view of the US. "All that's needed is to study the history of US and Western imperialism from the point of view of those who have been on the receiving end. The problem with Iran's intellectual circles and young people who want to copy being Western is that they have zero racial analysis," Reza says emphatically. "They think that the West will accept Iran and Iranians as equals. You can't understand the West or Western history without understanding that white supremacy is the bedrock of their entire project. But many Iranians believe we're white, isn't that true?"

Reza smiles and lets the question linger in the air while he puts a sugar cube in his mouth, taking a slow sip of his tea. A practiced professor who knows how to captivate his students, he is in no rush. Eventually, he continues, "It's a remnant of Pahlavi-era nationalist discourse—that we are the original Aryans. If you believe that, which many of my friends who hold opposing political views from us do, then you develop a huge blind spot when it comes to how Western power operates." He smirks a bit before he continues. "Many Iranians still believe we're white, not understanding that 'white' is a made-up category to keep Americans and Europeans on top. And so," he says after taking another sip of tea, "when we get sanctioned to the levels we have even when we didn't abandon the deal for a good eighteen months after Trump pulls out, and there's a Muslim Ban that predominantly targets Iranians, and Iranian students on valid student visas get deported from the US, and . . . and . . . and . . . then what happens? Our friends are all shocked and dismayed."

He continues, speaking with the air of someone who is confident in his analysis and used to defending it: "So when our side comes to power and says 'you can't trust the West,' our friends on the other side make us out to be rabid radicals. But it's their belief that the US will actually treat Iran as a sovereign nation and respect our desires to be free from their hegemony that's the radical idea. When has the US, or the West in general, ever let a country that's pushed out imperialist powers and taken control over its resources and decision-making to go without punishment? Quite the opposite," he raises his finger to make his point. "The West has made an example of every third world country to stand up to it in order to dissuade others from even thinking of doing the same. Just look at Haiti, look at Cuba, look at Venezuela, look at Zimbabwe. It levies wars and economic sieges to make populations who dared to rise up regret ever wanting independence. They try to make our lives miserable so no other third world population thinks to oust them from their affairs."

When Zarif received heavy criticism from hardline camps inside Iran for not pursuing a *meydaan* mentality, he retaliated with the critique that a battlefield point of view would only lead to further conflict. Musa, an Iranian-Lebanese fighter who serves as one of the conduits for strategy building between the Iranian Revolutionary Guard and the Lebanese Hezbollah, crosses his arms and shrugs his shoulders at the mention of the leaked Zarif tapes and his critique of the battlefield mentality. "Look, I respect Zarif and think he's a very skilled diplomat. But he sees one reality, and we see a completely different reality on a daily basis in Iraq, Syria, Lebanon, Yemen. The US says one thing in the diplomatic world, it's echoed loudly by all Western media outlets and their people in the region, and on the ground it acts completely contradictory to what it proclaims."

Hadi, a Lebanese member of Hezbollah who fought in Syria and spends months at a time in Iran to receive training, interjects to support Musa's point: "The reality is that the US and Israel thought they could overpower Iraqis, Lebanese, Iranians, Palestinians, and Syrians easily. It's precisely on the battlefield where we've shown them that not only can we fight back, but we can strike decisive victories and soil their plans to dominate the entire region. We're the only forces since the establishment of Israel to force Israel to retreat militarily, and to establish serious detente."

Musa jumps back into the conversation. "In the minds of the Americans and Israelis, that's not supposed to happen. In their minds, we're some backwards terrorists who should be no match for their self-perceived sophistication and military might. In reality, we've developed into groups that are not scared of them and we have our own means of defending ourselves. This is unacceptable to them."

Hadi nods along, adding, "So, when Iran and the axis of resistance are able to keep Bashar al-Asad in power against the dirty war the West and their allies played with all their mercenary jihadist groups, the US, Israel, and Saudi Arabia want to try everything they can to weaken Iran and its allied powers. They not only impose harsh sanctions on Iran, but they also heavily sanction Syria, they sanction Hezbollah, they make ri-

diculous demands of the Lebanese political elite to disarm us, they pour
money into heavy media campaigns against us across the region. So, yes,
we are in an active battlefield with them on many terrains."

Reza, the university professor and administration official in the
Raisi administration, concurs with this line of thinking. For him and
his colleagues from the more conservative elements of the political establishment, it is impossible to formulate effective national security and
diplomatic positions without the *meydaan* being front and center.

Even for someone like Hasan, the writer and professor who believes
in cultivating a "culture of peace" in Iran given the horrors of war, the
assassination of Soleimani and the intensified multipronged attacks
against Iran by the US and its allies since the imposition of "maximum
pressure" have pushed him to accept certain points by Reza and other
conservative colleagues. "I pushed back very heavily in a public way
against what I found were baseless attacks against Zarif and the JCPOA
up until the assassination of Soleimani. But with that assassination, I
agree with my conservative colleagues—before we can even begin to
think about maintaining a stable Iran, we need to make sure Iran exists
in the face of all of this pressure and shadow wars that seek to ravage the
country and create yet another failed and broken Middle Eastern country. This is, in my opinion, the tragedy of this strategy of the Americans
and Israelis. It's justified a total militarization of Iranian politics."

Could attempting to resolve issues with the US, Saudi Arabia, and
other neighboring countries decrease the need for a *meydaan* mentality
to be a central component of political decision-making? "Zarif tried with
the JCPOA," Reza, the university professor responds. "And before that,
there were other attempts at rapprochement between us. Look, I don't
deny there are people within the US political establishment that want to
decrease tensions with Iran. But there are very powerful forces that want
this conflict to continue—"

"On all sides, including ours," Hasan interjects.

Reza continues: "Yes, on all sides. But take one look around the
region. Since the US became the dominant power in the region, it's left
it in destruction. Nearly every country is in shambles. We've tried our
best to keep Iran out of that destruction. And to be perfectly honest, as
long as Iran is a state that believes in national sovereignty and will not
kowtow to outside forces, we will continue to be on the brunt end of de-
structive US policy. If it's not the nuclear issue, it's our ballistic missiles.

If it's not our ballistic missiles, it'll be human rights. If it's not human rights, they'll find another reason. Just look at every third world country that's dared to question Western imperialism—from Haiti ousting French colonialists to today."

Hasan sighs, nods his head, and looks down before he mumbles, "Unfortunately, yes."

Resistance Economy

To combat the notion that Iran will be sanctioned by the US for a myriad of issues even if the nuclear sanctions are removed, Iran's supreme leader, Ali Khamenei, has called for the entry of the young generation of revolutionaries into leadership roles, reiterating that "the solution to these problems lies in the strong, responsible and lively implementation of the policies delineated by the Economy of Resistance that need to be outlined, followed up and acted upon by administrations."[7] In other words, the goal is to figure out how to make the economy resilient in the face of continued sanctions.

Khamenei calls the increased sanctions regime against Iran an "imposed economic war" (*jang-e eghtesaadi-e tahmili*), echoing language used to describe the eight-year Iran-Iraq War of the 1980s. In both instances, Khamenei is clear that it is the US imposing these wars to isolate and weaken Iran and force it to capitulate. Iran's response to the war with Iraq in the 1980s was to build asymmetric capabilities and develop its own expertise in weapons, logistics, and strategy, at a time when it was isolated internationally. In the "imposed economic war" of today, Khamenei has called for similar tactics, with asymmetry and expertise extended into the realm of trade and operationalized by men tied to certain sectors of Iran's Revolutionary Guard.

Throughout the four-decade history of the Islamic Republic, a key discourse has been economic sovereignty and self-sufficiency. In 2010, Khamenei expanded on this discourse, formulating the notion of a "resistance economy" (*eghtesad-e moqavemat*) in the face of US sanctions and the global financial crisis of 2008–9. In a series of official meetings and speeches, Khamenei asked scholars, economists, and businesspeople to pursue policies that will leverage Iran's international trade, diversify markets, increase manufacturing, move away from dependence on oil revenue, and encourage development of Iranian industry and technology. The resistance economy, much like other developments in Iran since the 1979 revolution, was not announced as a fully formed idea but presented as an aspirational model to be perfected along the way by revolutionary loyalists.

Many of the business ventures that began to create a "resistance economy" did so under the Ahmadinejad government. Ali, a 55-year old businessman, met Venezuelan and Cuban officials in his spacious office on Argentina Square, one of Tehran's business districts populated with high-rise office buildings. Ali had a long-standing relationship with officials from Cuba's biotechnology and pharmaceutical entities, spoke conversational Spanish, and was interested in expanding his ties to Venezuela, which, unlike Cuba, had economic resources that could lead to significant profit margins for his businesses.

Ali hailed from a working-class family in a central province of Iran, but over the years he had created a fortune for himself and his family. He was 16 years old when the revolution began and 17 when he volunteered to fight after Iraq invaded Iran in 1980. When the war ended, Ali was 25; he desired a world beyond his provincial town. Taking advantage of one of the many educational opportunities available to veterans, he entered one of Tehran's most prestigious universities to study civil engineering. Upon graduation, he was employed in a new business created by a former commander of his from the war.

Many of these ventures created by former Revolutionary Guard members often outsourced the work, in the first two decades, to engineers and scientists who came from the professional classes. Yet many of these individuals, though not radical critics of the state, were not regime loyalists. Although this practice continues, there has been a concerted effort to increase the number of competent professionals in a variety of sectors who are also loyal to the Islamic Republic.

When Ali decided to venture out on his own, he lacked the capital to start a new business. But his former boss told him to take advantage of a new opportunity opening up with the Cuban biotechnology industry. At a time when Iran was working to lure European and East Asian investments, "No one really paid any attention to me and gave me a small smile of sympathy when I told them I was working with Cuba," he says. They doubted this relationship would go anywhere and knew how strapped Cuba was financially due to the US embargo. "But my former boss reminded me that we had to seek business partnerships all over, and he said to me, wisely, 'We need to learn how Cuba has created a biopharma- ceutical industry in the face of US sanctions.'"

At the time that Ali started to create the connections with Cuban state biotechnology entities in the 1990s, Iran's special relationship with Latin America had not yet been developed. When Ahmadinejad and Chavez began giving the green light to such ventures and supporting them with significant state resources, Ali was in an ideal position. Over the years, he and his sons eventually expanded their businesses to Venezuela; later, they became involved in different Revolutionary Guard–linked businesses, building residential units and infrastructural projects. Ali's businesses took him all around Syria, Afghanistan, and Iraq, in addition to Latin America. From the point of view of Khamenei, Iran's resistance economy is predicated on people like Ali and the younger generation of regime loyalists.

Ultimately, sanctions have enriched—by orders of magnitude— certain Revolutionary Guard enterprises. But it is impossible to provide exact numbers, given how sanctions-busting requires trade on the black market with attendant bribes and kickbacks. Perhaps more importantly, sanctions have weakened the independent businesspeople who had more ties to the West.

Mahmood is a wealthy businessman from a landowning family, who chose to continue his many businesses in Iran after the revolution. He fared very well, until Obama began comprehensive sanctions in 2011. Mahmood and his friends, many of them also wealthy business owners and manufacturers, now mourn the drastic loss in revenue and influ- ence. "Over the past ten years, the economy is being eaten up by those tied to the Revolutionary Guards," laments Mahmood. "They've been around since the end of the war, but until Obama and Trump sanctions, we independent business owners still held a lot of clout inside Iran. Over the past ten years we're being wiped out—sure, we're still running our businesses, but we don't have nearly the same kind of power we did before. Our traditional business partners outside the country are afraid to do business with us because of the sanctions, so these businesses run by those with the Revolutionary Guard step in and forge ahead because they can take risks to break sanctions that we just don't have enough capital or political clout to do so."

The 1979 Iranian Revolution completely upended the political, social, and cultural makeup of the country. Massive economic changes ensued,

and big business and manufacturing elites left the country or were executed. Even so, wealth was partially co-opted by the new political for-
mation of the country. Indeed, independent business owners continued
to hold substantial sway and lobbying power throughout the Islamic
Republic.

The imposition of comprehensive sanctions on Iran is changing
this dynamic. Massoud, a longtime friend of Mahmood's and himself
a wealthy business owner not tied to the regime, sums up the state of
affairs: "These sanctions are allowing the Islamic Republic to do something that they couldn't since the revolution: make those loyal to them
the complete winners as far as wealth concentration and creation is concerned. The sanctions have created the economic revolution that makes
those tied to the Revolutionary Guard and Khamenei's inner circle the
owners of the vast majority of wealth inside Iran."

This also means that some within the ruling establishment favor
the continuation of sanctions because it generates massive wealth for
them. Hasan contextualizes this phenomenon: "So much of what you see
play out publicly, or what Western observers call the 'factionalism' of
the system in Iran, goes back to who sees themselves as rightful heirs of
this revolution and therefore as beneficiaries of the political and business connections Iran creates around the world. The sanctions have
only exacerbated this situation because it drags so much of the trade
into the black market, which means it ultimately benefits the Revolutionary Guard and those tied to Khamenei." As that happens, creating new
social classes with wide-reaching consequences, ordinary Iranians have
gotten poorer, the domestic sphere has become even more militarized
and securitized, and the battlefield mentality has come to dominate both
domestic and foreign policy decision-making in Iran.

THREE

When Iran Was Sanctioned

Since the moment it was established in 1979, the Islamic Republic of Iran has been subjected to a steady stream of sanctions. Over the years, their depth and breadth have dramatically increased: often gradually, at times by leaps and bounds. The existing patchwork of sanctions reflects diverse policy objectives and disparate legal frameworks, developed and evolved over forty-four years and implemented by different governmental and institutional bodies.

The most important element, however, is that sanctioning Iran is now a seemingly permanent fixture of US policy toward the Islamic Republic. This chapter recounts the history of escalating and increasing sanctions, broken into four major phases, spread out over nearly half a century. Moreover, it reveals how this sanctions regime has not just failed at its ideal outcome, which is to change the nature of Iran's government to one amenable to the West, but has also failed to force Tehran to capitulate at the negotiating table.

In fact, the history of sanctions demonstrates that Iran's attempts to negotiate have been smashed, above all, by Washington's recourse to sanctions. Moreover, here as in chapter 2, it shows how sanctions have mostly *strengthened* Iran's resolve to oppose US policy objectives. Worst of all, this recalcitrance has been achieved, as the previous chapter showed, at the expense of the Iranian people.

Ultimately, this chapter reveals how sanctions as a tool of coercive diplomacy are effective only within a narrow field: specifically, imposing sanctions is effective only in proportion to *the prospects of relieving them* in exchange for policy shifts. As such, their measure of efficacy lies in what can be obtained when they are removed, not what happens when they are imposed.

Therein lies the dilemma. Sanctions have become so extensive and so intricately woven that it will be difficult to offer significant, concrete relief, short of a major turnaround in key aspects of Tehran's domestic and foreign policies. Reaching that threshold for removing US sanctions is difficult to imagine. What is not difficult to imagine is Iran looking at the last four decades of sanctions, and concluding that the only policy choice more perilous than suffering the toll of sanctions is surrendering to them.

The Sanctions Toolkit

There are different ways to categorize sanctions. Although sanctions are usually analyzed as an economic tool, they could also be *diplomatic/ political, military, technological.*[1] *Diplomatic or political sanctions* impact a state's international reputation and standing rather than cause economic loss, which can be implemented by excluding the state from international organizations or limiting travel for its leadership.[2] *Military sanctions* are meant to cause strain by denying the state's access to military hardware and technical assistance.[3] *Technological sanctions* are usually aimed at impairing the technological development of a state, stunting economic growth.[4] *Economic sanctions* are the most common type of sanction and damage a state's ability to receive and implement economic resources, thereby "inflicting punishment."[5]

The United States employs sanctions that are enforced and regulated by the Treasury Department's Office of Foreign Assets Control (OFAC) by way of five different sources. The first source is *statutes*. There are six major legislations directly targeting Iran. But there are other more general ones that apply to Iran as well. Since 1977, most sanctions have been imposed under the statutory authority of the International Emergency Economic Powers Act (IEEPA). IEEPA authorizes the president to implement economic sanctions, with the intent to deal with any usual and extraordinary threat, which has its source in whole or substantial part outside the United States, to the national security, foreign policy, or economy of the US, if the president declares a national emergency with respect to such threat.[6] These measures regulate US citizens and lawful permanent residents, wherever located; entities organized under US law (e.g., corporations or nonprofits); all entities and persons located in the US; and entities owned or controlled by US citizens.

Executive orders are another source of sanctions. There are twenty-six of them targeting Iran. These are issued by the US president and can be rescinded by the executive branch. It is, however, important to consider that executive orders cannot overcome legislative action. The third source of sanctions, US Justice Department civil lawsuits, aims at seizing Iranian assets to pay compensation to victims of terrorism, currently amounting to billions of dollars.[7] The fourth source is states' divestment acts. Thirty-two states and the District of Columbia have enacted divestment legislation or policies, directing state pension administrators to divest from companies that meet with, have significant trade ties to, or invest in Iran.[8] Given the importance of some of these states in the global financial system (e.g., New York), they carry a significant weight. They also increasingly have their own enforcement mechanisms, operating in parallel with federal authorities. Finally, there is the private sector, to whom compliance with sanctions is essentially subcontracted; this sector often overcomplies with these restrictions, which it views as more economically expedient than inadvertently crossing a red line.

Traditionally, economic sanctions are country-based sanctions, which prohibit virtually all activity and transactions involving a certain country, like Iran. These sanctions generally bar trade in goods and services, as well as financial transactions with persons who ordinarily reside within the country or are affiliated with its government. There are often general licenses that allow humanitarian trade, the exchange of information and informational materials, personal communications, and legal services. The use of country-based sanctions has decreased with the advent of more flexible list-based (or smart) sanctions, which allow more precise targeting of persons and groups who pose a threat to US national security interests. OFAC prohibits transactions between US individuals and entities with organizations on the Specially Designated Nationals and Blocked Persons List, or SDN list, which is amended on an "as-needed" basis. It targets persons involved in terrorism, weapons proliferation (particularly weapons of mass destruction), narcotics traf-

ficking, transnational organized crime, human rights abuses, and genocide. Between these two, there are sanctions that target specific sectors
of the sanctioned country's economy (e.g., US sanctions imposed in 2014
to punish Russia for its invasion and annexation of Crimea). Starting in
the late 1990s, Washington has also used extraterritorial and secondary
sanctions to target non-US persons who do business with Iran. These
measures regulate US markets by restricting foreign financial institutions' correspondent accounts in the United States, if they have any ties
with individuals and entities sanctioned by the US.[9]

No country in the world has been the target of this array of sanctions
to the extent experienced by Iran over the past four decades.

Weaving the Spiderweb

In February 1979, Iran's Islamic Revolution toppled the ruling monarchy
of the Shah Mohammad Reza Pahlavi, who was a staunch US ally. Since
then, sanctions have been a significant component of US policy toward
Iran. These measures were imposed by different US administrations in
four waves: 1979–95, 1996–2006, 2006–16, and 2018–present. Taken together, these ever-increasing waves demonstrate the US commitment
across bipartisan presidential administrations to punish, contain, and
coerce Iran through economic warfare.

The turning point in US-Iranian relations occurred on November
4, 1979: in response to President Jimmy Carter allowing the deposed
shah—exiled in Mexico—to enter the United States for cancer treatment,
fifty-five American diplomats were taken hostage in Tehran. The Carter
administration responded, in part, by banning the importation of Iranian crude oil.[10] Over the course of the following contentious months,
a string of executive orders froze $12 billion worth of Iranian govern-
ment assets within the jurisdiction of the United States,[11] barred exports
of US goods to Iran, severely restricted financial transactions with the
country, banned all Iranian imports,[12] and prohibited US citizens from
traveling to, or conducting business with, Iran.[13] The same year, the labeling of Iran as a "state sponsor of terrorism" triggered several financial
sanctions.[14]

Starting, then, with Carter's first unilateral sanctioning of Iranian
crude oil, this *first wave of sanctions (1979–1995)* originated as a US
response to the embassy hostage crisis, Tehran's more broadly anti-

American policies, and its support for violent groups that threatened US allies in the region. These sanctions (unlike the third and fourth waves) were largely confined to restricting material transfers to and from Iran, not blocking financial transactions and third-party investment in Iran. But while US sanctions were intended to compel Iran to cease supporting acts of terrorism and anti-American acts more generally, they also had a broader strategic purpose: to limit Iran's power and influence in the Middle East.[15]

In 1981, the Algiers Accords formally resolved the United States–Iran hostage crisis, and established the Iran–United States Claims Tribunal at The Hague (which continues to arbitrate government-to-government cases resulting from the 1980 break in relations and freezing of certain of Iran's assets).[16] The accords led to the removal of the most punitive measures against Iran by President Ronald Reagan, after the hostages were released on his inauguration.[17] Thus, less than two years after Carter's initial response, the US sanctions regime seemed to have ended.

Yet a few years later, in January 1984, sanctions were reimposed, when the State Department designated Iran as a state sponsor of terrorism, for its alleged involvement in the 1983 bombing of US Marine barracks in Beirut.[18] The designation denied Iran, in the midst of its war with Iraq, access to financial aid, dual-use technology (that is, technology with both civilian and military applications), and US defense exports.[19]

Previously, the 1961 Foreign Assistance Act and the Arms Export Control Act barred US foreign assistance to countries listed by the State Department as sponsors of terrorism. Successive foreign aid appropriations laws since the late 1980s have banned direct assistance to the Islamic Republic, with no waiver provisions. The US Export-Import Bank cannot finance any entity that, among others things, was sanctioned under the Iran Sanctions Act. In August 1986, Congress passed the Arms Export Act, barring Iran from receiving US arms and spare parts.[20] The following year—invoking continued Iranian aggression against US-flagged vessels in the Persian Gulf and Tehran's purported support for terrorism—President Reagan issued an executive order banning all imports of Iranian crude oil, goods and services, although without banning the trading of Iranian oil overseas.[21]

Next, at the end of the Iran-Iraq War in 1988, Washington sought to blunt Tehran's efforts to reconstitute its conventional military capability. The Iraq Sanctions Act of 1990 provided for a "presumption of denial"

for all dual-use exports to Iran, which could be waived only if "essential
to the national interest."[22] In 1992, Congress passed the Iran-Iraq Arms
Nonproliferation Act, prohibiting other countries from selling conventional and unconventional weapons to Iran.[23] Should another country
violate the 1992 act, the result would be suspension of US assistance,
technical exchange, co-production agreements, and sales of US arms to
the incriminated country for a period of one year. That same act even
requires US representatives to vote against international lending to that
country for a period of one year.

Iran has not received any significant international financial loans
since 2005. Even in 1993, the United States voted its 16.5 percent share
of the World Bank against loans to Iran of $460 million for electricity,
health, and irrigation projects. Nonetheless, the loans were approved by
a majority vote.[24]

Yet the Clinton administration took even more punitive steps, on
account of Iran's alleged support for violent movements in the Levant
(primarily Hezbollah and the Palestinian Islamic Jihad), as well as its
signing of a contract with Russia to complete the Bushehr nuclear power
plant.[25] In 1994, the administration began by targeting more Iran-related
entities to be sanctioned.[26] In 1995, it proscribed all US investment in
Iran's oil and gas sectors,[27] and subsequently, all involvement by US
firms in developing,[28] or helping to develop, Iran's oil industry.[29] Shortly
thereafter, an executive order barred all US trade and investment affiliated with the Islamic Republic,[30] as well as re-export by third countries
of US products to Iran.[31] And then, in March 1995, President Clinton, in
a "state of emergency" declaration with respect to Iran, added a prohibition on US companies knowingly exporting goods to a third country for
incorporation into products destined for Iran.

Since then, every US administration has extended the "state of emergency" status on an annual basis. Ironically, the period preceding the
1995 embargo had witnessed a sharp rise in trade between Iran and the
United States. The US had then become Iran's sixth-largest source of imports, with nearly $2.2 billion worth of trade from 1991 through 1994.
But this did not stop the Clinton administration. Instead, its regime of
sanctions exacerbated Iran's marginalization internationally. Perhaps
more worryingly, Clinton's actions also forced Iran to increasingly look
to the East, particularly to Russia and China, as a means of surviving
Washington's relentless economic onslaught.

The Long Arm of Sanctions

Yet in Washington there was growing frustration with the limited impact of sanctions on Iran's policies at home and abroad. Cognizant that without cutting off third-party exchanges with Iran, US sanctions would have only limited effect, Washington focused on the extraterritorial reach of its measures.

Thus came the *second wave of sanctions (1996–2006).* Enacted in August 1996, the Iran-Libya Sanctions Act (later renamed the Iran Sanctions Act, or ISA) was the first dramatic example of these new efforts to deter foreign companies from investing in Iran's energy sector through extraterritorial sanctions.[32]

ISA constituted a penalty that was meant to last. The prohibition was scheduled to expire, unless extended, on December 31, 2016. After its inception in 1996, legally, in order for the United States to terminate sanctions, ISA stipulated three necessary elements: (1) The president must certify that Iran has ceased efforts to design, develop, or acquire nuclear, chemical, and biological weapons, as well as ballistic missile technology, (2) Iran must be removed from the US list of state sponsors of terrorism, and (3) Iran must not pose a significant and foreseeable threat to US national security interests or its allies.

European countries vehemently opposed these secondary sanctions, both as a matter of principle and because they were engaged in a process of "critical dialogue" with Tehran at the time.[33] An ISA waiver was issued, in order to avoid penalizing European companies like Total, Gazprom, and Petronas for investing in Iran. Even so, ISA was a powerful prohibition both on companies doing business with Iran and on US officials themselves from ending the sanctions.

There have been brief moments that punctuate the continuing increase in sanctions. In 1999, for example, President Clinton used his waiver power to authorize the sale of medicine and food to Iran. And he did so again in 2000 to enable the import of pistachios, carpets, and caviar from that country.[34] Since April 1999, in fact, regulations on food and medical exports have permitted US sales of food and medical products to Iran as long as they were labeled humanitarian items. An April 2000 regulation relaxed the import ban for ten years. But Iran's growing difficulties in accessing the global financial system meant that the exemptions were increasingly futile, as international banks considered the cost of conducting due diligence to deal with Iran not worth the benefits.

Yet further alleviation of economic pressure was not forthcoming. Instead, heightened US concern over Iranian-Russian nuclear cooperation quickly closed this brief window of lessening, not increasing, sanctions.

In 2000, Congress passed the Iran Nonproliferation Act, ordering sanctions on foreign entities assisting Iran in developing weapons of mass destruction (WMD) and its ballistic missile programs.[35] Following the Bush administration's condemnation of the "rogue states" aligned in an "axis of evil," the 2000 Iran Nonproliferation Act later became the Iran–North Korea–Syria Nonproliferation Act (INKSNA) after the enactment of laws expanding its provisions to Syria (2005) and North Korea (2006). Even so, since 2000, INKSNA has authorized sanctions on foreign persons (that is to say, nongovernment actors) who are determined, in a report by the administration, to have assisted Iran's WMD programs. Sanctions imposed include a prohibition on US exportation of arms and dual-use items to the sanctioned entity, as well as a ban on US government procurement and on imports to the United States from the sanctioned entity. INKSNA also banned US extraordinary payments to the Russian Aviation and Space Agency in connection with the international space station, unless the president certified that the agency had not transferred any WMD or missile technology to Iran within the preceding year.

After the 9/11 attack on the United States, sanctions targeted not only Al-Qaeda but also, subsequently, Iran. An executive order by President Bush froze the US-based assets of institutions suspected to have been supporting international terrorism.[36] Additionally, it implemented a ban on US transactions with these entities. Under INKSNA, many institutions were blacklisted following the attack.[37]

During George W. Bush's presidency, attention shifted squarely to concerns about Iran's potential for making nuclear weapons. After Iran's covert uranium enrichment activities were brought to light in 2002, the EU-3 (France, United Kingdom, and Germany) engaged in a partially successful diplomatic effort with the Islamic Republic. The two sides reached an agreement,[38] pursuant to which Tehran suspended enrichment and allowed intrusive inspection of its sites through implementation of the International Atomic Energy Agency (IAEA) Additional Protocol.[39] In return, the EU-3 promised economic and energy cooperation.[40]

Yet the United States sidelined these EU negotiations, instead imposing a new set of sanctions in June 2005, which blacklisted individuals and entities supporting Iran's nuclear and missile programs.[41]

From Unilateral to Multilateral

By January 2006, unable to bridge differences between the two sides, the EU-3's diplomatic initiative ended in failure. Consequently, Iran resumed its uranium enrichment activities, and, subsequently, the IAEA referred the situation to the UN Security Council.[42] *This led to the third wave of sanctions (2006–2016),* marked by multilateral measures and financial sanctions to coerce Iran.

Partly, then, in response to reports that Iran was making progress in its nuclear program, the US Congress passed the 2006 Iran Freedom Support Act (IFSA).[43] It codified previous executive orders banning investment in and imports from Iran; also, "promotion of Iranian democracy" became official US policy. But the most significant innovation of the 2006 act was the decision to turn to financial sanctions, as a complement to more traditional measures Tehran had appeared able to circumvent.[44]

The US Treasury Department began blacklisting major Iranian banks, and pressuring and cajoling other states to follow suit.[45] During 2006–16, the department conducted a campaign—termed as "targeted financial measures"—to persuade foreign banks to cease transactions with Iran. As part of this effort, Treasury officials briefed banking officials around the world on Iran's use of the international financial system to fund terrorist groups and acquire weapons-related technology.[46]

This period is characterized not only by US-imposed financial sanctions but also by the UN Security Council sanctioning Iran. Three UN Security Council resolutions (1737, 1747, and 1803) imposed sanctions on Iran's nuclear program and WMD infrastructure. Resolution 1929 (June 9, 2010) asserted that major sectors of the Iranian economy supported Iran's nuclear program, and, in response, authorized UN member states to sanction civilian sectors of Iran's economy. It also imposed binding limitations on Iran's development of nuclear-capable ballistic missiles and imports and exports of arms. The UN sanctions on Iran were enacted by the Security Council under Article 41 of Chapter VII of the UN Charter and applied to all UN member states.

Barack Obama's 2008 election appeared to herald a greater emphasis on engagement, rather than simply punishment, in Washington's approach toward Iran.[47] Still, the two-track policy remained at the core of Obama's approach: the belief being that a good-faith invitation to dialogue needed to be complemented by continued—and even sharpened—pressure, if it were to produce results. This was seen as all the more relevant after Tehran appeared to spurn the first US entreaties.

Consequently, on November 6, 2008—that is, the week of Obama's election, more than two months before his inauguration—new regulations were imposed, which barred foreign banks or persons from accessing the US financial system to acquire dollars for any transaction involving Iran (known as "U-turn transactions").[48] There was no blanket ban on foreign banks or persons paying Iranian entities in US dollars, provided that no bank accessed the US financial system to replenish its supply of dollars to accomplish their transactions with Iran. Even so, with many financial institutions worldwide halting their business with Iran, and the United States barring Iranian banks from dealing in dollars, Iran virtually became a financial pariah.[49]

Accordingly, between 2009 and 2012, the United States both toughened its own pressure and turned to the UN Security Council for additional measures. In fact—partly in response to developments such as Iran's post-2009 presidential election crackdown and the failure of an effort to swap a portion of Iran's stockpile of enriched uranium for nuclear fuel rods,[50] partly in response to pressure from Congress—the Obama administration devised ever more comprehensive economic penalties.

These culminated in 2010 in the adoption of the Comprehensive Iran Sanctions, Accountability, and Divestment Act (CISADA), which targeted individuals and entities aiding Iran in developing its energy sector, took aim at Tehran's ability to import petrol, and restricted its ability to engage in financial transactions.[51] CISADA includes a "special rule" pursuant to which firms that pledge to verifiably end their business with Iran and forgo any future contracts with the country are exempted from sanctions. It also meant to expand a bottom-up democratization of Iran by sanctioning alleged human rights abusers and facilitating freedom of speech on the internet.[52]

The United States benefited at this time from a significant diplomatic and political alignment with its European counterparts. After the 2010 passage of Resolution 1929, European Union (EU) sanctions on Iran became nearly as extensive as those of the US. This shift contrasted with earlier periods, such as when the EU countries refused to join the 1995 US trade ban on Iran.

Over time, the Obama administration issued more executive orders to penalize Iranian officials for their suspected role in nuclear and missile programs; human rights abuses;[53] and alleged financial and operational assistance to the Syrian regime in suppressing antigovernment protests. An International Atomic Energy Agency (IAEA) report in late 2011 detailing the possible military dimension of Iran's nuclear program added to the momentum for more pressure.[54] Targets included Iran's petrochemical industry and, again, persons tied to its missile and nuclear programs.[55]

In 2011, the Obama administration began to focus on sanctions to disrupt Iran's finances, a decision that would reverberate over a decade and affect millions of people's lives (as seen in the previous chapter). Given US dominance in the now fully digitized global financial system and the power of the US dollar, Washington could curb Iran's access to the global banking system in ways that were previously unfathomable.

The Obama administration took banking restrictions to a new level, labeling the entire Iranian financial sector—including its Central Bank (CBI)—a "jurisdiction of primary money laundering concern."[56] Significantly, on December 31, 2011, under congressional pressure and after obtaining flexibility for incremental implementation to mitigate any impact on global energy prices, Obama signed the National Defense Authorization Act of 2012 (NDAA 2012), in which section 1245 bars foreign banks from processing oil receipts through the CBI, with the goal of gradually depleting Iran's revenues.[57]

Equally important, the administration ordered domestic financial institutions to impound all remaining Iranian governmental assets and sanctioned any third-country purchase of Iranian oil and petroleum products,[58] save for countries already exempted under the National Defense Authorization Act of 2012.[59] Expressing frustration at what it considered to be continued Iranian defiance, on August 1, 2012, Congress passed the Iran Threat Reduction and Syria Human Rights Act (TRA or ITRSHRA), which codified several previous executive orders; expanded both the list of sanctionable activities and attendant penalties; banned the provision of messaging services for conducting financial transactions and shipping insurance; and prohibited repatriation of Iran's oil receipts.[60] ITRSHRA required reports on electronic payments systems, such as the Brussels-based Society of Worldwide Interbank Financial Telecommunications (SWIFT), that process transactions for Iranian banks. That law also authorizes, but does not mandate, sanctions against SWIFT or against electronic payments systems.

Despite purported White House objections—based on concern that it "threaten[ed] to undercut and confuse" other sanctions—2012 concluded with adoption of yet another harsh measure, the Iran Freedom and Counter-Proliferation Act of 2012 (IFCPA).[61] It blacklisted the entire energy, shipping, shipbuilding, and port-operating sectors in Iran as "entities of proliferation concern." This set of decisions was strengthened by monitoring sanctions evasions and punishing those who breach the US decisions.[62]

None of these 2011 economic measures (as we examine in subsequent chapters) were effective in ending Iran's nuclear program. But they were devastatingly effective in inflicting pain on the country's economic well-being.

Then, in Iran's 2013 presidential elections, Hassan Rouhani—a pragmatic politician—was swept to victory. In response, the United States pushed the pause button in imposing new sanctions on Iran. And eventually, after more than two years of arduous negotiations, the two sides in July 2015 concluded the Joint Comprehensive Plan of Action (JCPOA).[63]

A Heavy Lift

The prolonged process that led to JCPOA was tortuous. It took more than a decade of diplomatic fits and starts and a perilous sanctions-versus-centrifuges race for Iran and the P5+1/E3+3 (the UN Security Council's five permanent members plus Germany) to agree to a core compromise: acceptance of a limited and tightly monitored uranium enrichment program on Iran's soil in return for reintegration into the global economy.[64] More than two years of grueling multilateral diplomacy culminated in a meticulously parsed 159-page accord that received unanimous Security Council endorsement on July 20, 2015.[65] The agreement then went through a trial by fire in the US Congress and the Iranian parliament. Once it emerged unscathed, it entered into force on October 18, 2015—designated as Adoption Day per JCPOA's calendar. This triggered the start of Iran's rollback of its nuclear program and cooperation in resolving the International Atomic Energy Agency's long-standing questions about its past nuclear activities.

Implementation Day occurred on January 16, 2016, after the IAEA certified that Iran had fulfilled its key commitments under the agreement, which prompted sanctions relief. The quick progress surprised most observers and dismayed accord critics. Its Iranian detractors were concerned that President Rouhani's eagerness for sanctions relief had led him to hasten rolling back the nuclear infrastructure, irreversibly damaging it and depriving Tehran of leverage to ensure that the West delivered its end of the bargain.[66] US opponents of JCPOA were deeply dissatisfied with how the IAEA closed the file on allegations of the program's past military dimensions, saying the JCPOA Joint Commission (the seven negotiating parties, coordinated by the EU) had made exemptions that allowed Iran to skirt some obligations.[67]

The criticism missed the bigger picture. Speeding implementation accelerated the core trade-off that motivated the deal: unshackling Iran's economy from sanctions while closing all potential pathways for weaponizing its nuclear know-how. The decisions to grant exemptions, known as memorializations, are standard for implementing a technically complex agreement; none impinged on the constraints that rendered nuclear weaponization virtually impossible.[68] Their confidential nature—likewise, hardly exceptional in the nonproliferation field—was the result of the procedural requirement that all eight Joint Commission members approve publication of internal documents. Several refused: some out of concern for a political backlash over details of what critics on both sides viewed as additional concessions, and others not wishing to politicize the IAEA's work.

A vast array of US, EU, and UN nuclear-related sanctions on Iran were relaxed on Implementation Day. In the ensuing months, the impact on Iran's economic performance became increasingly tangible: oil production and exports returned to pre-sanction levels of 3.85 million barrels per day, of which around two million were exported; the country absorbed more than $11 billion of foreign direct investment, the highest annual level in nearly two decades; trade with the EU increased by 42 percent; Iran regained access to $55 billion of previously frozen assets; inflation dropped from a peak of 45 percent in 2013 to less than 8 percent in December 2016; Iranian companies signed contracts worth $150 billion with major European, Asian, and even US firms. The International Monetary Fund (IMF) forecasted that the economy would grow 4.5 percent during the 2016–17 fiscal period, up from 0.5 percent the previous year.[69]

Still, sanctions relief fell short of its promise. Perhaps most important, Iran struggled to restore normal international banking relations. While some second- and third-tier international banks resumed providing financial services, first-tier banks did not.[70] This hampered reintegration into the global economy, which, along with low oil prices, dashed highly inflated public expectations of a rapid recovery. Each side blamed the other. Iranian foreign minister Javad Zarif complained:

> [The US Treasury] goes out and tells people that "it's OK to do business with Iran, but" . . . and then there are five pages of ifs and buts. So at the end of the day, the banks say, "we'll take the safe road" . . . As far as the United States government is concerned . . . it took [it] seven months to issue licenses for seventeen out of the 118 planes Airbus plans to sell [to Iran].[71]

US officials pointed to the unprecedented complexity of untangling the sanctions and to their extensive efforts: publishing hundreds of pages of guidelines; dozens of multi-agency trips to explain sanctions relief to Iran's trading partners; and even then–secretary of state John Kerry's efforts, including personally encouraging European banks to engage Iran.[72] Never before had the United States repealed so many sanctions at once and needed to demonstrate results in a short period of time. So, of course, unanticipated complexities abounded.

The primary US embargo, which since the 1980s has broadly prohibited US persons from engaging in transactions with Iran, remained in force, though with a few exceptions: now, US-Iran trade could include civilian aviation, food and humanitarian goods, Iranian caviar, pistachios, and carpets. So too did secondary US sanctions remain, specifically those related to Iran's regional policies, ballistic missiles program, and human rights record.[73] Moreover, thirty-two US states and the District of Columbia maintained their own sanctions against Iran that targeted contracting, public trust, and insurance divestment and banking.[74] There were also sanctions of individuals and entities: of the 600 sanctioned pre-JCPOA, more than 200, including ones with links to the economically omnipresent Islamic Revolutionary Guard Corps, remained blacklisted by the Treasury Department's Office of Foreign Assets Control (OFAC).

Navigating this complex web of residual sanctions within Iran's opaque economy proved difficult. Due diligence is costly and cumbersome, and its standards are ill-defined. This adversely affected businesses' risk-reward calculus of trying to comply while operating within the Iranian economy's opaque ownership structure. The costs, after all, are not theoretical: since 2004, the United States has levied more than $15 billion in fines for violations.[75]

One of the most challenging sanctions was the ban on Iran's access to the US financial system. There had been various workaround attempts—OFAC clarifications (as obtuse as the restriction is severe); Iran's efforts to circumvent by denominating its trade in other currencies; symbolically significant deals like Boeing's sale of eighty civilian aircrafts, the largest Iran-US contract in thirty-seven years—that both sides hoped would have a snowball effect. None did much to resolve the problem.[76]

These difficulties bring to light the challenges of effectively removing US sanctions and dissipating their chilling effect. Practical considerations also stand in the way. Even assuming Iranian willingness to compromise, the standard for lifting US sanctions is high. The president can modify or revoke an executive order, but most of the sanctions have been codified by Congress, thereby limiting even an amenable president's room to maneuver.[77] The president can exercise their waiver authority or order greater flexibility in enforcing the penalties, but such short-term and easily reversible steps are unattractive to the sanctioned country, which often mistrusts Washington.[78] So even after JPCOA's implementation, at a seeming moment of triumphant diplomatic accord, the sanctions' chill stayed stubbornly in place.

The Pendulum Swings Back

A shadow was cast over the accord's survival in November 2016 with the election of Donald Trump, an avowed JCPOA critic. In the Trump administration's first year in office, contradicting the spirit of JCPOA, Congress enacted the 2017 Countering America's Adversaries through Sanctions Act, which imposed sanctions on individuals and entities associated with Iran's ballistic-missile program, or with the sale or transfer to Iran of military equipment.[79] For its part, the Trump administration blacklisted nearly a hundred Iran-related individuals and entities for their involvement in Iran's ballistic-missile program, for Iran's support of nonstate actors, and for the country's human rights violations.[80]

The US also labeled Iran's Islamic Revolutionary Guard Corps as a Foreign Terrorist Organization (FTO). This was significant not only because it was the first time an official branch of a state's armed forces has been designated as such by the United States. It was also significant because, as will be seen in the next chapter, the IRGC maintains an expansive role in Iran's opaque economy.[81] The Trump administration managed to turn the IRGC into the pariah organization par excellence, making it the most-sanctioned entity on the SDN list.

By the summer of 2017, Iran's economic growth stalled due to uncertainties around JCPOA's fate that drove away much-needed foreign investment and left the market in limbo. Then, on May 8, 2018, Iran's worst fears were realized: the Trump administration officially ended US participation in JCPOA.[82] Without the United States, JCPOA's entire balance of give-and-take was disrupted. And Iran stood to lose most—if not all—of the economic dividends the deal had promised it.

Then came the *fourth round of sanctions (2018–present)*. These "maximum pressure" sanctions of the Trump administration arrived in two major tranches: an initial set of non-oil sanctions on August 7, 2018, and a second, more significant batch on November 5 against over 700 persons and entities, including around 300 new targets.[83] As per previous sanctions (2010–13), these latter sanctions targeted Iran's lifeline: its oil exports.

Officially aimed at reducing these exports to zero, the Trump administration's maximalism helped it remove as much Iranian oil from the market (approximately one million barrels per day) on its own, as its predecessor did with international support in the years before JCPOA.[84] More damaging to the Iranian economy than the reduced volume of oil exports was a new requirement under US sanctions: the oil exports' proceeds—which constituted 35 percent of government revenue, as per the annual budget at the time—remained locked in escrow accounts, which can only be used for imports from those countries.[85] (The United States did grant exemptions to eight Iranian oil customers, but only as long as they continued to significantly reduce the volume of their crude imports.)[86]

On April 22, 2019, the US State Department announced that no additional waivers would be granted after May 2, in order to drive Iranian oil exports as close to zero as possible. Iranian officials dismissed Washington's ability to achieve its objective of zero exports. Still, the measure proved effective in precipitating a sharp drop in Iran's crude oil sales, which fell from around 2.5 million barrels/day (mbd) in April 2018 to under 0.5 mbd in December 2019.[87] Throughout the year, the United States continued to expand and enforce its sanctions designations.[88] Among the most significant of these amplified sanctions were: labeling the IRGC an FTO (April); sectoral sanctions against Iran's metal industries and major petrochemical firms (May–June); targeting Supreme Leader Ali Khamenei's office (June), as well as Foreign Minister Javad Zarif (July); blacklisting the Central Bank of Iran, as well as the country's national development fund, less than a week after the attacks against Saudi oil facilities (September); designating many of Iran's remaining unsanctioned banks for sanctions, in order to more comprehensively shut Iran's banks out of the international financial system (October); and designating a sanction of the company Islamic Republic of Iran Shipping Lines (December).[89]

In response to the US killing of the IRGC's General Qasem Soleimani on January 3, 2020, Iran fired ballistic missiles into Iraqi bases hosting US troops. Subsequently, on January 10, 2020, the Trump administration announced a new executive order, which imposed sanctions against Iran's construction, mining, manufacturing, and textile sectors; and it designated eight additional senior Iranian officials, and blacklisted more than two dozen firms and ships, linked to Iran's metals trade.[90]

Using the same executive order, Washington designated Iran's financial sector writ large for penalties, including the eighteen banks that remained connected to the global financial system.[91] Although the United States underscored humanitarian exemptions to the sanctions, the Europeans expressed misgivings about the decision to sanction the entire financial sector.[92] The Treasury Department also blacklisted the Mostazafan Foundation, a revolutionary foundation that acts as a massive economic conglomerate in Iran.[93] Other sanctions singled out firms active in sectors ranging from energy to metals and shipping.[94]

Also targeted were nuclear- and defense-related individuals, entities, and goods, ranging in scale and specificity from the Atomic Energy Organization of Iran to dual-use aluminum with possible military applications.[95] The United States designated senior Iranian political figures, including members of the Guardian Council, the interior and intelligence ministers, and security forces associated with human rights violations. After it became clear that the UN Security Council would not support US efforts to extend the Resolution 2231 ban on arms transfers to and from Iran, which expired on October 18, 2020, the United States imposed unilateral sanctions aimed at achieving the same objective.[96]

In February 2020, as the COVID-19 pandemic gripped Iran, the Treasury Department issued a General License to permit transactions with the Iranian Central Bank for purchase of humanitarian items.[97] The Trump administration even offered Iran assistance, via the World Health Organization, to help it battle the COVID-19 outbreak in early 2020. Perhaps it was to be expected that Iran refused what it saw as charity by a country that had impeded, with unwarranted and unilateral sanctions, its own ability to fight the pandemic.

All in all, the Trump administration levied over 1,500 sanction designations against Iran as part of its "maximum pressure" campaign, either by restoring designations lifted under JCPOA or introducing new ones against both nuclear and nonnuclear targets.[98] Indeed, throughout 2020, the Trump administration continued its policy of placing unilateral US sanctions on Iranian and Iran-linked targets: blacklisting key sectors, companies, and individuals, either through new designations or redesignations using additional authorities.[99] These sanctions appeared designed, at a minimum, to complicate the process of their repeal by a future US administration.[100]

When Joe Biden came to office in January 2021, many hoped that JCOPA would be rapidly restored.[101] At the time of this writing, however, the Biden administration has left the Trump-era sanctions untouched and has built on them. It is true that the Biden administration is negotiating over the scope of sanctions relief it might offer as part of a revived nuclear deal. But it has also kept the inherited sanctions in place. In some cases, it even expanded these penalties, placing emphasis on increased enforcement as JCPOA talks grounded to a halt in September 2022.[102]

With key Iranian economic sectors already blacklisted, the United States added to its sanctions against particular individuals and companies. These were mostly unrelated to JCPOA and Iran's nuclear activities. On March 9, 2021, the Biden administration unveiled its first Iran-specific sanctions, designating two men identified as IRGC interrogators, who allegedly committed human rights abuses during Iran's 2019–20 protests.[103] In December, it sanctioned a further thirteen persons and entities on human rights grounds.[104] For its part, the EU sanctioned eight individuals in April, including the IRGC commander and paramilitary Basij force head, and three Iranian prisons for allegedly helping suppress demonstrations in November 2019.[105] In September 2021, the US Treasury Department sanctioned four Iranians indicted for plotting to kidnap a US citizen, and in November designated six more persons and one company for alleged involvement in cyber-activity meant to disrupt the 2020 US presidential election.[106] In October, the United States issued sanctions targeting what it described as Quds Force networks raising revenue for the Revolutionary Guard's drone program and Middle East activities.[107]

In June, the Justice Department seized nearly three dozen websites linked to Iran's previously sanctioned radio and television union. In July, the Commerce Department blacklisted eight entities for Iran-related export violations; in December, it targeted companies in four countries "for diverting or attempting to divert U.S. items to Iran's military programs."[108]

There were several instances of Washington revisiting existing sanctions designations. In June 2021, the United States delisted five individuals and entities linked to the Iranian petrochemical trade, citing "a verified change in behavior or status," and in July and October, following legal challenges, removed sanctions against several individuals and companies designated in 2020 for links to Iran's ballistic missile program.[109] The Biden administration continued Trump-era sanctions waivers for Iraqi energy imports from Iran.[110]

With evidence coming to the fore of Iran's military support for Russia's war of aggression against Ukraine and its proliferation of drones and missiles throughout the region, the Biden administration started imposing more targeted sanctions. In March, the Treasury Department revealed sanctions against one Iranian individual and four entities for engagement in ballistic missile–related procurement following Iran's missile strike in Erbil and Huthi attacks in Saudi Arabia and the UAE.[111]

In May, Washington announced sanctions against an international network that sold hundreds of millions of dollars through oil smuggling and money laundering for both the IRGC-QF and Hezbollah, additionally emphasizing involvement of the "Russian Federation government and state-run economic organs."[112] Then, in July, the United States announced an executive order imposing financial and travel sanctions on people responsible for unjustly holding US nationals.[113] In response, the Iranian foreign ministry blacklisted sixty-one US officials and lawmakers in July, alluding to their support for the dissident group Mojahedin-e-Khalq.[114] From late May to August, the United States added four sets of energy-related sanctions.[115]

Following the death of Mahsa Amini on September 16, 2022, the Biden administration and many Western countries resorted to sanctions to condemn the regime's brutal crackdown against the protestors. The United States sanctioned Iran's "morality police" and seven senior Iranian security officials.[116] Additionally, on September 23 it issued a general license to facilitate greater access for Iranians to the internet and other online platforms due to the government's restriction of internet access, following their suppression of protests.[117] On October 10, the UK sanctioned the "morality police" along with five senior security and political figures.[118] On October 17, the European Union designated the "morality police," as well as Iran's information minister, condemning the use of force against the peaceful protesters.[119]

The following months saw a constant increase in sanctions from the international community. In November 2022, the United States sanctioned three Iranian entities, including the IRGC Aerospace Force, in a larger set of designations involving Russian- and UAE-based companies implicated in the transfer of drones (also known as UAVs, unmanned aerial vehicles) being used in Ukraine.[120] Additionally, the European Union approved sanctions against thirty-two individuals and entities over the Iranian government's iron-fisted approach against the protesters as well as UAV provisions to Russia; the UK in parallel sanctioned two dozen Iranian officials.[121] On January 6, 2023, Washington targeted sanctions at half a dozen individuals, including the director, linked to an Iranian company allegedly responsible for Iran's ballistic missile programs.[122]

A One-Way Ratchet

This history shows that sanctions have become so extensive and so intricately woven that it will be hard to offer significant, concrete relief. Short of a major—and improbable—turnaround in major aspects of the Islamic Republic's domestic and foreign policies, then, reaching the threshold for removing US sanctions in particular is hard to imagine. That leaves the option of a time-limited suspension or waiver, which, in turn, is likely to prompt at best time-limited and reversible Iranian reciprocal steps. JCPOA's sorry fate has deepened Iran's mistrust in the utility of such ephemeral economic reprieves.

The impact of sanctions, moreover, has acquired a life of its own, one that will outlast the measures themselves. This is because important trading and consumption patterns already have changed. Companies and countries that have shifted away from Iran—often at considerable expense—are unlikely to rush back, at least short of solid assurances that any decision to remove the penalties will be lasting rather than temporary.

Finally, there is another, considerable risk. Because the United States has placed all of its eggs in the sanctions basket, failure may appear to leave no other option for the US but war.

None of this is meant to indict sanctions as a policy tool. Even in the Iranian case, it is plausible that, in their absence, Tehran might have advanced further along the nuclear path. And they remain a preferable option to military confrontation.

But, at a minimum, it argues for a more nuanced understanding of sanctions and their efficacy. The history of Iranian sanctions, then, compels one to exhibit greater prudence and judiciousness in imposing them, and to resist piling on more sanctions when those already in place do not succeed. It demands constantly assessing and reassessing sanctions' social and economic consequences. Perhaps most of all, this history requires that the United States preserve sufficient nimbleness so that sanctions can be used—including through their removal—to advance negotiations in a diplomatic process, where a scalpel, not a chainsaw, is required.

FOUR

When an Economy Is Sanctioned

In 2011, President Barack Obama substantially changed the nature of US sanctions by preventing other countries from trading with Iran. Obama's sanctions prohibited the sale of Iran's main source of foreign exchange earnings: oil. The sanctions also cut off Iranian banks, including the Central Bank, from the international financial system. Even if Iran could export oil—or any other good—it would have difficulty in receiving the proceeds. Iran would have to settle for items a country was willing to sell (like tea from Sri Lanka), and receive such items through barter or by accepting indefinite IOUs.

This chapter presents two main arguments. First, *in tandem with sanctions, all economic indicators point to a sharp change from growth to stagnation or decline.* This shift is evident in aggregate economic data as well as in household-level indicators of incomes and employment obtained from survey data. It is evident in the rising ranks of the poor since 2011 and the decrease in the size of the middle class. Analysis of the data leaves little doubt that, while sanctions have hurt government finances, they have done greater harm to ordinary Iranians, impoverishing millions. This account contradicts arguments asserting that sanctions have not hurt ordinary people or, while admitting the opposite, blaming the impoverishment on the incompetence and corruption in Iran's ruling elite. Second, *reliance on markets, especially decisions to allow prices of*

74

foreign currencies and most goods to rise, explains why a decade of harsh economic sanctions has failed to instigate economic collapse, or change the regime or its behavior. Contrary to predictions of economic collapse, Iran's economy had enough flexibility to adjust to the loss of oil exports and prevent serious loss of output. To be sure, the adjustment entailed substantial loss of the average living standard, but the flow of goods and services continued and images of empty store shelves and long lines at distributions centers, characteristic of command economies, were rare. The argument that sanctioning one more individual or entity can do what the proverbial straw does to the camel's back—that is, to turn a failed sanctions policy into a success—has not proven to be true.

When the Obama sanctions took effect in 2011, oil prices were at their height and Iranians were enjoying rising living standards thanks to robust economic growth. Sanctions brought the oil boom to an abrupt end, leaving little doubt that they had reached their target. The stated purpose of the sanctions was to immiserate the Iranian people, so as to indirectly pressure Iran's leaders to limit their nuclear ambitions. But others in the West also saw these sanctions as an important tool to contain Iran by scuttling its economic growth. The oil boom of the 2000s saw Iran growing at a robust pace, which enabled Iran to project its power across the Middle East and challenge US hegemony. From this perspective, the objective of inflicting a persistent economic crisis on the Islamic Republic seemed at least as important as containing its nuclear program. Indeed, opponents of the Joint Comprehensive Plan of Action (JCPOA) relied on exaggeration: complaining about the economic benefits of giving Iran $150 billion as part of the nuclear deal, three times the actual size of the country's frozen assets abroad.[1]

In both views, the key to the success of the sanctions was how Iran's economy would respond to them. For those policymakers who wanted to contain Iran, economic crisis was the goal. For those interested in changing Iran's nuclear and regional policies, the crisis had to make life for ordinary Iranians hard enough to draw them into the streets, and then to elicit concessions from their leaders or force them out of power.

But as this chapter will argue—and as seen in the resiliency of Iranian society in chapter 1—economic collapse was never in the cards. Presenting quick collapse and regime change as a likely outcome, however, did prove useful in attracting support for the US sanctions from many quarters, including Iranians inside and outside Iran who would not have

approved of a policy that imposed economic misery for decades. Still, a
significant recession was unavoidable.

Pressure on the living standards of ordinary Iranians was always at the
core of the logic of sanctions, which in turn would lead them to exercise indirect pressure on the government to change its behavior. Although limits
on oil exports would first hit the government's purse, it was believed that
the shock would soon reach people's budgets. Two assumptions proved
false. First, that the blow would be so large as to send people into the
streets, risking their lives. In fact, there was at most a 15 percent reduction
in living standards (similar to what Argentines have experienced recently
for reasons internal to their economy). The protests in the fall of 2022 that
followed the tragic death of Mahsa Amini in police custody may not have
happened in the absence of the social restrictions that have sown resentments due to decades of social and legal discrimination against women,
although dissatisfaction with the economic conditions was certainly a
factor. While rising inflation provided an important backdrop to the uprisings, unlike in previous protests, social demands—beautifully captured
by the slogan "Women, Life, Freedom"—dominated the protesters' chants.
Linking the protests to economic sanctions, as some observers have done,[2]
is weakened by the fact that in 2021 the economy was growing and household incomes outpaced inflation by 11 percentage points.[3] Unemployment,
which affects youth especially hard and might have triggered more protests, had remained stable throughout the sanctions period.

The second assumption was that the people would blame their own
government, and not the United States. This assumption also proved
unrealistic, at least as far as blaming hardliners who had the last word
on Iran's foreign policy was concerned. Opinion polls taken in 2021
showed that after several years of sanctions, the popularity of pro-West
politicians such as Hassan Rouhani (president, 2013–21) and Javad Zarif
(foreign minister to Rouhani, 2013–21) declined as the popularity of conservatives like Ebrahim Raisi (president, 2021–) rose.[4] But, as the 2022
protests against forced hijab revealed, a year after Raisi had taken charge
of the government, the popular rage against the conservative ruling elite
was mainly directed at their social policies rather than policies that had
triggered the sanctions.

This chapter will show that living conditions for ordinary Iranians
have indeed declined significantly, back to where they were two decades
ago. The ranks of the poor have expanded and those of the middle class

narrowed. But if sanctions aimed to create a more politically moderate Iran, they failed.

To evaluate the impact of sanctions, this chapter begins with an account of their timing and intensity. Before 2011, the economic impact of sanctions was muted and difficult to distinguish from other factors that shook the economy. These included disruptions such as the war with Iraq (1980–88) and reconstruction (1989–97), which was followed by an oil boom in the 2000s.

But, starting in 2011, with oil prices at their peak, sanctions became the dominant factor, reducing oil exports and disrupting the country's international trade. In 2013, oil exports—the main source of foreign exchange and government revenues—were down by two-thirds (shown later in Figure 3). Financial sanctions added to the large negative shock from the cut in oil exports by isolating Iran from the global banking system and forcing Iranian traders to find workarounds for the secondary US sanctions at considerable cost. It was during this time that the United Arab Emirates (UAE) emerged as the main entrepôt for Iran's international trade. Financial restrictions deepened the economic blow in more complex and concealed ways, especially by encouraging corruption. As chapter 1 has shown, the consequence of these impacts has been widespread misery and social unrest.

Proving that Iran's current economic crisis stems from such financial sanctions is difficult. Separating the effect of the sanction from other factors is complicated by the fact that postrevolution Iran is not a stranger to economic turbulence. From 1980 to 1988, for example, the war with Iraq caused significant destruction and reduced Iran's oil exports to a trickle, clearly overwhelming any effect sanctions might have had. Together with the 1979 revolution itself, the war cut the GDP by one-third (see Figure 1).[5] Economic restructuring after the war initiated by President Rafsanjani (1989–97) produced its own shock, as markets replaced widespread rationing, causing living standards to stagnate from 1992 to 1995 (shown later in Figure 7). These market reforms provided the springboard from which the economy grew at a whopping 10.4% per year in the following two decades, although growth in the 2000s was mainly the result of the oil boom.[6]

Consequently, if sanctions played a role before 2011, their impact was overwhelmed by other factors, such as the Iran-Iraq War and the reconstruction effort that followed. As Figure 1 shows, postwar reconstruction

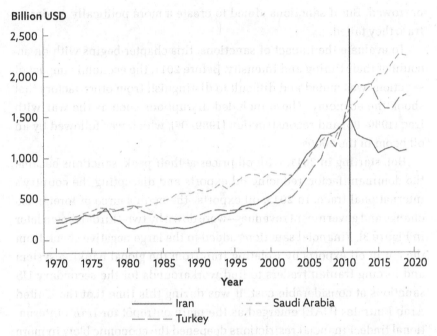

FIGURE 1. Economic growth in Iran, Saudi Arabia, and Turkey. GDP is in billions of constant international dollars (2017 PPP). PPP dollars use US prices to evaluate GDP in different countries. Source: Penn World Tables, version 10.0.

generated impressive economic growth before oil prices rose in the early 2000s, despite the sanctions that were then in effect.

Prior to Obama's 2011 financial sanctions, the 2008 global financial crisis caused a temporary decline in the world price of oil and halted Iran's economic growth. Still, the economy resumed its growth quickly. Just a few years later, in 2014, the world price of oil again fell (this time, from above $100 to about $40 per barrel); Iran's economy was hurt, but the impact was overshadowed by the effect of sanctions, which had pushed the country into recession since 2012. (The dip in Saudi GDP at this time, as seen in Figure 1, reveals the impact of the oil price collapse on Saudi Arabia.)

The timing of the impact of sanctions on Iran's economy is more easily established by considering the fluctuations in Iran's crude oil production and exports (see Figure 2).[7] As noted in the last chapter, oil exports fell from about 2 million barrels per day (mbd) in 2011 to less than half of that amount as sanctions tightened. Of more immediate relevance to the economy is the size of oil revenues in constant dollars and per capita.

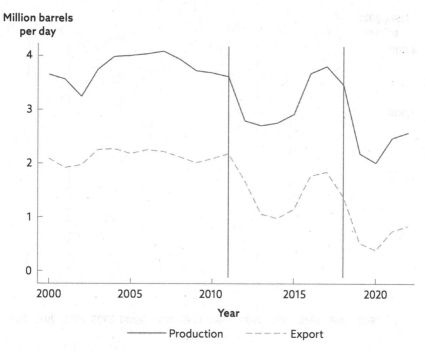

FIGURE 2. Crude oil production and exports (millions of barrels per day). Source: Federal Reserve Economic Data (FRED).

Figure 3 shows the relative size of the two oil booms enjoyed by Iran, in the 1970s and 2000s, and the fact that since Trump's sanctions, oil revenues per capita have been lower than they were in the 1960s.

Finally, further evidence of the detrimental effect of sanctions on the economy is found in the quick economic recovery that Iran enjoyed when sanctions eased briefly, during 2016–17, with the 2015 nuclear deal (JCPOA) in effect. The economy grew by 13% in 2016 and 7% in 2017 as oil exports and revenues increased. As Figure 2 shows, oil exports quickly bounced back to 2 mbd, the level before sanctions, and revenues in 2017 were nearly twice their level in 2015 (Figure 3).

Trump's withdrawal from JCPOA in 2018, followed by his "maximum pressure" campaign, put a quick end to this recovery. These actions cut oil exports by half and GDP by 6%, plunging the economy deeper into recession (shown later in Figure 4). Following Biden's election, oil exports increased to about 1.2 mbd in 2021, in part because Trump's departure weakened compliance by China and a few other recipients of Iranian oil and in part because Iran found more ways to get around the sanctions.

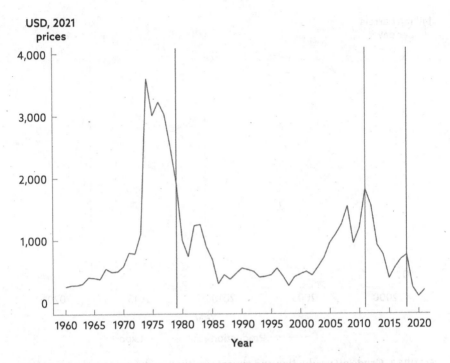

FIGURE 3. Oil revenues per person (2021 USD). Dollar values of oil revenues are deflated by the US CPI to bring their purchasing power to 2021, before dividing by population. Source: Central Bank of Iran and OPEC Annual Statistics.

However, the economy continued to suffer, as financial sanctions prevented Iran from easy access to the proceeds from these exports.

The Cost of Sanctions

How much has Iran and its economy lost from the sanctions? One method is to compare Iran's GDP to those of similar economies that were not sanctioned. For a simple comparison, consider the GDP of Iran alongside those of Saudi Arabia and Turkey in Figure 1.

Evaluated in international dollars (PPP), the three economies produced the same output around 2011; but after Obama's sanctions Iran's economy stalled, while its main regional rivals continued to grow. As a result, Iran's GDP today is much less than that of Saudi Arabia and Turkey. Other GDP measures that do not use PPP dollar values, such as

Iran's own official national accounts, show a less dramatic decline in Iran's GDP than the Penn World Tables data used in Figure 1, but they all tell the same story of the sudden emergence of a gap and the role of sanctions in Iran's economic stagnation after 2011. While this simple comparison leaves little doubt about the timing and general impact of the sanctions, it does not allow us to measure the size of the loss.

To measure how much Iran has lost because of the sanctions, we need a counterfactual. That is, what the economy *would* have done had there been no sanctions. Neither Saudi Arabia nor Turkey is a good counterfactual for Iran. The gap between Iran and Turkey post-2011 certainly exaggerates the size of Iran's economic loss, because Iran's GDP would have faltered with the decline in the price of oil even in the absence of sanctions, as did Saudi Arabia's GDP. Moreover, for a more accurate measurement, the comparator countries should be similar in economic complexity and government policies, which no single country is.

To measure the cost of sanctions more formally, we should use a group of countries with appropriate weights attached to the GDP of each. This is known as the synthetic control method (SCM), which constructs a "synthetic Iran" as the counterfactual.[8] The weights are calculated so as to minimize the distance between Iran and its synthetic counterparts for the period before sanctions. Gharehgozli and Ghomi employ SCM to estimate that the loss of GDP in Iran, respectively, was 17.1% over three years (2011–14) and 19.1% over four years (2011–15).[9] These are low compared to the 50% that has been reported in the case of Iraq sanctions in 1991.[10]

While SCM improves on the arbitrary selecting of comparator countries, the popularity of the technique should not hide its fragility. Changes in the list of countries or predictors (variables that predict the GDP) often yield different estimates. More generally, constructing counterfactuals for countries that differ from Iran in unquantifiable respects— institutions, level of corruption, and policy effectiveness—is hazardous. As the rise of China has taught us, in many ways each country has to carve its own unique path to economic growth.

Another approach, employed by Laudati and Pesaran, uses Iran's own past data to predict what the economy would have done in the absence of sanctions instead of relying on a set of comparator countries.[11] They employ a time-series structural model and data over the entire post–Iraq war period to estimate the impact of sanctions. Their estimate of the impact of sanctions over the period 1989 to 2019 is a loss of 2% of growth per year. This estimate is substantially lower than what Figure 1 or SCM studies indicate for the period of intense sanctions after 2011, when the growth rate fell by much more than 2% per year. For example, the change in the annual growth rate from before (2003–11) to after sanctions (2011–19) implied by Penn World Tables (PWT) data in Figure 1 is from 7.4% to –3.4%, over 10% per year. Iran's own official data for the same period record a drop from 5% to 1% (shown later in Figure 4).[12]

Estimates of the cost of sanctions in terms of lost economic growth can easily vary with the assumptions one makes about what might have happened in their absence. But what is not in dispute is that sanctions were instrumental in ending Iran's robust growth of prior decades. The discontinuity in a host of indicators noted above—oil exports, investment, currency value, and the growth rate of the GDP—leaves little doubt that sanctions dealt a serious blow to Iran's economy.

Oil and Vulnerability to Sanctions

Iran is unusually vulnerable to sanctions because it is a fairly open economy and it is a single commodity exporter. For the past two decades, imports have amounted to about 20% of GDP and its trade dependence (imports plus exports as % of GDP) to about 50% of GDP, which is about the same as Turkey or Russia. It is also highly reliant on oil exports, which makes Iran even more vulnerable to sanctions. In the past, crude oil exports accounted for more than 50% of all exports but have averaged about half as much in the past decade. Government revenues from oil, which can be thought of as the main target of sanctions, dropped from about 40% of all revenues in the proposed budget for 2010 to less than 30% under sanctions.

Oil exports are more easily tracked, stopped, and their proceeds frozen than exports of a variety of manufacturing goods, such as those from China. Government revenues from oil also determine the level of investment because most investments, public and private, can be traced to oil income as their source. Historically, government savings from oil revenues have been the largest determinant of economic growth in Iran. Private investment has played an important role as well, before and after the revolution, but it has generally followed government's lead. Government investment in infrastructure, and the credit it makes available to

private investors, are the most important determinants of overall investment in the country.

In the decades before 2011, high levels of investment, especially
public investment in infrastructure, reached about one-third of GDP and
enabled robust growth before sanctions. As a revolutionary country, Islamic Iran's business climate has not been conducive to private investment.[13] Nevertheless, before 2011, private investment grew by 8.8% per
year, faster than public investment at 5.4% per year.[14]

Both public and private investment proved highly vulnerable to sanctions. Public investment fell because sanctions reduced oil revenues,
and funds allocated for development expenditures are the first to be
sacrificed for more urgent current expenses. In 2018 and 2019, public
investment fell by a whopping 23% and 22% in real terms, much faster
than private investment, which fell by 6.6% in 2018 and registered zero
growth in 2019.[15] Private investment fell because it usually follows the
government lead and because sanctions increased economic uncertainty
by disrupting Iran's international trade, the exchange rate and inflation
(see below). As a result, total gross investment has averaged about 13% of
the GDP since 2018, about half its value in 2011, which is barely enough
to repair old capital (SCI national accounts data). The harsh lesson from
letting development outlays drop below replacement is being learned as
supplies of electricity, natural gas, and drinking water, once a source of
pride for the Islamic Republic, are disrupted. In winter 2023, the government had to cut natural gas to Iran's heavy industries, like steel, to maintain the supply to homes. Nevertheless, social media buzzed with the
news that the clock had turned back a century as animal dung replaced
natural gas in heating some homes in eastern Iran.

Resilience of the Non-oil Economy

Despite the vulnerability of oil exports to sanctions, Iran's economy has
proved more resilient than proponents of sanctions had anticipated. This
resilience is seen more clearly in the behavior of non-oil sectors, which
add up to what is called the non-oil GDP. The overall impact of sanctions
is better understood by focusing on the non-oil GDP, which accounts for
the output of some 95% of Iranian workers. Figure 4, which uses data
from the Statistical Center of Iran (SCI) that distinguish oil and non-
oil GDP, shows that under sanctions the non-oil GDP did much better

than the GDP with oil. In 2021, nonoil GDP was 26.0% higher in real terms than in 2011, compared to 10.2% for the total GDP. Figure 4 shows that under sanctions the gap between GDP and non-oil GDP shrank. In 2006, non-oil GDP was 71% of the total GDP rising to 86% in 2021. The growth of the non-oil GDP under sanctions, though very modest at 2.3% per year, is in sharp contrast to the dramatic accounts of economic collapse based on currency crashes, inflation, and loss of oil exports. The relative stability of the non-oil GDP has been a source of confidence for Iran's hardliners, who have tried to show that the Islamic Republic can not only withstand sanctions but can also grow. Later in this chapter, the reasons behind the relative stability of the non-oil GDP will be discussed and the potential for Iran's economy to grow while under US sanctions reassessed.

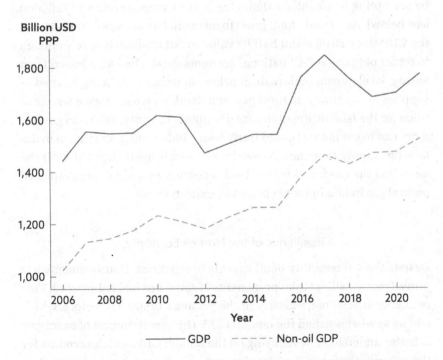

FIGURE 4. GDP and non-oil GDP in constant 2011 international dollars. Values reported in rials are converted to international dollars using the PPP conversion factor for 2011, equal to 5,855 rials per dollar. Source: Statistical Center of Iran.

How Sanctions Affect the Economy

For three decades, US sanctions targeted Iran's top officials and its government. As these sanctions failed to deliver results, their scope widened. In 2011, Obama's crippling sanctions extended to target the entire economy. While the impact of sanctions on the government and the rest of the economy cannot be cleanly distinguished, it is useful to look at the two separately. The former impact is easier to describe in terms of loss of oil revenues, but its scope goes beyond the government's operation. Because of its large role in the economy, what happens to the government affects the rest of the economy significantly. The government is responsible for incomes earned by the large civil service, about 15% of the labor force. Its anti-poverty welfare covers about one-tenth of the population, and its other transfers reach nearly everyone. Historically, the government has directly carried out the bulk of investments and supplied credit to the private sector for its investment. So, when its revenues shrink, everyone feels it.

Since the 1970s, government revenues have played a large role in the economy, although this dependence has diminished as the economy has become larger while oil exports have declined. In 2010, before sanctions, oil exports accounted for about 40% of all government revenues, and taxes about 30%. In 2020, oil revenues reached their lowest point, after Trump's maximum pressure campaign, while taxes had increased to 35%. A decade after sanctions had constrained its main source of income, the government had not found a replacement for the lost revenues. The government has recently improved its ability to borrow from the public. In 2020, it had reached a record 27%, rising from less than 10% a decade earlier. The sale of government properties, first as privatization and more recently to supplement revenues, has been controversial and marred with charges of corruption. In 2023, by order of the supreme leader, a commission was created and granted legal amnesty in order to expedite the sale of public property "not in use," expected to raise about 5% of the total revenues. The rest of the shortfall has been paid for with new printed money, which explains the rising rate of inflation during the decade.

Setting aside the impact of sanctions on the government, to describe the impact of sanctions on the population at large goes well beyond dependence on the public purse, involving the more complex mechanism of various markets. To describe this mechanism, it is helpful to start with the transmission of pressure—devaluation in the market for foreign currencies—and follow it to domestic prices and incomes in other markets.

The best way to see the close relationship between sanctions, devaluation, and inflation is with two graphs, Figures 5 and 6. In Figure 5, changes in the nominal exchange rate (rials per USD) are depicted with its real value, known as the real exchange rate, which are the nominal rates expressed in 2021 rials (the role of the real exchange rate is discussed later in this chapter). The timing of large devaluations—sudden increases in the nominal exchange rate—closely match the timing of sanctions. In a matter of a few months, the 2011 Obama sanctions doubled the value of the US dollar in terms of the rial. The devaluation unleashed inflation, which further reduced the value of the rial. By 2013,

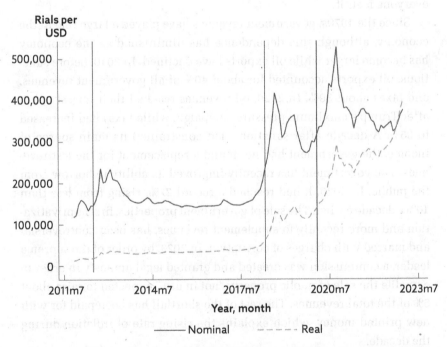

FIGURE 5. Shocks to the nominal and real exchange rates. Real exchange rates are nominal rates divided by the ratio of Iran's CPI to that of the US, both normalized to 100 in 2022. Source: Nominal exchange rates are taken from tgju. com (www.tgju.org/chart/price_dollar_rl/2).

when Iran agreed to meet the world powers to discuss limiting its nuclear program in return for the lifting of sanctions, the rial had lost two-
thirds of its value in 2010. The next big collapse of the rial occurred in
2018, when President Trump withdrew from the nuclear deal and reimposed sanctions, trebling the value of the dollar again. The COVID-19
pandemic dealt its own blow to the economy in 2020, further weakening
the currency.

The transmission of external shocks to the currency markets is rather
quick and sometimes occurs before the event itself. Each bout of sanctions first arrived as news of an impending drop in oil revenues, which
initiated a drop in the value of the rial in the free currency market as
individuals tried to move their savings into assets with rising value—
foreign currencies.

As unwelcome as devaluations generally are, they are necessary if the
economy is to adjust to the loss of oil exports. This is especially true of
an oil economy in which, as is explained later, the local currency is often
overvalued, discouraging the production of non-oil products that generate most of the jobs. To shield the local economy from these shocks, the
government distributed its own earnings of foreign currency at a large
discount. The multiple exchange rate system has been a large source of
corruption without fully protecting the economy from the shock of sanctions. How else to explain the sharp increases in the general price level
that closely followed devaluations?

Despite the subsidies, devaluations have quickly transmitted to all
sectors of the economy as local prices adjusted to the new price of foreign exchange. Figure 6 shows the movement of the general price level
in the last decade, which exhibits close correlation with the timing of
episodes of large devaluations. The changes in the rate of inflation since
Trump's maximum pressure campaign testify to the damage it has done
over and above depriving Iran of its oil income.

The proposition that the correlation between sanctions, the exchange
rate, and inflation implies causation running from sanctions to exchange
rate to inflation is difficult to prove. An alternative reading minimizes
the role of sanctions and instead blames endemic budget deficits resulting from internal pressures for social expenditures, which expand the
money supply, causing inflation, which devalues the rial. Such a reading of the evidence shifts the blame for Iran's economic problems from
sanctions to mismanagement. While no doubt this interpretation carries

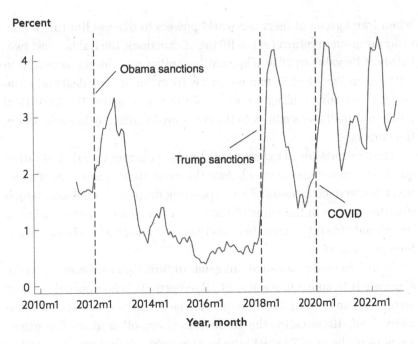

FIGURE 6. The timing of episodes of inflation. Three-month moving averages are the average of inflation in three consecutive months, the month before and after each month. Inflation measures the percent increase in CPI per month in urban areas. Source: Central Bank of Iran.

some truth, it is difficult to reconcile it with the timing of the violent movements of the exchange rate and inflation displayed above.

The Market for Foreign Exchange

Most of the time, Iran operates with multiple exchange rates. Including them all in Figure 5 would overcrowd it. The government has at different times used lower rates intended for specific purposes. The free-market rate is of interest because it reflects the expectations of millions of private actors and is therefore more informative about the impact of sanctions. The official rates are rigid, stay the same after sanctions have reduced the supply of foreign currencies, and do not affect local prices the same way that the free-market rate does. Having said that, the free-market rate often exaggerates the impact of sanctions, and its price does not reflect the true scarcity of foreign exchange, because it is a narrow market, and some buyers use it to move their wealth abroad. Most essential commodities, like food and medicine, are imported with the official, often subsidized, rates, so it is a mistake to interpret devaluations in the free market as an indication of reduction in average living standards. Some estimates put it at less than 10% of all foreign exchange transactions.

Because of its transparent and often exaggerated response to measures taken by the United States, the Iranian authorities are not always happy with the high visibility of the free-market rate, and from time to time have tried to suppress it. One reason for the continued operation of the free market is that not all transactions take place inside Iran and can be easily controlled. Some markets are outside Iran (Herat in Afghanistan, Soleimanieh in Iraqi Kurdistan, or Dubai) and operate the *hawala* system. In this system, no money changes hands and traders match the buyers of US dollars, usually located in Iran, with sellers abroad. The prices "discovered" by these parallel transactions are quickly reported in the Iranian media, setting off price increases in the local currency markets.

The unregulated free market allows purchases for speculation, capital flight, and foreign travel. A regulated market, called Nima, has been set up for licensed importers and exporters, and a highly subsidized market allocates foreign exchange for import of basic necessities. In the last few years, for example, when the free-market rate reached as high as 300,000 rials per USD, importers of medicine and essential foods could buy foreign currency from the Central Bank at 42,000 rials, a sixth of the organized market, which hovered around 250,000 rials. In practice, the free-market rate seems to affect prices in Iran the most; so, for the most part, market signals do their work.

Once foreign currencies rise in value in the official and unofficial markets, import prices rise quickly, which turn to full-fledged inflation when the Central Bank injects cash into the system to prevent bankruptcies. Eventually, wages and other personal incomes decline in real terms, as expected after an aggregate loss of resources, as markets transmit the aggregate shock to the household level. This is how sanctions threaten current prosperity, during the year they are in effect. But their cost extends beyond the current year because diminished resources and dim prospects for business reduce private investment, negatively affecting future incomes and employment.

For the most part, how sanctions lead to economic contraction follows the standard economic analysis of the impact of adverse aggregate shocks, such as loss of export revenues. Where Iran's experience differs from the standard case is the simultaneous loss of revenues for the government as the main exporter (oil), which reduces its ability to lead a recovery or assist the poor and affected businesses. A second and more important difference is the role of sanctions in inhibiting the market response that, in standard cases of loss of export revenues and devaluation, comes to the country's rescue by helping it to expand other exports and to produce domestically what it previously imported. These beneficial changes help limit the loss of revenue and in some cases can increase employment. Financial sanctions that prevent Iranian producers from repatriating their sales abroad is the main reason why Iran has not been able to take advantage of the market flexibility it has tolerated so far by allowing depreciation, movement of capital, and imports to continue.

Iran is not a poster child for a market economy, but markets play a significant role in its economy. Market signals, though often distorted by government actions, are nevertheless the main mechanism for the allocation of resources. What young people study, where the family lives, or how the family stores its savings are all guided by market prices, even though government influence distorts these decisions—investment in human capital is guided by publicly set wages and tenure rules,[16] interest rates have little to do with scarcity of capital,[17] and the exchange rate is manipulated to subsidize import of essential commodities.

In this respect, Iran's experience with sanctions differs from that of other heavily sanctioned countries, like Cuba and Venezuela. In Cuba, the rigid communist economy has stagnated under sanctions for decades. In left-leaning, populist Venezuela, fears of inflation and their adverse effect on incomes of the poor prompted its leaders to resist devaluation and resort to price fixing, which emptied the supermarket shelves from consumer goods and led to hyperinflation. The analogy with Venezuela may have led some analysts to predict hyperinflation in Iran.[18] So far, Iran's inflation has not turned into hyperinflation, which occurs when, fueled by the runaway printing of money, inflation continues to rise after the initial shock has passed. In populist regimes, the state prints money to protect the purchasing power of its social base, usually the poor. As Figure 6 shows, inflation has been high but not rising at a steady pace. After each period of intense prices increases, inflation came down, although the amplitudes have been rising and there is no guarantee that the government can control the pace of future price increases, especially if sanctions continue as tight as they have been.

Markets are not part of the ethos of the Islamic Republic. During its first decade, when the war with Iraq raged, the war economy naturally expanded the role of the state at the expense of the market. Coupons replaced market prices as the mechanism for the distribution of goods, and mosques replaced markets as the place to get your building materials and the new refrigerator. Today, as sanctions exacerbate economic uncertainty and rock the market system, the experience of the war years casts a dark shadow over private economic activity.

After the war, with the return of economic stability, markets revived under the leadership of President Akbar Hashemi Rafsanjani (1989–97). Coupons were discontinued, local chambers of commerce sprang up around the country, and markets regained their primacy. Critics from the left and the right dismiss Rafsanjani's reforms as the origin of the neoliberal economy they associate with the reformist administrations of Mohammad Khatami and Hassan Rouhani.

As luck would have it, the first test of the market's primacy arrived when the conservative administration of President Mahmoud Ahmadinejad (2005–13) was in office. Far from a pro-market reformer, Ahmadinejad identified with the populist policies of Hugo Chavez and Nicolas Maduro of Venezuela rather than his predecessors, Rafsanjani and Khatami. In 2012, when pressures from the tightening Obama sanctions were being felt in Tehran's currency market, the rial was gradually depreciating but then suddenly caved in October 2012, losing half of its value in a matter of few weeks (Figure 5). The government ordered security forces to round up money changers who loitered on the sidewalks of Ferdowsi Avenue near the Central Bank. In the ensuing chaos, as trade in the more organized foreign exchange markets (*sarrafis*) was disrupted, threatening the country's international trade, the government relented. The deputy governor of the Central Bank in charge of foreign transactions announced that money changers were welcome to operate legally while the official rate remained fixed. In an apologetic statement, she thanked traders for their service to the economy. The market had reasserted itself and from then on would lead the adjustments to sanctions.

Two years later, in July 2015, Iran and the Group of 5+1 would reach the nuclear accord known as JCPOA, which allowed for a short period of economic stability, exemplified by a relatively stable nominal exchange rate (Figure 5) and mild inflation (Figure 6). If Trump had not withdrawn the US from the 2015 nuclear accord, the course of Iran's adjustment to sanctions would have been very different and Iran sanctions might have been known as a case of success. To see this alternative reality, just cover the right side of the graphs in Figures 5 and 6 (beyond year 2017) and imagine that the trends would continue.

Sanctions and Living Standards

Viewed from this perspective, which is common among observers inside and outside Iran, the history of Iran's economy under sanctions is one of unmitigated decline. According to the devaluation-inflation recorded in Figures 5 and 6, the currency has lost value continuously and the CPI climbed unceasingly since the start of sanctions in 2011. But economic performance is not summarized by the behavior of the exchange rate and the CPI. To be sure, devaluation and inflation are highly disruptive, but what happens to living standards is not observable from the behavior of monetary measures alone.

As noted earlier in this chapter, the most popular measure of living standards is GDP per capita. But a more accurate measure of what appears on people's dinner table (*sofreh mardom*, a common refrain of Iranian politicians) is personal consumption as reported in household surveys. For example, inflation of 40%, which is the current rate in Iran, need not reduce the living standards of a minimum wage worker if his or her wage rises by 57%, the legal minimum announced for 2022, or if the person receives rent income, which is rising faster than inflation (about 7% of households report rent income).

As noted above, measures of living standard from GDP data vary depending on the source, though all show decline in GDP per capita. According to PPP data from Penn World Tables, GDP fell by an average of 3.8% per year during 2011–19 (Figure 1), and GDP per capita by 5.0%. According to Iran's official national accounts data, during 2011–21, GDP increased by about 0.5% while GDP per capita fell by about 1% per year. The difference arises because PPP uses US prices, which differ from Iranian prices. The World Bank, which estimates its own 2017 PPP data, shows no change in Iran's per capita GDP for the decade 2011–21, which is closer to Iran's own official data.

But GDP per capita underestimates the decline in purchasing power felt by ordinary Iranians, because GDP includes parts of government expenditures, such as those for defense, that ordinary people do not consider as contributing to their living standard. For a more accurate assessment of the latter, we turn to the annual household expenditure surveys. These surveys record expenditures of over a thousand items for thousands of households and offer a detailed view of household consumption. Figure 7 presents the average real consumption expenditures per person for three regions of Iran—rural and urban areas with the urban areas of Tehran province grouped separately.

The trends in per capita consumption expenditures closely reflect the changes in GDP noted above: the twenty-year period of economic growth before sanctions followed by stagnation and decline (Figure 1). During 1990 to 2010, average consumption nearly doubled; urban areas outside the Tehran province led the increase (2.4 times) while rural areas lagged (1.6 times). In contrast, the period of sanctions (2010–21) exhibits divergent behavior, with Tehran experiencing an increase of 25% in per capita

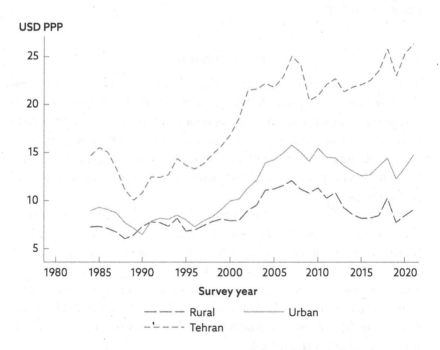

FIGURE 7. The fall and rise of living standards, by region. Real expenditures per person per day in constant 2021 prices. Source: Authors' calculations, Household Expenditure and Income Survey, Statistical Center of Iran.

consumption over the period, while rural areas did the worst (down by 20%), and other urban areas lost 4.6%. The better performance of Tehran under sanctions suggests that sanctions favored households living closer to the center of power, beating smaller urban areas that had done much better in the preceding twenty years. The national average rose by 5.1% in ten years, an annual increase of 0.04% per year, which is in sharp contrast with the 3.4% increase before sanctions. In 2021, real per capita household expenditures were down by $1 PPP per day compared to their peak in 2007, but higher by the same relative to 2010, just before sanctions (using the World Bank's PPP conversion factor of about 40,000 rials per USD). This is closer to GDP estimates supplied by Iran's own national accounts.

Although multiple factors affect average living standards and poverty, the role of sanctions stands out, both in the rise and fall of average consumption before and after 2011, and in the temporary uptick during 2016–17, when JCPOA was in effect. The harshness of the Trump maximum pressure campaign is also evident in the acceleration of the deterioration after 2018.

Impact on Nutrition

The most important damage from the economic crisis is to health, especially that of the poor. Although food and medicine have been exempted from sanctions, overzealous policing of Iranian trade after 2018 dissuaded banks from processing payments for most transactions, even those including food and medicine.[19] Iran depends on imports for a quarter of its food supply.[20] But for the poor, the aggregate food supply may not be the critical issue.

Even if food were available, the poor's shrinking income—because of the economic crisis brought about by sanctions—may put certain foods outside their reach. On the flip side, various food subsidies and substitutions by households between food and nonfood expenditures have surely ameliorated the negative impact of the economic crisis on nutrition. There is a direct subsidy for bread and indirect subsidies for basic food items, like chicken, through the preferential exchange rate for imports of food and animal feed.

Despite the subsidies, the ratio of food in total expenditures—which is closely correlated with living standards[21]—increased from 29.9% in 2010 to 32.7% in 2020 (however, this is still lower than its value at the end of the war with Iraq, about 45%). For the poorest quintile, the share of food fell from 53.8% in 1984 to 42.7% in 2010, then rose to 44.4% in 2020. According to the literature on food insecurity, households with food shares below 50% are not considered vulnerable nutritionally, since they have room to cut back their nonfood expenditures.[22]

Still, digging deeper into the data from expenditure surveys confirms the adverse impact of the economic crisis brought about by sanctions on the nutrition of the poor. Figures 11 and 12 (shown later) plot the calorie and protein contents of consumption expenditures by quintiles of per capita expenditures.[23] The trends in average intake of these nutrients, as well as for phosphorous and vitamin B12 (not shown in these figures), are all downward and for all quintiles.[24] In 2011, the average person in the lowest quintile consumed 2,064 calories and 68 grams of protein per day, compared to 1,818 calories and 61 grams of protein in 2020. Much of the decline in protein was due to cutbacks in the consumption of red meat, which has occurred for all income groups but more severely for the poor. Their average consumption of red meat fell by 60% in the last decade, from 0.27 kg per person per month in 2011 to 0.10 kg in 2020. During the same period, their poultry consumption remained constant, at 1 kg per person per month, which partially stabilized their total intake of animal protein.

It is difficult to ascertain the degree to which sanctions directly contributed to the fall in nutrition. It is often noted that food imports are not sanctioned, although the difficulties that sanctions created for the movement of funds between Iran and the rest of the world implicate sanctions in the diminished food consumption and nutrition. The downward trend in consumption of red meat has been a global trend, at least since 2007, which an arid country facing a decade-long drought, like Iran, cannot avoid.[25] But the economic crisis that sanctions precipitated no doubt reduced Iran's ability to import food and for the poor to purchase it.

Furthermore, there is a perceptible acceleration in the rate of decline in calorie and protein consumption around 2011. Before 2011, these trends were rather flat and fell with different speeds afterward. For calories, even before sanctions, the average intake for the lowest quintile was below the 2,100 minimum calories per person per day, a standard that is commonly used in defining poverty. Thus at least half of this group, or 10% of the total population, have been calorie-poor for the entire last decade. However, after 2011, malnutrition worsened, as pressure from sanctions caused the average calorie intake for this group to drop by 11%. The situation for protein was better, in the sense that at the beginning of the decade the majority of those in the bottom quintile received the 60 grams minimum level of protein intake, indicated by the horizontal line in Figure 12 (shown later). But by 2020, about half of them suffered from protein deficiency according to this criterion. These trends are consistent with the rise in poverty rates noted earlier.

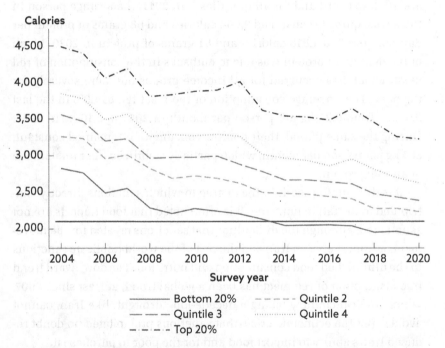

FIGURE 8. Caloric intake has been declining, but after 2011 fell below the minimum requirement for the lowest 20%. Source: Authors' calculations, Household Expenditure and Income Survey, Statistical Center of Iran, and the National Institute of Research on Nutrition and Food Industries, Tehran, Iran, for caloric content of individual food items.

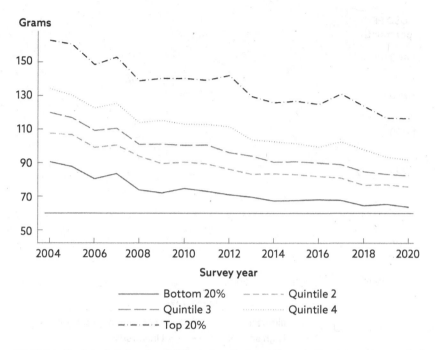

FIGURE 9. Protein intake also fell but stayed above the minimum recommended standard for all income groups. Source: Authors' calculations, Household Expenditure and Income Survey, Statistical Center of Iran, and the National Institute of Research on Nutrition and Food Industries, Tehran, Iran, for protein content of individual food items.

Wages

When a large negative shock hits the economy, no amount of flexibility or adjustment can prevent private consumption from falling. The first stop in the search for how an aggregate shock cuts the average household budget is the real wage, which is the main source of income for the majority of Iranians. In order for the economy to adjust to a lower level of consumption, real wages must fall, which is to say nominal wages cannot keep up with inflation.

Figure 10 depicts the real wages for workers with different levels of education. As with household consumption, real wages for all education groups peaked around 2007, which was the height of the oil boom and before sanctions hit. Between 2007 and 2011, the floodgate of imports reduced demand for Iranian products and workers and prevented nom-

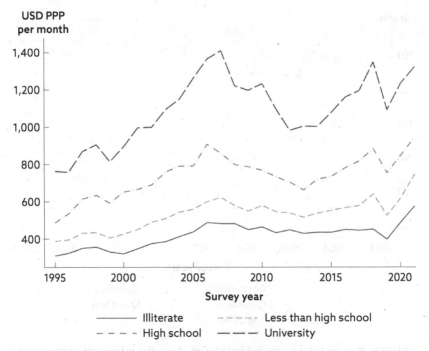

FIGURE 10. Real wages by education level, constant 2021 prices. Nominal average wages are deflated by the CPI and converted to PPP dollars using the 2021 World Bank conversion factor of 46,020 rials per international dollar. Source: Authors' calculations, Household Expenditure and Income Survey, Statistical Center of Iran.

inal wages from increasing as fast as inflation. The oil boom caused the rial to appreciate, making imports cheap and Iranian labor costs high. This is a well-known malady that afflicts oil-exporting countries, known as the Dutch Disease, after the de-industrialization of the Netherlands following rising natural gas exports in the 1960s. In Iran, this is reflected in the fact that real wages were on their way down several years before sanctions tightened in 2011 and suggests a more complex relationship between sanctions and real wages than between sanctions and oil exports or GDP. More evidence of this complex relationship is the recovery of wages after sanctions arrived in 2011 (seen later in Figure 12). Real wages bottomed out in 2013 as the effect of the rial's drastic devaluation of 2012 showed up in the labor market. The later rise of wages, especially during 2016–17, is likely the result of the 2015 nuclear deal (JCPOA).

Wages stalled in 2018, when Trump sanctions begin, but resumed their growth in 2019. It is difficult to predict if this later rise is a trend or will fall prey to dimming prospects for sanctions relief in light of the 2022 protests and Iran's support for Russia in the Ukraine war.

Impact on the Middle Class

The economic crisis of the last decade has affected living standards across income groups. Figure 11 shows the relative share of four income groups: the poor, lower middle class, middle class, and upper middle class. The poor are defined as those below the poverty line of $6.85 PPP per person per day in 2017, suggested by the World Bank for upper-middle-income countries (raised to $7.60 in 2021); the lower middle class is between the poor and the middle class. Middle-class status is defined as having per capita expenditures between two and five times the poverty line, and the rich as those above five times the poverty line. As in most developing countries, Iran's rich families rarely participate in income surveys, so the upper-middle-class label used in Figure 11 is more appropriate.

First, notice the contrast between the pre- and post-sanction periods, which we have seen in other graphs. During two decades of economic growth, 1990 to 2010, the middle class rose from one in five to more than half the population. At the same time, the ranks of the poor shrank considerably, from one in two to one in five. The share of the other two groups did not change much, so the shifts in income classes can be summarized as a substantial shift from the ranks of the poor to the middle class. After sanctions, this process of social change came to a halt. At some point, between 2011 and 2019, some 9 million people lost their middle-class status and joined the ranks of the lower middle class and perhaps even the poor. While the middle class suffered losses as sanctions shrank the economy, the poor suffered the most. The 9 million people who became poor between 2011 and 2019 could ill afford any loss of income. Significantly, in the last two years, about half of these individuals have regained their previous higher status. This is consistent with the upturn in average household consumption noted in Figure 7.

Naturally, the middle class and the poor resent their loss of income, but they pose different challenges for the government. The Islamic Republic, too, regards them differently. The founder of the Islamic Republic, Ayatollah Ruhollah Khomeini, considered the poor (*mostasafin*) as

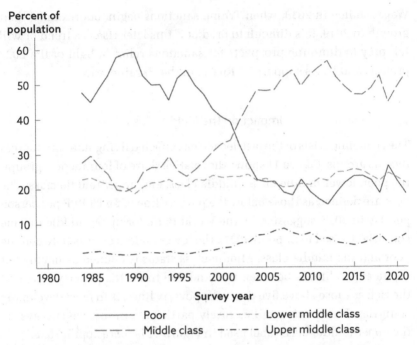

FIGURE 11. Social classes defined according to per capita household expenditures. The poor are defined as those below the poverty line of $7.60 PPP per person per day; the lower middle class below 1.5 times the poverty line, the middle class below 5 times the poverty line, and the rest are the upper middle class. Source: Authors' calculations, Household Expenditure and Income Survey, Statistical Center of Iran.

the natural social base for a populist and anti-imperialist revolution. He often referred to them as "the light of my eyes." Postrevolution governments had their greatest success by implementing policies that targeted the poor, especially in rural areas. They have also put in place a fairly extensive social protection system that assists the poor, which has come under stress as sanctions have bankrupted the government.[26] In Iran, the poor benefit from extensive income transfers, and are seen as a natural ally of the populist and anti-imperialist Islamic Republic. In contrast, the middle class often finds itself at odds with the socially restrictive Islamic laws and is therefore a more serious source of political pressure than the poor who, though harder hit, are more easily reached with income transfers.[27] As such, those in the middle class are viewed by the hardliners with suspicion: because of their taste for Western lifestyles and distaste for authoritarian rule, which seem inconsistent with how the Islamic Republic defines itself.

Social Protection

The poor sailed through the first wave of sanctions and devaluation. They did so because, starting in 2011 as sanctions tightened, they received substantial cash transfers from a program that was partially linked to sanctions. One of the first places sanctions aimed was import of gasoline. At the time Iran competed with Venezuela for the country with the lowest gasoline price and as a result demand was rising by 7% per year. To limit its consumption, the Ahmadinejad government took the difficult decision of removing the hefty subsidies for energy and bread. In return, to prevent protests, it paid generous cash transfers amounting to more than 20% of the median income.[28]

The program proved popular with the poor but not with upper-income Iranians, who consumed the bulk of the subsidized energy but received the same amounts in cash transfers as the poor. The redistributive subsidy reform program had even less appeal because it was identified with President Ahmadinejad, whom they considered illegitimately reelected in 2009. In addition, the program generated high inflation, which angered the salaried class. Higher energy prices had hastened inflation because of its direct impact on cost of production and the fact that the government had to print money to fill the shortfall in the program's revenues.

The government of President Hassan Rouhani that succeeded the populist Ahmadinejad government in 2013 was very critical of the cash transfers, and let their value diminish with inflation. In 2011, they were worth about $90 per person per month (PPP), falling to $15 in 2021. A gasoline price increase by the Rouhani government in November 2018 was announced without mentioning any compensating increase in cash transfers. Unsurprisingly, it was met with urban riots that engulfed most Iranian cities.[29] The budget allocations show more spending on health and education, but not in direct income transfers.[30] Cash transfers were back in the government's good graces in 2022. This time, the second conservative administration, led by President Ebrahim Raisi, offered cash transfers in compensation for removing subsidies for foreign exchange allocated for food imports.

Cash transfers are a logical and proven type of income assistance that helps the government address poverty during sanctions. Domestic energy use had expanded after the revolution considerably, creating an additional reason to use prices to control demand. Before the revolution, Iran produced about 7 mbd of crude oil, from which it earned record revenues, making the government and the country oil-rich. After the revolution, and despite sanctions, Iran produced about the same amount of oil and gas equivalent barrels per day, but more than two-thirds of it was used domestically. Before the Ahmadinejad subsidy reform program, the government was revenue-poor because it sold this energy at very low prices. If the government could sell this oil and gas at international prices—that is, with no subsidy—it could afford to finance more generous cash transfer programs. Estimates of the amount of energy subsides ran as high as 20% of the GDP and thwarted government expenditures. Most commodity subsidies are distributed unevenly, especially energy. Gasoline is the most regressive, with the top decile receiving about ten times as much of the subsidy as the bottom decile. The same ratio of subsidies going to the top and bottom deciles for natural gas and electricity is 3 and 4, respectively.

This is why the replacement of energy subsidies with cash transfers in 2010 lowered poverty and inequality in 2011 and 2012, despite the tightening of sanctions.[31] It was the failure of the Rouhani government to do the same during his tenure that forced him to run large budget deficits, as Trump sanctions reduced government revenues from oil exports. His successor, Ebrahim Raisi, repeated the Ahmadinejad experiment when he replaced foreign exchange subsidies for food imports with cash transfers. Like energy subsidies, selling foreign exchange at a third of its market price was unequal, inefficient, and added a new space for corruption. For example, red meat imported with the subsidized exchange rate did not always reach consumers at prices that reflected the subsidy, and the benefit of the subsidy for the richest decile was 2.5 times that of the lowest decile (corresponding to the ratio of their per capita consumptions). The reform raised inflation to historic levels (in June 2022 inflation reached a 300% annual rate) and was widely criticized. For this reason the Raisi administration has ruled out energy price reform for the foreseeable future, even though it can add to efficiency in the use of hydrocarbons and increase equity substantially.

Employment

Economic crises are almost always associated with loss of employment, but, in the case of Iran, if anything, employment increased under sanctions. In the past decade, employment fell only once, in 2020, due to the disruption of the COVID pandemic. As in most other countries, COVID hit the service sector the hardest (Figure 12). Three reasons explain the stability of employment under sanctions. First, nearly half of all workers in Iran are self-employed, and thus do not quit during stagnation. Second, wage labor employment in Iran is rigid because labor laws discourage employers from laying off workers. Finally, those who lose their jobs often move to the large informal economy. Unemployment insurance covers only 4% of workers, so there is no financial benefit from declaring being unemployed. For these reasons the unemployment rate is not a good indicator of the conditions of the labor market and therefore the impact of sanctions in Iran. Table 1 shows the unemployment and labor force participation rates of prime-age workers (ages 25–54). For the last fifteen years, male unemployment rates have remained in the 7–9% range; for women, 11–18%. There is more variation in the labor force participation rates, which includes those working and seeking work. If anything, sanctions appear to have increased participation. During 2005–11, when oil income was abundant, participation rates fell, for men from 92% in 2005 to 86.3% in 2011 and for women from 23.3% to 17.4%. This is not surprising. It is well known that an increase in nonlabor income reduces participation in market work. Sanctions appear to have had a small positive impact on men's participation, perhaps because oil income diminished, but women's participation rate fell back to below 18% in 2021.

The continued increase in employment during the decade of sanctions tells the same story as discussed earlier regarding the resilience of non-oil production—the non-oil GDP. Employment conditions for young people, who have been in the forefront of anti-regime protests in recent years, have never been good, but have not deteriorated much under sanctions. Limiting the age range in Table 1 to 20–34 doubles the unemployment rates but leaves the trends the same.

Year	Unemployment			Labor Force Participation		
	Men	Women	All	Men	Women	All
2005	6.8	11.5	7.7	92.0	23.3	57.5
2006	7.0	11.1	7.8	91.1	22.8	56.9
2007	6.6	11.6	7.6	90.8	21.6	56.1
2008	6.6	11.9	7.5	89.2	18.8	53.6
2009	8.3	13.3	9.3	88.9	19.8	54.1
2010	9.0	16.0	10.3	87.6	19.2	52.9
2011	8.3	16.7	9.8	86.3	17.4	51.2
2012	8.3	16.0	9.8	86.8	19.0	52.0
2013	7.0	16.5	8.6	87.5	17.3	52.1
2014	7.3	16.8	8.9	87.2	17.2	51.9
2015	8.0	17.1	9.6	87.9	18.8	53.1
2016	9.2	18.7	11.1	88.8	21.2	54.6
2017	9.2	17.8	10.9	89.4	22.6	55.9
2018	9.4	17.3	11.0	90.1	22.6	56.0
2019	8.2	16.1	9.7	89.9	22.0	55.7
2020	7.6	14.6	8.9	88.4	18.4	53.0
2021	7.1	14.6	8.4	89.2	17.7	53.0

TABLE 1. Unemployment and labor force participation rates of prime-age workers (25–54 years old), by gender. Unemployed are defined as those having worked at least one hour in the week before the interview and individuals are in the labor force if they are employed or are actively seeking employment. Source: Authors' calculations, Labor Force Surveys, Statistical Center of Iran.

The resilience of employment under sanctions is due to more than rigidity in Iran's labor markets. As explained in the next section, devaluations stimulated the production of substitutes for imported goods, which limit the loss of jobs due to the loss of oil income. This is seen in Figure 12, which shows employment in industry to be rising after sanctions, albeit very moderately.

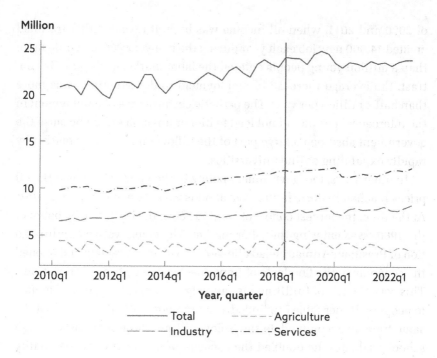

FIGURE 12. Employment has been stable and slightly increasing in industry. Source: Authors' calculations, Labor Force Surveys, Statistical Center of Iran.

Reversing the Dutch Disease

For insight into the surprising trends in employment and non-oil GDP under sanctions, this chapter earlier looked to the well-known theory of economic growth for oil-rich countries (in the section "Wages"), known as the Dutch Disease. As seen in Table 1, Iran's oil boom was not good for employment. During the period of rising oil revenues in the 2000s, unemployment increased and labor force participation declined. According to the Dutch Disease theory, employment in tradable sectors suffers because abundant foreign exchange lowers the price of foreign currencies and imported goods, encouraging the substitution of imports for locally produced goods. For the same reason, export of non-oil products becomes uneconomical. Compelling evidence for this theory is found in the change in national employment between the national censuses of 2006 and 2011, when oil income was high. It revealed that Iran had created 14,000 new job each year during the five-year period, while more than a million young people entered the labor market each year. By contrast, the average increase in employment under sanctions was more than half a million per year. The pathetic performance of employment in the intercensal period did not lead to higher unemployment because the government absorbed a large part of the inflow into the labor market by rapidly expanding online universities.

In other ways, too, government policy in the late 2000s, when the oil prices reached historic highs, was at odds with its demographic reality. At the time, the largest cohort of Iranians born during the baby boom of the 1980s was entering the labor market. The conservative administration of President Ahmadinejad allowed the rial to appreciate and opened the economy to the floodgate of imports—the Dutch Disease on steroids. This was his way of fulfilling his campaign promise to "bring oil money to people's dinner table," intended as a pro-poor, anti-elite slogan. At the same time, to accommodate the inflow of Iran's largest cohorts of high school graduates, he doubled the capacity of universities while quality declined. The result would haunt his successor, Hassan Rouhani, four years later when the unemployment of college-educated youth sharply rose.

If the Islamic Republic was intent on developing a bomb or scaling up its nuclear enrichment to the level that would trigger US sanctions, the economic policies it pursued in the years beforehand did nothing to prepare it for the eventual standoff.

The inflow of oil money in the decade before sanctions ill-prepared the country for coping with sanctions in different ways. Besides making domestic production uncompetitive, the falling value of foreign currencies encouraged closer integration of Iranian production into the global economy. Producers increased the use of imported inputs in production, making Iranian industries more vulnerable to sanctions that would arrive in 2011. More than half of all imports were intermediate products. A good example of how the oil boom further integrated Iran's economy into the global economy and thus weakened its ability to cope with sanctions is the story of a sugar factory in the eastern industrial city of Neishabour, where one of this book's authors grew up. Ghand-e Neishabour, one of the country's oldest sugar factories, established in the decade of rapid industrialization in the 1960s, had encouraged sugar beet farming in the region, engaging thousands of growers and lorry drivers, who transported the crop to the factory. During the harvest season, lorries would line up on the road to the factory's door waiting to unload. But, in the 2000s, with the oil boom in full swing, the line of lorries started to shorten and then stopped up altogether as rising costs and cheap foreign exchange made the use of the local sugar beet uneconomical. The factory cut its purchases from local farmers and instead imported raw sugar, which it processed and packaged for the local market.[32] The factory stayed afloat but only by integrating itself into global trade.

While the flood of imports rapidly modernized the kitchens and livings rooms of Iran's rising middle class, it failed to prepare them for the kind of sacrifice their hardline leaders would ask of them just a few years later. Iran's middle class, which in repeated elections had expressed its preference for global engagement and respectability, was the wrong citizenry to sacrifice its living standards in a standoff with "global arrogance," the term their leaders used for the United States. In recent years, Iran's conservative leaders have been preaching frugality and making do with less, while in his Nowruz speeches the supreme leader named the new year as one dedicated to production. The appeals have fallen on deaf ears in a country whose people are more eager to embrace a middle-class lifestyle through consumption than in a global competition of skills and productivity.

Distortions caused by the Dutch Disease are not irreversible. In principle, as oil exports decline and foreign currencies become expensive, domestic production can become more advantageous. Devaluation raises the price of traded goods (agriculture and manufacturing) relative to nontraded goods (mainly services and goods difficult to transport), setting off restructuring in favor of manufacturing and improved employment. Much of the economic history of Iran in the last two decades can be told with the help of the movement of relative prices, which is at the core of the Dutch Disease model of oil-induced lopsided development.

Figure 13 shows the far-reaching swings in the ratio of two price indices, that of traded goods to nontraded goods (as defined by Iran's SCI). Both indices are set at 100 in 2016, so their ratio, referred to here as the terms of trade index, was equal to 1 in that year. During the oil boom, the index fell by one-third, triggering the "de-industrialization" of Iran. But as sanctions took effect and oil incomes decreased and the rial experienced multiple devaluations, traded goods regained their advantage. The

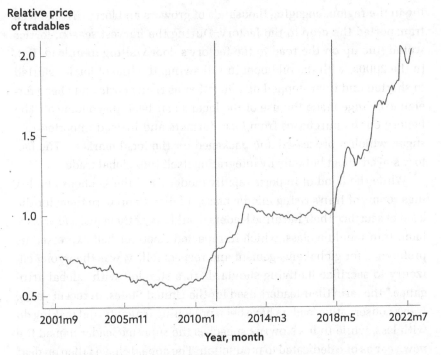

FIGURE 13. Relative price of tradable goods increased with devaluation. Source: Statistical Center of Iran, monthly inflation reports.

terms of trade index had doubled in six years. These changes are easily linked to the movements of the real exchange rate in Figure 5, themselves driven by changes in oil income and the intensity of the sanctions.

No oil-rich country has voluntarily given up the benefits of rising living standards with oil income. Oil revenues feed an addiction, which is why oil is often seen as a mixed blessing, or a "poisoned well" as the late Fuad Ajami referred to oil.[33] In this regard, sanctions may have done Iran a favor by forcing it to come to terms with the eventual disappearance of hydrocarbon incomes, either by the exhaustion of reserves or by technology and climate change rendering them unusable. The oil-rich neighbors of Iran to the south in this sense lag far behind, having resorted to foreign labor to produce at home those services that cannot be imported, like childcare and domestic services.

Between the two bouts of sanctions, Obama's in 2011 and Trump's in 2018, inflation erased a good part of the devaluations so the real exchange rate, which adjusts the nominal rate by changes in the relative rates of inflation in the US and Iran, fell by about 80% (Figure 5). Trump's assault on the nuclear deal and Iran's economy extended the life of the reverse Dutch Disease process.

Returning to the real side of the economy, one looks for the consequences of the improvement in the terms of trade in favor of traded goods, the reversal of the Dutch Disease, to show itself in the composition of the national output and in the non-oil GDP, which is what the vast majority of Iranian workers produce. Indeed, as seen in Figure 4, there is an upward trend in non-oil GDP, which, this chapter argues, accounts for the resilience of the Iranian economy under sanctions.

In principle, such large changes in relative prices should encourage restructuring of production to reverse the ill effects of the Dutch Disease. Some change in this direction is evident: Non-oil exports have increased—in 2022 they were $48 billion, twice as much as crude oil exports. But the bulk of the increase in non-oil exports has come from heavily subsidized petrochemicals, which are capital intensive and do not create many jobs. Relative price changes have also stimulated the substitution of domestic goods for imports, and Iranians are taking more vacations inside Iran than in neighboring countries, and shiny new shopping malls are springing up in Tehran and Iran's largest cities. Substitution of locally produced goods for imports has also increased without making a big dent in joblessness. The increase in manufacturing output and employment has been modest but notable. Manufacturing employment grew by 11.6% during 2015–20, despite harsh sanctions in place since 2018, reversing the decline of 16.0% that occurred during 2011–15.

But for the restructuring to be complete, at least four important preconditions must hold. First, some economic stability must prevail for producers to plan and undertake the necessary investments in production of newly profitable traded goods. This will not happen unless the future of trade with the rest of the world becomes more predictable. In recent years, especially since Trump's withdrawal from the nuclear deal, every month's news raises hopes of the resumption of talks to revive the nuclear deal, which are then quickly dashed by some official's tweet. News of negotiations rocks the exchange rate and local prices, shaking business confidence in economic stability. Second, producers must have access to credit to finance their investments. Iranian banks have been in a state of near bankruptcy for several years and are unable to lend to producers, especially small producers who create most of the jobs. Third, to restructure, producers must have access to global markets to import new technologies and to procure new inputs. Finally, sanctions have suppressed domestic demand, so production increase should be directed toward external demand—exports. As with access to technology, access to external markets requires sanctions against movement of goods and money to ease.

So far, there is no sign that restructuring is steady or even accelerating. If anything, progress toward removing these obstacles has slowed. The anemic restructuring appears to have convinced many in the conservative camp that they are witnessing the green shoots of the resistance economy that the supreme leader has envisaged for an Iran cut off from the Western economies.

To sum up, to date the economic impact of sanctions has been far from what the hawkish US conservative establishment had predicted. To be sure, sanctions ended two decades of steady economic growth and caused widespread economic distress among the population. But they did not cause the economy to collapse nor did they cause mass uprisings to put serious pressure on the government. The relative flexibility of the economy, and the decision to allow the currency to depreciate, helped initiate—so far a very modest—economic restructuring away from oil exports and toward domestic production. Despite its much-diminished resources, the government used its social protection mechanism to shield the poorest households from hunger and a descent into severe poverty. While there have been numerous protests, so far they have not reached the level that would threaten the regime or force it to submit to US demands.

FIVE

What Sanctions Cost the United States

Iran is not the only country to have endured prolonged economic sanctions. But it does have the distinction of being subject to one of the most extensive and thoroughgoing application of sanctions. Therefore, the case of Iran is a valuable examination of both the efficacy and cost of using sanctions as an instrument of foreign policy.

The proliferation of sanctions on Iran as a principal tool for managing its perceived threats has signaled the greater prominence of economic statecraft in US foreign policy. There is a growing body of work examining the impact and implications of this trend for American interests.[1] When it came to Iran, economic sanctions were not deployed merely as punishment for specific Iranian actions and policies. Instead, as shown in earlier chapters, they were used to define an enemy; they were used as a strategic tool to manage Iran, and even change the character of the country and profile of its regional role.[2]

Iran has lived under various US sanctions for over four decades. However, since Iran embarked on building a nuclear program in 2003, sanctions grew in scale. That trend coincided with the deepening of the US Treasury's investment in financial tools after 2001 to combat terrorism. Those tools, in turn, made economic sanctions on Iran both more expansive and more effective.[3] The Treasury has continued to develop its arsenal of sanctions tools, a process not unlike the Pentagon's never-ending investment in more lethal weaponry. In this process Iran, more than any other country, has served as the target that has justified the Treasury's development of its "economic statecraft."[4]

The underlying assumption here is one that has long guided international relations: the greater the economic pressure and the more vulnerable the economy of the target country, the more likely it would respond to demands for change.[5] In reality, however—as also shown in earlier chapters—Iran found ample ways to survive under sanctions, and has by and large resisted accommodating US demands, even as sanctions became more punishing.[6]

The sanctions regime has had its ebbs and flows. But it was during the Trump administration when sanctions crossed a Rubicon, posing hitherto unanticipated costs and consequences for US foreign policy. The case of Iran therefore raises questions about the effectiveness of sanctions as a tool of foreign policy, but with added questions about its costs to the country that imposes them.[7]

Sanctions and Nuclear Diplomacy

The Trump administration's escalation of economic pressure on Iran assumed that sanctions would replicate—and even enhance—what they had achieved during the previous administrations. This was incorrect.

The way that the Bush administration responded to Iran's nuclear program was to shun negotiations. Instead, it applied economic pressure to compel Iran to end its nuclear program. Soon after the US invasion of Iraq, Iran's president at the time, Mohammad Khatami, sent a letter to the Bush administration via the Swiss Embassy in Tehran. In that letter he offered direct talks with the United States.[8] But Washington rejected the overture, believing that the fall of Baghdad would soon be followed by the collapse of the Islamic Republic in Tehran.[9]

Washington also assumed that Tehran's offer of talks reflected fear of coming economic pressure. Despite Washington's rejection, in 2003 the EU-3 (France, Germany, and the UK) sought to avert a nuclear crisis with Iran by negotiating a deal to halt its nuclear program. Washington dismissed the agreement, believing it had only proved that Iran was desperate and susceptible to pressure. And if that was the case—the thinking in Washington went—then why not escalate pressure rather than settle for a deal now?

That approach did not yield the desired result.[10] First, the US at the time demanded Iran give up its nuclear program altogether but did not offer to lift sanctions in return; instead, it only threatened Iran with even more economic pressure. To use Washington's own terminology, what was on the table was all "stick" and no "carrot." Second, Washington's European allies—already jilted by the Iraq war experience and unhappy with US rejection of their nuclear deal with Iran—were reluctant to follow Washington's lead. They were worried that Washington had already used one nuclear threat to start a war with Iraq, and, unrepentant, was now eyeing Iran's nuclear program as an excuse to barrel toward another war with Iran.

Washington's reliance on escalating sanctions in lieu of a deal at the diplomatic table only convinced Iran to continue to build its program—that is, to build more leverage. Clearly their program was too small to persuade Washington to take it seriously enough to put economic incentives on the table. Washington, on the other hand, remained convinced that economic pressure alone would compel Iranian compliance with its demands. From its perspective, it was not a matter of whether sanctions would work, but simply how much was needed to move Iran.

A decade later, that approach would find additional credence in Washington, after the United States and Iran joined nuclear talks in 2013. It became a widely held belief that it was the successful tightening of economic pressure on Iran during Obama's first term as president (starting in 2011) that compelled Iran to agree to the diplomatic negotiations that led to JCPOA.[11] The bombastic rhetoric of Iran's president at the time, Mahmoud Ahmadinejad, was likewise important in providing public support in both the US and Europe for additional sanctions. Facing an obdurate Iran, President Obama took advantage of European enthusiasm for his presidency to win support for tighter sanctions on Iran. Unlike with Bush after the Iraq invasion, Europeans trusted that Obama did not want war or regime change and was genuinely interested in boosting the chances for diplomacy.

During the first term of the Obama administration, expansion of Iran's nuclear program was met with additional economic sanctions, including at the United Nations. And, indeed, the sanctions that the United States imposed on Iran between 2010 and 2013 were the most comprehensive and biting that Iran had confronted since 1979.

Such international support for those sanctions sent a powerful signal to Tehran. The Islamic Republic was then reeling from nationwide Green Movement protests—discussed in chapter 2—and felt especially vulnerable.[12] Tehran did not want escalating international pressure at that point and needed to focus on consolidating power at home. The Obama administration had been careful to signal to Tehran that it was not after regime change. Furthermore, its message to allies was that its sanctions policy was not designed to ratchet up tensions with Iran and pave the way to war, of which the Bush administration stood accused. Instead, the Obama administration's intended goal was to force Iran to engage in serious negotiations over its nuclear program. In effect, sanctions were depicted as an alternative to war, and, as such, a less costly path to achieving US diplomatic goals.

To that end, Obama even encouraged Brazil and Turkey in early 2010 to pursue a nuclear deal with Iran, although he demurred accepting it when it was concluded.[13] Perhaps he had not expected Brazil and Turkey to succeed, expecting instead their failure to isolate Iran further. Or he felt that Iran was unlikely to abide by a deal with only Brazil and Turkey and that Congress was unlikely to endorse a deal the US had not been privy to. Still, the exercise underscored American interest in diplomacy and that Iran would have to engage the United States to resolve the crisis. And to compel Iran to talk, the US followed its dismissal of the Brazil-Turkey deal with greater sanctions on Iran, combined with an offer of diplomacy.

With the United States still mired in the Iraq war quagmire, a diplomatic path to resolve a major crisis was compelling. The historian Nicholas Mulder writes of the time when the "economic weapon" was first conceived after World War I; it was considered the preferred tool to compel states to observe rules of the international order, because those who used the weapon were immunized from confronting the costs and consequences of its use.[14] As he puts it, "The coercive power [of economic sanctions] was administered not out of the cockpit of a bomber or through the bench of a cannon but from behind a mahogany desk."[15] The "field of operations," he cites an American observer of the time explaining, "is not a visible terrain; but a force is exerted just the same."[16]

To put together the toughest economic sanctions on Iran to date, Obama used the power of presidential executive orders, combined with new comprehensive congressional legislation and fines levied on third parties, including levying of fines on major European banks.[17] The strategy yielded results. First, the sanctions proved effective: Iran's economy contracted by 17% between 2010 and 2012, as economic growth fell by 7.6%, oil exports fell by 50%, and inflation rose by 65%.[18] Second, the sanctions yielded the intended policy result. In 2013, the United States and Iran engaged directly: first through secret talks,[19] and then through formal diplomatic negotiations under the aegis of the five permanent members of United Nations Security Council plus Germany (the so-called P5+1).[20] Iran's leaders were no doubt surprised and alarmed by the scale and effectiveness of the new sanctions, and the international support Obama had garnered for them. They also concluded that Obama was serious about diplomacy, but that the United States would not agree to any deal unless it was a party to it. Therefore, there was a plausible way to reduce sanctions through negotiations.[21]

The United States concluded that the only reason why Iran had agreed to serious negotiations was because of sanctions pressure. Sanctions had worked, obviated war, and defused a conflict that could have potentially entangled the United States in a prolonged and costly military conflict, which would have dwarfed the Iraq war in scale. Even Iran acknowledged that the 2015 deal—according to which Iran would significantly reduce the scope of its program, in exchange for the lifting of US and UN sanctions that had been imposed after 2010—proved to be the only occasion when a country had exited the UN's Chapter 7 sanctions without war and regime change.[22]

It is important to note, however, that Obama coupled added economic pressure with a clear statement: first, the United States was not after regime change in Iran, and, second, it was serious about a negotiated deal. The latter meant that Obama relied on the removal of sanctions to incentivize Iran to negotiate. It was not the threat of more sanctions that compelled Iran to talk and cut a deal. Rather, it was the prospect of earlier sanctions being lifted.

This important lesson of the 2015 nuclear deal was lost on the Trump administration. The threat of sanctions is a deterrent. And yet, once imposed, its power of persuasion ultimately lies in lifting them; and that is where the US sanctions strategy is weakest. Its political and legal ability to lift sanctions lags behind the alacrity with which they are imposed.

Still, at the time, the 2015 nuclear deal was successful. In short order, Iran implemented its commitments under the deal, coined the Joint Comprehensive Plan of Action, or JCPOA.

But the US would find it more difficult to implement its own part of the deal. First, the perceived success of sanctions in getting Iran to a deal created an appetite for holding on to them for as long as possible, so as to extract further concessions from Iran. Furthermore, economic sanctions proved more difficult to dismantle than nuclear infrastructure, as shown in chapter 4. Rescinding sanctions required political support at multiple levels in the US government; even then, it would require political will at the highest level to defend the decision. Many businesses found the sanctions rollback too slow and fraught with pitfalls, and, as such, were not willing to risk the wrath of the US Treasury to do business with Iran.

Still, Iran's economy got a boost from the deal. Between $50 and $56 billion in Iran's foreign reserves were released; the economy grew by 17%, creating 3.5 million jobs.[23] The Rouhani government estimated that, over a ten-year period, the deal would have increased the size of Iran's middle class by 35%.

But despite these gains, even in 2015 Iranians realized that the quid pro quo they had signed on to at the negotiating table was not that at all. Iran would quickly abide by its side of the deal; but although some US sanctions were removed, the bulk would continue to restrict Iran's economy.

In the United States, the foreign policy establishment saw the nuclear negotiations and JCPOA in simple formulaic terms. The lesson drawn from the experience was that where low-level sanctions do not work, higher-level sanctions will, and can achieve goals that had hitherto been the domain of war. The logical conclusion was as simple as it was false: *Why remove all sanctions? In fact, why stop escalating them?* Sanctions could not just achieve immediate objectives but maximal goals. That became the basis for criticisms against JCPOA as soon as it was signed: Why had the United States not gone further to disarm Iran altogether, end its missile program, liquidate its proxies, and extricate it from the Arab world? According to critics, there was no limit to what sanctions could have achieved. Rather than being credited for success at the negotiating table, the Obama administration was instead excoriated for settling for too little, for not using the sanctions weapon to its fullest effect.

These arguments were all based on the assumption that imposing stringent economic sanctions on Iran bore no cost to the US economy, and that going further with sanctions too would be cost-free. American companies were not involved in Iran, although European companies had interests in the country and would bear a cost. There was much European carping, but their reaction would not dent the perception in Washington that the United States did not have to worry about the cost of escalating sanctions. Furthermore, Iranian energy exports were not sufficiently large to sway global markets. As the 2011 sanctions began, for example, European countries swiftly reduced oil imports from Iran, replacing their needs with imports from other producers—and would eventually cease to import oil from Iran altogether. There was little worry that there would be an oil supply shortfall. Oil markets were fungible enough to absorb reduction in Iran's energy exports. Iran alone would shoulder the cost of sanctions—at least, so it was believed—and would do so even if they were reimposed and escalated.

It was these assumptions and conclusions that led the Trump administration to place little value on the 2015 nuclear deal and to decide that the United States could walk away. In its place, they chose to simply escalate sanctions to exact more concessions from Iran, and believed that doing so would have no cost to the United States—the US could simply get a better deal by increasing economic pressure. The Republican Party and a notable segment of the Democratic Party had already bought into this argument when they criticized JCPOA in 2015.

Therefore, criticisms of Trump for undoing Obama's deal did not include serious questioning of the underlying assumption of his policy. Such critiques do not contend with the idea, for example, that sanctions are a facile and cost-free tool, which, if deployed at scale, can achieve its intended policy goals.

Iran, the Perfect Target

There were clearly consequences to over-relying on sanctions. But these concerns were overshadowed by acid views of the Islamic Republic in the US Congress and media, as well as a broad swath of the American public. The Islamic Republic had long been viewed as an intractable enemy, a country that had held American diplomats hostage in a humiliating ordeal in 1979–80, and had since lost no opportunity to make a display of its anti-Americanism. Iran had come to be seen as the fountainhead of terrorism in the Middle East, and a root cause of instability in that region. More recently, Iran's role in supporting militias in Iraq and waging a bombing campaign to undermine the US in Iraq, which had claimed a large number of American casualties, had hardened those views. All of this made only the timing and extent to which sanctions could be escalated worthy of discussion.

At the core of this outsized view of "Iran as enemy" is Iranian enmity toward Israel, its support for Hezbollah and Hamas, and the potential threat posed by Iran's nuclear program to Israel. Given that support for Israel is important to domestic American politics, opposition to Iran has become an article of faith among American politicians, especially in the Republican Party. That creates a situation in which lifting sanctions on Iran would exact notable political cost, while imposing them would accrue political capital and political contributions.

This problem emerged in 2022 at the conclusion of the Vienna talks directed at restoring JCPOA, when Iran's demand that the designation of Foreign Terrorist Organization (FTO) imposed by the Trump administration on the Islamic Revolutionary Guard Corps be removed. That request became the rallying cry for opponents of deal-making with Iran, threatening to undo the nuclear negotiations. A designation and sanction that was imposed to persuade Iran to return to talks had—thanks to US domestic politics—turned into an obstacle.

From the outset, sanctions on Iran were designed to signal the international community's disapproval of Iranian policies and to deter and punish those policies. Iran's insistence on challenging the United States and threatening its neighbors invited more sanctions, which punished the state without deterring it. This challenged some of the fundamental assumptions behind the use of sanctions: that isolation dejects a population, and that fear of economic ruin deters aggressive action. President Woodrow Wilson once said that the true power of economic sanctions was psychological; they worked because "it is the soul that is wounded much more poignantly than the body."[24] Those feelings, however, did not dissuade Japan from attacking the United States in 1939. In fact, American sanctions likely encouraged that course of action.[25]

In Iran's case too, the disapproval of the international community did not compel the population of Iran into action in ways that the United States had hoped. This was, in some measure, because for many years revolutionary fervor made such communication with the Iranians futile. Sanctions did not deter the Islamic Republic either. Its anti-Americanism and revisionist challenge to the regional order continued unabated.

Still, for US policymakers, a key value of using sanctions to manage

Iran is that the practice did not stir up any domestic opposition. No sol-diers are placed in harm's way, no military operations are funded by taxpayer money, and no American businesses are impacted by disrup-tions to trade and commerce. American businesses do not protest, and the public does not see the impact.

There were also important innovations to the structure of the sanc-tions regime during the Obama era that made them more attractive. As discussed in chapter 4, one effective innovation was to extend sanctions to third-party actors—those who were engaged in the economic activ-ities that primary sanctions intended to halt. Equally important was closing down Iran's access to SWIFT (Society for Worldwide Interbank Financial Telecommunication), the widely used international messaging system for banking transfers, which further limited trade with Iran that was not impacted by sanctions.

This showed that US control over critical nodes in an interdependent world gave it inordinate power to pursue its foreign policy goals through nonmilitary coercion by extricating a country from the international economic system.[26] While this represented a significant display of the power that sanctions afforded US foreign policy, it also made it difficult to avoid the danger of overreach.[27]

Even before Trump was elected, as we have seen, the 2015 nuclear deal was facing challenges. Meanwhile, in Tehran, the slow pace of sanc-tions removal was eroding support for the nuclear deal and encouraging the belief that, unlike classic arms-control deals, the implementation of a sanctions deal would disfavor Iran in lopsided fashion. In fact, the re-silience of sanctions on Iran would ultimately complicate any diplomatic negotiations with an adversary, because it changed the give-and-get cal-culation, along with the sequencing and speed of implementation. Iran would learn those lessons only after the ink dried on JCPOA. How it reacted would, in turn, make US use of sanctions more problematic.

But the United States saw only unlimited possibility in deploying sanctions. The lesson of Obama's negotiations with Iran—that sanctions impact only the targeted economy, do so quickly and with devastating effect, and, in turn, produce fruitful negotiations—clouded the Trump ad-ministration's view. It saw no cost in abandoning the deal, and believed a stronger deal could be made in short order. When skeptical European allies warned Washington about the consequences of scuttling the hard-fought 2015 deal, the Trump administration's answer was that Europeans should not worry: "It would be a matter of a few months before Iran would be crawling on its knees begging for another deal."[28]

In May 2018, President Trump formally withdrew from JCPOA and imposed a bevy of new sanctions on Iran. During the following two years, the number of sanctions on Iran grew from 750 to over 1,500.[29] This represented an unprecedented surge. Iran quickly became the most economically sanctioned country in the world.

Reimposing sanctions was easy and did not bear any immediate and obvious political or economic cost for the United States. Iran had already rolled back its nuclear program, shipped its stockpile of enriched uranium to Russia, and dismantled its cascades of centrifuges. The sanctions gave the US the means to demand renegotiation of a deal after its successful implementation had altered the balance of power that had yielded the original deal. Iran had given up tangible physical assets that it had built over time and at great cost, whereas the US had merely agreed to rescind laws that it could one day reinstate. There was no meaningful cost to lifting sanctions, nor to reimposing them. In effect, President Trump showed sanctions to be a particularly versatile weapon, one that could be waged much more swiftly than the hard assets of the adversaries.

The power of sanctions, however, could work only once. It had worked in 2013–15 to get the original deal, but it was not going to work again regardless of the severity of their impact. Even if Iran agreed to fresh negotiations—as it would eventually do in 2021—diplomacy would become more difficult. Iran would now try to calibrate what it gives up and how quickly to account for the US ability to reimpose sanctions.

And yet, when Trump withdrew from the deal, the expectation was that Iran would quickly comply with new American demands. The potential costs of piling on more sanctions would not become apparent for a while longer.

Domestic Anchor of Sanctions

Sanctions allow the US government to pursue a coercive foreign policy without demanding sacrifices in blood and treasure from Americans. In fact, sanctions as a foreign policy tool gained attraction after World War I, explains the historian Mulder, exactly because European powers exhausted by war (yet compelled to assert the writ of the League of Nations) found economic statecraft to be an expedient substitute for war.[30] Similarly, America's reliance on sanctions has increased in recent decades, on pace with the growing antiwar mood that followed in the wake of the Iraq war of 2003.

However, sanctions are not a simple substitute for war. First, although the US Congress declares war, the president as commander-in-chief oversees the actual conduct of the war: including when hostilities start, how they unfold, and when they cease. Furthermore, although it is Congress that decides whether to invoke the War Powers Act, they do so only pursuant to the president's request, and are not independent from the executive branch of the US government. More important, wars are ended by presidents, and Congress cannot continue a war in defiance of the presidency.

That does not hold true for sanctions. Congress can pass its own sanctions, as it did in 1996 with the Iran-Libya Sanctions Act. The president can suspend the application of sanctions, but that would amount to a temporary reprieve, a ceasefire. When it comes to sanctions, Congress has the ability to wage war on par with the presidency and even in defiance of it.

To avoid wrangling between the executive and legislative branches of the government, the White House would have to negotiate with Congress over the removal of sanctions, and that demands of a president both time and precious political capital, which reduces the presidency's maneuverability when conducting foreign policy. Iran fully understands that entrenched opposition to its policies in Congress goes beyond the fate of the nuclear deal. As such, the executive branch and American diplomats cannot be fully trusted to deliver on the promises that they make, in this case, on lifting sanctions in exchange for capping the nuclear program.

Meanwhile Iran also understands that sanctions are reducing the likelihood of America resorting to war to achieve its policy objectives. Therefore, since sanctions obviate war but are unlikely to be fully lifted, the question for Iran—or any country subject to US sanctions—is how to arrive at a manageable level of sanctions: where Iran would avoid war but be able to tolerate sanctions. That happy medium will—in contrast with stated US policy goals—actually require Iran to *sustain* its nuclear leverage and keep regional pressure on the US.

In effect, rather than resolving the problem, sanctions freeze it. Sanctions have locked the US and Iran in complicated calculations, in which both Iran's nuclear program and sanctions remain in place. The equilibrium will avoid an outright crisis. But it will be a situation in which the glass is half full for Iran and half empty for the US.

Economic sanctions are rapidly imposed and lifted only slowly, and often not at all. After the signing of the 2015 nuclear deal, it took Iran six months to fulfill its obligations under the deal, including the dismantling of a plutonium enrichment reactor. But years later, when the Trump administration left JCPOA in 2018, the United States had still lifted only a fraction of the sanctions it had promised to. Why?

First, the labyrinthine legal process for delisting is time consuming, and often involves Congress, which could impose hurdles or reimpose the same sanctions under a different pretext. Second, lifting sanctions on trade or investment proved meaningless, since sanctions on financial and banking systems—either because Iranian banks had been sanctioned for other reasons or were not signatories to the Financial Action Task Force (FATF, which combats money laundering and illicit uses of financial networks)—remained in place. One set of sanctions would make the lifting of other sanctions immaterial. In Iran's eyes, a nuclear deal would produce little sanctions relief unless the Islamic Republic changed other policies too—that is, until the regime itself changed. Thus, if full compliance on Iran's part would result in only partial compliance on the US side, then Iran too should either comply less or seek greater leverage to compel greater compliance by the United States. That is exactly the attitude Iran adopted ahead of nuclear negotiations in Vienna in 2021.

Congress's ability to exercise outsized influence on sanctions, far more than what it can do in the case of military operations, gives to special interests the incentives and the means to influence US foreign policy. It also gives individual members of Congress the ability to shape both Congress and the administration's respective positions. This reduces the room to maneuver that the president and his diplomats need to conduct effective foreign policy.

Even President Trump, his near total control of the Republican Party notwithstanding, did not remain immune. He was eager to negotiate with Iran but dithered at key junctures. He asked Japan's prime minister at the time, Shinzo Abe, to go to Tehran in July 2019 to persuade Iran to engage with the US in nuclear talks, but then couched that step with new sanctions on Iran's petrochemical sector to avert criticism from his conservative allies. The new sanctions were put in place shortly before Prime Minister Abe's trip. Even before Abe had arrived in Tehran, the supreme leader cited the new sanctions in a tweet on June 23, 2019, addressing the prime minister directly: ".@AbeShinzo U.S. president met & talked with you a few days ago, including about Iran. But after returning from Japan, he immediately imposed sanctions on Iran's petrochemical industry. Is this a message of honesty? Does that show he is willing to hold genuine negotiations?" Trump had felt it necessary to assuage hawks in Congress and his own party that he remained steadfast in pressuring Iran. That attempt, however, sabotaged fruitful diplomacy with Iran.

The problem is even greater when it comes to lifting sanctions. For instance, maximum pressure sanctioned economic institutions in Iran, including the country's Central Bank. The Trump administration also insisted on imposing as many sanctions as possible, not solely concerned with the nuclear issue but also linked to support for terrorism and violations of human rights. As a result, to lift those sanctions, the president in effect would have to vouch that those institutions, such as Iran's Central Bank, have never supported terrorism and will not do so in the future. That is risky for any president. Nor would the White House be comfortable arguing that Iranian state institutions may have supported terrorism or violated human rights, and could do so in the future, but, nevertheless, still insist that it is necessary to lift sanctions on them. At a fateful juncture, with the success of the Vienna talks at stake, President Biden refused to lift the Foreign Terrorist Organization designation or other sanctions imposed on the IRGC. This problem became even more pronounced as protests engulfed Iran after Mahsa Amini's death. The protests were led by young women challenging the Islamic Republic's forcible imposition of head coverings on women. The bravery of protesters defending their fundamental rights in the face of a harsh government crackdown captured the world's imagination. The Biden administration concluded that the lifting of sanctions would face a severe public backlash, which meant that nuclear diplomacy was at a dead end. In fact, the administration, and its European allies, added new sanctions in response to Tehran's crackdown on the protests. Sanctions are intended to act as a coercive foreign policy tool, but domestic public opinion holds a veto over whether they can be lifted.

Sanctions lifting will either fail, or exact considerable political cost. That makes any US administration reluctant to agree to sanctions lifting; and even if an administration agrees to do so, it is unlikely to see it through as promised. Iran, and other US adversaries, know this. Thus, they approach talks with the United States having already factored in US inertia, at least when it comes to sanctions lifting.

If countries must either change completely to get rid of sanctions or remain subject to them, they lose any incentive to arrive at agreements. And yet, such agreements are the aim of American foreign policy. Which means that, rather than making US goals more achievable, sanctions *solidify* the problems that caused the United States to impose sanctions in the first place.

Escalation of sanctions against Iran between 2018 and 2022 led Iran to seek closer ties with Russia. The new cooperative relationship between the two manifested itself in Iran's military support for Russian invasion of Ukraine, which incensed Europe and the United States, inviting additional sanctions on Iran, and making a nuclear deal even more unlikely. In effect, American sanctions had helped engineer a fundamental strategic shift in Tehran, moving from a semblance of neutrality that reflected the "neither east, nor west" mantra of the 1979 Revolution to align Iran decidedly with Russia.

In wars, the two sides can agree to a ceasefire. With sanctions, such an agreement is an arduous and lengthy process, which means that conflicts can slow, but will not end.

SIX

What Sanctions Cost Iran—and the World

President Trump's "maximum pressure" showed, once again, the inability of economies large and small to avoid the US use of so-called secondary sanctions (directed at countries and companies that violate US sanctions on Iran).[1] Trump dispensed with the Obama administration's façade of rallying allies to support sanctions. He showed that the United States did not need to do so. Instead, all it had to do was to impose sanctions, and demand that all countries abide by them, threatening punitive action even against violators outside of US legal jurisdiction.[2] The world might complain over this exercise of extraterritoriality, but it would have no choice but to quickly fall in line.

However, as will be discussed below, the scale and brazen manner of implementation of "maximum pressure" was so drastic that it did provoke reaction among allies. They may not have had a choice but to accept American policy, but they did not do so without reservation. That resistance would cost the United States.

To start with, Washington's European allies refused to leave JCPOA and used whatever means at their disposal to keep it afloat and resist American policy where they could. Trump's Iran policy had assumed that Europeans too would leave the deal, forcing its formal collapse. Even though Europeans had no choice but to abide by the US sanctions, they were not compelled to follow the US on the diplomatic front. The clearest example of this came in September 2020, when European powers refused to vote in support of the US drive to reimpose arms embargo sanctions on Iran at the United Nations.

At the outset, however, "maximum pressure" was seen in the US as a resounding success. So much so that a common refrain in Washington in 2018–19 insisted this success proved that the US was more powerful on the world stage and more capable of imposing its will than policymakers and academics had previously understood. America did not really need allies or adversaries to agree with its policies; they had no option but to do so. Such hubris would only further American reliance on sanctions.

The efficacy of economic sanctions, however, proved to follow a "reverse J-curve"—whereby an economic trend first dips before it rises—not a straight shot to the moon. At a certain point, that is, sanctions proved counterproductive. The Trump administration imposed severe sanctions on Iran with the expectation that Tehran would quickly surrender and agree to negotiate with the US on a new nuclear deal, but also agree to fundamental changes to its regional policies. The eruption of social unrest in Iran in December of 2017, continuing into early months of 2018, perhaps convinced the administration that the Islamic Republic was about to buckle under pressure. The White House decided that it should not settle for a nuclear deal and should instead push for regime change. That is certainly how Tehran interpreted the intent of maximum pressure. The twelve-point list of demands put forth by Secretary of State Mike Pompeo went far beyond Iran's nuclear program and amounted to *de facto* regime change. However, although the maximal flexing of American power went unchecked, it failed to achieve the goal for which it had been deployed.

As the chapters in this book show, maximum pressure buffeted Iran's economy and society, but the Islamic Republic did not crumble, nor did it come to America on its knees ready for a new nuclear deal. Why was this the case and what have been the costs of that outcome?

Moral Hazard

Since the humanitarian catastrophe of the Biafran war in the late 1960s, concern for human rights and the welfare of the people has been a prominent component of American foreign policy.[3] US foreign policy claims a moral high ground and takes issue with how governments treat their citizens. It criticizes and levies sanctions on those who brutalize their population and deny them their basic constitutional and human rights. After the genocide in Rwanda in 1994, the idea of "responsibility to protect" became a buzzword of American diplomacy. It guided American intervention in Libya in 2011.

Broad-based economic sanctions, however, belie this vaunted concern for the welfare of the people.[4] Sanctions inflict pain on people to influence the behavior of their government. This was the explicit reason why economic sanctions were first conceived of and used after World War I. Then, the architects of economic sanctions were open about the intent and effect of sanctions: they aimed "to instill fear in civilians."[5] At that time, however, the explicit goal of sanctions to make people suffer was viewed as a deterrence to aggression. As the use of sanctions becomes routinized, policymakers no longer acknowledge sanctions' impact on individuals. The nomenclature surrounding sanctions today (rather than explicitly "inflicting pain on a population" or "instilling fear" in them) conveniently obfuscates *who* the sanctions impact.

A century after the League of Nations conceived of sanctions as an enforcement tool, how the tool works has not fundamentally changed. The population is punished for its government's behavior, and the population is tasked to compel the government to change its ways; even though, all along, the sanctioning government acknowledges that undemocratic and brutish governments are impervious to public opinion and pressure from below. American sanctions on Iran and later Russia unfold in tandem with the widespread belief that Iran's rulers and Russia's president Vladimir Putin are "brutal dictators," deaf to public opinion and ready to crush any sign of opposition. And yet the underlying assumption of sanctions is that popular disgruntlement and unrest will force dictatorships to change course. Sanctions are not generally levied on democracies, where the popular will matters. They are an instrument mostly deployed to bring dictators to heel, even though, by their nature, dictatorships resist and suppress dissent.

Thus, there is a moral hazard in the assumptions relied on by sanctions. They are premised on making life difficult for civilians, who are themselves helpless to change their fate. Prolonged and severe sanctions damage societies and economies in ways that cannot be easily reversed when and if sanctions are lifted. The more severe the sanctions, the greater the moral quandary. The case of sanctions on Iran bears this out.

The impact of sanctions on Iranian society has been detailed in earlier chapters of this book. Maximum pressure showed that US sanctions
could decimate an economy. The evidence from Iran is compelling.
Between 2018 and 2021 Iran's economy contracted by 12% and its per
capita income by 14%, poverty rose by 11% and average living standards
fell by 13%.[6] Inflation ravaged the economy. Food prices rose by 186%
and healthcare by 125%.[7] As disposable income shrank, Iranians spent
30% less on education and 32% less on entertainment.[8] In 2017, 45% of
Iranians could be considered middle class; that number fell to 30% by
2020.[9] The economic downturn affected all aspects of Iranian society.[10]
The impact was even worse during the COVID-19 pandemic, especially
as the United States decided not to provide effective exceptions for importing necessary pharmaceutical and humanitarian goods to deal with
the pandemic.[11] Iran could technically buy medical and pharmaceutical
goods, but, owing to financial sanctions, it could not pay for them.

The pauperization of Iran under maximum pressure was one reason
why the 2022 protests did not explode into a massive movement that
could overwhelm the Islamic Republic. The protests reflected popular
anger—especially among youth—toward the cultural strictures and political repression that dominated their daily lives. The discontent toward
the country's dire economic situation was even more widespread. However, the thin margins that Iranians were forced to survive on dissuaded
them from joining protests and strikes that could disrupt their liveli-
hoods. Too many Iranians lived day-to-day and depended on government
assistance—by one estimate 75% of Iranians in 2022 needed government
economic assistance to make ends meet—to mount a revolutionary struggle.[12] Sanctions that were designed to encourage regime change were in
effect preventing it from happening.

Such a foreign policy—which aims to destroy the middle class, crush
people, and foster hardship and poverty among civilian populations—
simply is not morally superior to the targeting of civilians in warfare.
A central element of US policymaking is to question the moral values
of adversary governments like Iran, and then to rally the international
community to support those policies guided by moral values. However,
targeting civilians through sanctions erodes the American moral high
ground and increases the cost to its policy.

A further problem lies in the negative impact of sanctions on society.

Earlier chapters have detailed how maximum pressure has changed Iranian society in worrying ways.

It has long been an article of faith in Washington that Iran has the most "pro-American" population in a region where anti-Americanism has been rife. Iran is, after all, the only post-Islamist country in the region, one that has tried an Islamic revolution and lived under an Islamic state and is no longer enamored by its promise. The driving force in Iranian society for change, opening the country, and turning toward the West has been the middle class.[13] Yet US economic sanctions have shrunk the Iranian middle class, reducing its economic importance and political influence.[14]

This is counterproductive to American foreign policy. Sanctions have not changed Iran; instead, they have weakened the constituency within it that favored building ties with the West.[15] Sanctions, then, have only made dealing with Iran more difficult, as the social base for resistance and distrust of the West has grown larger and more influential.

There is also the lesson the United States should have learned in Iraq.[16] When punishing sanctions were first adopted as the instrument for containing and changing the Saddam Hussein regime, Iraq boasted the largest middle class in the Arab world, a population with economic means and know-how, and the greatest number of engineers per capita. Iraq then had a literacy rate, infant mortality, and life expectancy that was the envy of the Arab world. It was this impression that led American policymakers to expect building democracy in Iraq to be an easy task. But that middle class disappeared under sanctions.[17] When Saddam fell from power, the middle class was nowhere to be found. It was the disenfranchised and the poor that inherited Iraq.[18] Instead of democracy, the country was ravaged by extremism and civil war. It has become a threat to the region that continues to tax American foreign policy.

Something similar has started to unfold in Iran, as the middle class is sinking under the weight of sanctions, and the country's social infrastructure is atrophying.[19] The result has been a hardening of its politics, which has put the country on the wrong path. Rather than looking to move past the revolution to normalize its foreign relations, it is hunkering down within the citadel of its rejectionist views.

In fact, as we have seen in earlier chapters, Trump's withdrawal from JCPOA and his maximum pressure strategy undermined the argument for pursuing engagement with the United States. President Rouhani and his moderate faction had argued for trusting the US in negotiating a nuclear deal with the hope that it would anchor Iran's future in ties with the West, and boost Iran's middle class and its moderate proclivities.[20] By withdrawing from the deal, the US bolstered the argument of Rouhani's critics and rivals—that Rouhani had been naïve and that it was a mistake to have trusted the US. The supreme leader, who had tacitly supported nuclear talks and JCPOA, now distanced himself from the deal, saying that he had warned Rouhani all along.[21]

If in 2013 the supreme leader had concluded that moderates would do better negotiating with the US, which had helped the election of Hasan Rouhani to the presidency and Javad Zarif's appointment as foreign minister, in 2021 he resolved on the reverse. He decided that the moderates would not be able to lift sanctions, and intractable and trenchant hardlines could achieve that goal. Sanctions had hardened Iran, and that would ultimately prove costly to the United States in the longer run.

In June 2021 the hardline candidate Ebrahim Raisi was elected president, and the foreign policy team that had negotiated the 2015 nuclear deal was replaced by those who believed that the US would only respond to pressure and threat. Ali Bagheri Kani, the new Iranian chief negotiator, had long criticized JCPOA and Iran's approach to diplomacy. He believed that only an Iran on the threshold of nuclear breakout could elicit concessions from the United States, and ensure that sanctions would not return.

US reliance on sanctions had taught Iran that the way to combat and reverse sanctions was by becoming more threatening. How have these lessons played out since 2015?

Maximum Pressure Fails, then Backfires

Iran was initially shocked by the US withdrawal from JCPOA and its bevy of new sanctions. This was not because Iranians had a charitable view of President Trump's intentions. Instead, their disbelief came from their calculation that the United States would remain in the deal because it would be able to use the mechanisms of the deal to exert pressure on Iran. By leaving the deal, Washington abandoned that advantage. The Trump administration may have expected that its departure would provoke Iran to quickly reciprocate and also leave the deal. With no deal in place, Iran would be isolated and exposed. It would have no diplomatic protection for its nuclear program.

Witnessing popular unrest in Iran in late 2017 and early 2018, Washington may have also concluded that the Islamic Republic was teetering on the verge of collapse and thus scuttling the nuclear deal and adding economic pressure would hasten its collapse. Short of that, Washington assured its worried European allies that Iran would be on its knees looking for a deal within a matter of months, and the whole issue would be quickly resolved, thanks to the power of sanctions.[22]

Trump's assumptions proved wrong. Tehran resolved not to give Trump a quick victory by leaving JCPOA and acquiescing to new negotiations. And they had two good reasons for doing so.

First, quick success would not satiate Washington's desire for a stronger deal, but, rather, whet its appetite for deploying sanctions to ask for something beyond the nuclear deal—in effect, regime change. If Iran went to the table quickly, then Washington would see it as weak and push harder. Secretary of State Pompeo's twelve demands of Iran made it clear that Washington's agenda extended far beyond Iran's nuclear program to the nature of the Islamic Republic itself.[23] A few months later Pompeo would add human rights demands to his original twelve points,[24] making it clear to Tehran that the United States was after regime change. The more Washington policy looked like regime change, the less inclined was Tehran to engage, lest it encourage the pressure. When fresh protests erupted in Iran in 2019 and 2020, Iran's rulers suspected American incitement, the unfolding of a one-two punch of sanctions and covert action. That suspicion turned to conviction in 2022 as protests erupted across Iran in the aftermath of the death of Mahsa Amini. Iran's rulers openly accused the West of waging a "hybrid war" (*jang-e tarkibi*) against Iran. In that war sanctions prepared the ground, while the use of cyberattacks and information warfare through social media and exile television stations fomented uprisings.[25] The 2022 protests posed a significant challenge to Iran's rulers. They exposed the depth of popular discontent; anger not only at the economic situation facing the country but the authoritarian and theocratic nature of the Islamic Republic. The world cheered the protesters and reveled in the humbling of Iran's ruling order. Tehran, however, was determined not to engage in nuclear diplomacy from a position of weakness, especially since it saw the American hand behind the protests. Iran would not see engagement as beneficial until it convinced the West that hybrid war was futile.

Second, Iran had already cashiered the bulk of its nuclear program to secure JCPOA. It had no leverage in new talks. The question of trusting the United States in the first place, in 2013, had been a divisive political issue in Tehran. The government of President Rouhani had pushed for nuclear talks and then acceptance of JCPOA. The deal had proven to be ephemeral; its economic promises to the people, a mirage. Iranians were frustrated and angry that the United States had easily fooled Iran. There was no political support in Iran for new negotiations, not after Iran had fulfilled its part of JCPOA.

All this meant that Iran had to resist and survive maximum pressure rather than surrender to US demands. Iran decided to stay in the nuclear deal, an unexpected maneuver that immediately wrong-footed the Trump strategy. For the first time, it was the United States that was diplomatically isolated and subject to international criticism. Staying in the deal gave reason and time for Europeans to explore ways to address Iran's economic concerns. By staying inside the deal, Iran denied Washington the argument that Iran was in violation of the nuclear deal, after which Washington would need to seek the support of the international community to roll back the program, perhaps by military means. Iran also needed time to explore ways to sustain its economy despite the draconian new sanctions, and to build leverage for future talks. It could achieve those aims better if it stayed inside JCPOA.

All of this did not dissuade Washington from seeking to destroy JCPOA from the outside and force Iran into new negotiations. Again, the weapon of choice was sanctions. The United States launched a strategy of "maximum pressure," putting Iran's economy under unprecedented pressure by cutting Iran's oil exports, trade, and access to the international financial system. The number of sanctions on Iran would increase threefold in a matter of two years.

The Iranian economy, as earlier chapters show, would prove more resilient than Washington had assumed. The shock to the economy was severe, and social unrest was real. However, Iranians by and large blamed Washington for the sudden turn in their fortunes; hence, the full force of their wrath was not directed at their own government. Political protests rattled Iran on an ongoing basis but remained localized. They did not grow in a mass movement that could threaten the ruling regime, as they had during the Green Movement of 2009.

Iran gradually built the capacity to circumvent the sanctions, at least enough for its economy to stay afloat.[26] Iran continued to export oil, natural gas, and electricity to neighboring countries and, for a time, to India. Most importantly, it continued to sell oil to China.[27] Manufacturers who had relied on European capital and intermediary goods replaced trade ties with Europe with new ones with China.[28] That helped local manufacturers expand production to supplant some of the Western imports; but, more important for the long run, it also tied Iran's economy to a greater extent to China.[29]

If President Rouhani and his team had hoped that JCPOA would anchor Iran's economy and hence political future in ties with the West, maximum pressure had the opposite effect. Iran's rulers now saw economic ties with the West as a vulnerability and relations with China as necessary to their strategy of survival. It would be these burgeoning economic ties with China that would culminate in talks for a twenty-five-year strategic partnership between the two countries.[30] In the short run, an axis with China would help Iran resist maximum pressure. Yet in the longer run, this new partnership would open Iran to greater Chinese influence, at a time when the US was hoping to curtail Beijing's growing global influence.

Maximum pressure sanctions did not end Iran's oil exports altogether. In fact, exports went up from 400,000 barrels a day at the outset of maximum pressure to 700,000 barrels a day in 2020.[31] This was still far lower than the 2.5 million barrels a day before maximum pressure was put in place. The damage to the Iranian economy was significant enough to persuade Iran to favor a deal with the United States, but not any deal and not at any cost—a return to JCPOA as it stood in 2015 was unlikely. Iran had learned that it should build a bigger nuclear program before negotiating with the US, then negotiate incrementally, and give up nuclear assets slowly over a far longer period than it did in 2015, to compel the US to lift sanctions and dissuade it from reimposing them.

By May 2020, Iran's leadership was confident that the country had weathered the worst of maximum pressure. The long-run cost to Iran's economy and political stability was profound, but there would be no immediate threats to its ruling order. Tehran had concluded by then that, despite its best intentions, Europe was powerless in the face of American policy and would not be able to find any way around maximum pressure. This conclusion would only confirm Iran's strategic shift away from the US in China's direction.

Iran's leaders also concluded that the Trump administration saw no cost in applying maximum pressure and would continue to escalate pressure to get what it was after. Unless that perception was reversed, Trump was likely to continue the current course and seek to further tighten the economic noose around Iran's neck. That would inevitably lead to either war or regime collapse and mayhem inside Iran. Tehran had to deter Washington by imposing cost on its strategy. Those among the Iranian leadership who had argued for a more robust Iranian response to maximum pressure started to get the upper hand.

———

Washington was attracted to sanctions because it has been deemed as a facile alternative to war. But Iran's case showed that sanctions will eventually encourage a country under sanctions to react in ways that, instead, escalates the risk of war. This unfolded in Iran's case as maximum pressure sanctions started to cripple Iran's economy and destabilize the Islamic Republic; and as Washington looked poised to keep tightening the stranglehold on Iran. Tehran decided to make it clear that further pressure would lead to war, and that it would be costly to the United States and its Persian Gulf allies who had supported US policy.

The turning point came in April 2019 when President Trump, frustrated that maximum pressure had not yet brought Iran to its knees, decided to further tighten sanctions on Iran. He announced that the United States was going to reduce Iran's exports to zero: this meant ending waivers the US had given a few countries to continue to buy Iranian oil while they looked for alternatives. Washington would also pressure China to end its purchase of Iranian oil. With this announcement, Iran's "strategic patience" ended. Pressure would have to be met with pressure. The turning point shows that sanctions will not remain forever cost-free.

Iran reacted to Trump's announcement by declaring that, since the other signatories to JCPOA were no longer in compliance with the deal—as Iran was not receiving the economic benefits it believed it was entitled to—Iran too would reduce its own compliance but would remain in the deal. These steps away from full compliance were reversible but significant. They would happen gradually, with the aim of putting Europeans on notice that the deal was in real danger and the burden of saving it could not be shouldered by Iran alone. Tehran was also sending a signal to Washington that its economic pressure risked a major crisis.

By 2019, Tehran had concluded that despite his bombast Trump was averse to starting a new war in the Middle East, and much like his predecessor wished to reduce American entanglements in the region to focus on Asia. Trump might have thought that he could increase economic pressure on Iran without risking war or jeopardizing his pivot to Asia. Iran was now determined to disabuse him of this halcyon assumption.

In May 2019, four tankers were attacked off the cost of the United Arab Emirates (UAE) port of Fujairah on the Gulf of Oman.[32] Iran denied responsibility, but the attack sent a strong signal to both the US and UAE that Iran would no longer merely absorb maximum pressure and was determined to exact a price for sanctions. Instability in the Persian Gulf would threaten stability of energy markets and the global economy. The UAE and Saudi Arabia had supported the US withdrawal from JCPOA and US sanctions on Iran. Iran also intended to warn its neighbors of the cost of supporting maximum pressure. The UAE's main urban centers are a mere hundred kilometers from Iranian shores. They are in easy reach of Iranian missiles and drones, and that makes the UAE's energy and tourism sectors vulnerable to Iran.

The Fujairah incident was followed by additional attacks on tankers in the Persian Gulf. Then came an audacious Iranian downing of a high-flying US surveillance drone.[33] That act brought the US close to military retaliation. According to President Trump, US fighter jets and missiles were ready to commence attacks on Iranian targets, when he changed his mind.[34] The downing of the American drone showed both Iran's willingness and capability to escalate the crisis in ways that the US had neither anticipated nor wished to see unfold. In fact, President Trump's last-minute change of heart showed that he was not willing to countenance the rebounding costs that maximum pressure was setting before the United States.

With these attacks, Iran also showed that it had crossed a Rubicon. It had become more aggressive, risk-taking, and dangerous. This was a *consequence* of sanctions. The world would now understand that the prolific use of sanctions was likely to be met with hard power. Ultimately, sanctions were not an alternative to war but could be a cause of war.[35]

American response to Iranian aggression was to add to the sanctions. Iran responded by further aggression. In September, Iranian drones and missiles carried out a sophisticated attack on oil facilities in Abqaiq and Khurais in eastern Saudi Arabia. The audacity of the attack, and Iran's ability to go around Saudi and American radars and air defense systems, caught Washington by surprise. Iran was again signaling that it was not going to passively endure sanctions, but was also showcasing military capabilities that could prove deadly and which the United States may have not been aware of. In short, maximum pressure could lead to a war that could be more difficult and costly than the US might have assumed.

President Trump decided not to retaliate directly—although the US said that it carried out cyberattacks in response. Iran was again escalating conflict in response to maximum pressure and signaling that it had the capability of causing significant damage in the UAE and Saudi Arabia and to the stability of oil markets. Iran was becoming more dangerous, and Washington was dealing with its provocations by ignoring them. Iran was also showcasing its military technology to deter war. Tehran's goal was for the US to reassess maximum pressure. It was a risky gambit that would again bring the two sides closer to war. The brewing crisis also showed that, unlike in a military confrontation, the US could not reduce the scope of sanctions as a way of de-escalating a conflict.

Iran's decision to escalate regional tensions ultimately led to a near war standoff with the United States. In late December 2019 an Iranian missile attack on an Iraqi air base killed an American contractor.[36] The US retaliated with missile strikes on Iraqi militias that had carried out the attack and maintained close ties to Iran's IRGC. The incensed militias mobilized a mob to lay siege to the US embassy in Baghdad, demanding the withdrawal of American troops from the country.

Worried that the standoff would lead to an attack on the embassy—precipitating another "Benghazi" imbroglio, or worse yet, another "American hostage crisis" akin to 1979 in Tehran—the Trump administration decided to kill the commander of IRGC's expeditionary force, the Quds Force, General Qasem Soleimani.[37] Soleimani had a near-mythic reputation as the mastermind behind Iran's regional operations.[38] Eliminating him, concluded Washington, would both cripple Iran's regional policies and be a strong warning that it desist from aggressive policies.

The drone that killed Soleimani also killed the senior Iraqi militia commander, Mahdi al-Mohandes. Millions of Iranians took to the streets to mourn Soleimani's killing, turning the IRGC commander into a martyr and, for some, a folk hero. Similarly, Mohandes's killing incensed many Iraqi Shias. In both countries, there were calls for vengeance as a deep grudge against the United States set in.

Iran's supreme leader declared that the true revenge for Soleimani's killing would be an American departure from the region.[39] Still, Iran had to respond more concretely, not only to assuage domestic public opinion but also to deter further US assassination attempts. On January 8, 2020, Iran targeted the Ain al-Asad base in Iraq, which was home to some 1,500 US troops with close to a dozen ballistic missiles. The barrage was the largest missile attack US troops have ever faced. Surprisingly there were no US casualties.[40] The attack was the culmination of a tense forty-eight-hour period during which the two countries stood at the edge of war. That the missile attack did not lead to greater conflict owed to President Trump's decision to dismiss its scale and impact. Responding to questions about traumatic brain injuries some American soldiers may have suffered in the attack, Trump said, "I heard that they had headaches."[41]

Maximum pressure had brought the two to the verge of war, a war that failed to materialize only because the US president decided to back down. Iran, however, concluded that its show of force had worked; it had exposed the US aversion to war and compelled it to de-escalate. The killing had also gained sympathy for the Islamic Republic at home and abroad and energized the regime's resolve.[42]

The case of Iran had confirmed that sanctions could ultimately lead to war. And yet, this historical lesson seems lost on policymakers.[43]

———

Every step Iran took away from full compliance escalated pressure on the United States and Europe. Iran rebuilt its enrichment capability using more advanced cascades of centrifuges; it increased its stockpile of hard water and low enriched uranium; more worryingly, it commenced enriching uranium to 20%. In December 2020, the Iranian parliament mandated that the government match noncompliance with noncompliance: unless the United States and Europe took steps to fulfill their JCPOA obligations, Iran would resume enrichment and suspend cooperation with the United Nations' nuclear watchdog agency, the International Atomic Energy Agency (IAEA). These steps would reduce the breakout time—the time Iran needed to amass sufficient highly enriched uranium for one bomb—that JCPOA had established. Iran would not resume cooperation with the IAEA before February 2021.

In the run-up to American presidential elections of 2020 the Democratic Party candidates, President Biden included, had confirmed their wish to restore JCPOA. All Iran had to do was to wait out Trump. A US return to JCPOA would follow, along with the reestablishment of "compliance for compliance." Sanctions would be lifted on Iran, as it too would reverse steps it had taken away from its commitment under the nuclear deal.

However, once in office, the Biden administration dithered. It decided that there was no need to rush the restoration of JCPOA—or even seek to do so. The administration feared that a simple return to JCPOA would provoke bipartisan resistance. It had to elicit further concessions from Iran in the form of tighter nuclear restrictions, and curtailment of its program and regional activities—in short, what Secretary of State Anthony Blinken called "a longer and stronger deal."

Thus, maximum pressure failed to achieve its policy goal and wasted valuable trust and political capital, as well as time. JCPOA contained several provisions that would expire by 2023—the so-called "sunset clauses." In agreeing to this timeline, the Obama administration had assumed that successful implementation of JCPOA would build trust and generate momentum, which would pave the way for further negotiations that would address any unresolved issues and extend the deal well beyond 2023. Maximum pressure had instead destroyed trust and wasted four years, making the 2023 deadlines more ominous than they had been in 2015. The Biden administration had to contemplate returning to a deal that had limited shelf life, and it had to exchange sanctions relief just to get Iran back into full compliance with the deal. Once the US returned to compliance under JCPOA, it would have little leverage to persuade a jilted Iran to trust in new negotiations. The Biden administration was also confronting an important cost of sanctions, which was discussed in the previous chapter: namely, the inordinate ability of Congress and domestic pressure groups to resist the lifting of sanctions.

To solve this conundrum and get Iran to agree to accept additional restrictions, the Biden administration decided to hold on to maximum pressure for a while longer. It did not return to JCPOA soon after assuming office, as it had indicated during the presidential campaign. The new administration rejected a limited lifting of sanctions as a goodwill measure, even on vital medical and humanitarian trade amidst the pandemic, and decided to wait. In effect, the Biden administration adopted the maximum pressure strategy as its own, confirming the Trump-era belief in the efficacy of sanctions in achieving Iran policy goals.

There would be no immediate talks. Instead, the Biden administration conveyed to Tehran that Iran would have to return to full compliance before the US would consider doing so, and at best Washington would be willing to release Iranian funds frozen in Asian banks—payments for oil Iran had sold under JCPOA—in exchange for Iran's full compliance with JCPOA. Iran understood this to mean that the US wanted to buy its full compliance with "its own money," oil proceeds that were facilitated by JCPOA, but there would no lifting of Trump-era sanctions. Washington was going to use those to elicit further concessions from Iran on nuclear, missiles, and regional issues—to secure a so-called longer and stronger deal.

The realization that maximum pressure had now become bipartisan American policy—that is, that the Biden administration, too, was leaning on it for the same reasons as its predecessor—angered Tehran. In response, Iran decided to mount its own maximum pressure. Through the spring of 2021, Iran accelerated its nuclear program at an alarming scale. It suspended IAEA monitoring of nuclear sites and commenced enriching uranium first up to 60%, saying it would push that limit to 90%.

Under JCPOA, Iran was allowed only 202.8 kilograms of low enriched uranium at 3.67% until 2031. By 2021, Iran had enriched around 2.5 tons of uranium, of which 114 kilograms were enriched to 20% and eighteen kilograms to 60%.[44] It had deployed advanced centrifuges in contravention of JCPOA stipulations and hinted that it might leave JCPOA altogether to pursue a more secretive nuclear program. Under JCPOA, Iran was permitted to operate a limited cascade of first-generation centrifuges. By 2021, it was operating over 2,100, including more advanced second-generation centrifuges.[45] It was also testing even faster cascades with greater enrichment capacity.

The United States and Israel sought to slow the program through acts of sabotage at Iran's nuclear enrichment and centrifuge production facilities in Natanz and Karaj.[46] Israel also assassinated Iran's top nuclear scientist (and later other military officials and scientists),[47] and carried out debilitating cyberattacks against industrial facilities and Iran's energy and electricity grids. These were all done to warn the Islamic Republic, and to foment public discontent.[48]

These operations, however, did little to dent the expansion of Iran's nuclear program. The effect was, in fact, the opposite. Iran rebuilt damaged facilities quickly and accelerated its program.[49] Iran's breakout capacity started to shrink rapidly. It would soon get down to two weeks. And given the know-how Iranian scientists had gained, and the infrastructure they had built in the process, JCPOA restrictions would no longer be adequate to ensure that Iran remained two years away from breakout.[50]

It was after Iran flexed its muscles that the US dropped its strategy of Iranian compliance for release of Iran's frozen funds, and, instead, agreed to engage in indirect talks in Vienna in 2021 to fully restore JCPOA. It now faced an even more distrustful and obdurate Iran, one that demanded compensation and guarantees from the US.

It was not just Trump's *volte face* that had angered Iran. Now, most importantly, it was Iran's realization that the US had become comfortable with sanctions, and the ease with which they could be put in place meant that the barter of sanctions for nuclear assets was not an even one.

In 2021, Iran's leaders concluded that they had miscalculated in 2015. They had not fully understood the ease with which sanctions could return. They had gone into negotiations with the US too early and with too little leverage, and then had implemented their part of the deal too quickly. All of which had led the Trump administration to conclude that the US could withdraw from the nuclear deal without concern over Iran's nuclear capability, and then envision no cost to imposing maximum pressure on Iran. Instead, they expected sanctions to quickly result in new negotiations and a new deal.

If Iran's nuclear program had been more advanced in 2015—so the thinking now went in Tehran—Iran could have asked for more concessions while giving up less, and Washington would have shown a greater commitment to agreement. Thus, the lesson that maximum pressure taught Iran was that a nuclear deal will only be successful if Iran has enough leverage to force the United States to lift more sanctions, and then to think twice about breaking the deal.

The larger lesson of JCPOA, however, was that Iran gave up tangible physical assets that it had built over time and at great cost, whereas the US merely agreed to rescind laws that could one day come back into force. There was no meaningful cost to lifting sanctions, nor to reimposing them. It is to change this calculus that Iran decided to resist maximum pressure and demand that the US government pay compensation for abandoning the deal and inflicting economic pain on Iran.

Even while JCPOA was being negotiated, Iran's supreme leader reminded Iranian President Rouhani and his team of the fate of Muammar al-Qaddafi in Libya. When Qaddafi agreed to give up his nuclear program, the supreme leader told his audience, Libya received some sanctions relief, but no goodwill from the West. Instead, giving up the nuclear program played a hand in the toppling of the Qaddafi regime. In fact, this would be the same point made after Russia invaded Ukraine, reneging on guarantees it had given Ukraine when it separated from the Soviet Union and turned over its nuclear arsenal to Russia.

Once maximum pressure was imposed, Tehran worried that the aim was to use sanctions to weaken Iran, before more aggressive intervention could topple the Islamic Republic. Commanders of the IRGC started to argue that it was better for Iran to go to war with the United States while it still had its strength, rather than languish under sanctions that would hollow the Iranian state, as they did in Iraq under sanctions. War, they argued, would also rally the population to the flag, and deny Washington the breach between the people and the leadership that it coveted.[51]

Iran decided not to go to war. But, as sanctions bit hard into the economy, it did start to risk direct confrontation.

––––––

Iran's leaders have come to see regime change as the goal of maximum pressure—a hybrid war directed at toppling the Islamic Republic. They have blamed popular protests that have rocked the country over the past three years on outside interference—assuming Washington's strategy is to prod the population into unrest and then use its agents to light the fuse for a mass uprising. Would the United States have followed such a strategy had Iran not given up its nuclear program? The guardians of the Islamic Republic think not. The imperative of regime survival will remain a barrier to easy concessions in nuclear talks unless the fear of regime change subsides in Tehran.

The Biden administration hopes that a new nuclear deal with Iran will diffuse the crisis that was precipitated by the US withdrawal from JCPOA. However, maximum pressure has made a full return to the 2015 deal an elusive goal. Iran successfully reacted to American pressure by pressure of its own, in the form of a more assertive regional policy and acceleration of its nuclear program. Sanctions did not force the 2015 nuclear deal to crumble. Instead, the agreement was hollowed out, and only then did it provoke Iranian countermeasures. That forced the US to return to nuclear negotiations, facing a more bullish Iran further along on the path to advanced nuclear capability. The United States, which had wanted a "longer and stronger deal," now had to settle for a weaker JCPOA.[52]

Any deal that would leave Iran closer to a breakout point than in 2015 is likely to keep Iran under sanctions. But this will continue the vicious cycle of Iranian pressure to lift them, as well as American reliance on more of them to keep Iran at bay. That poses the risk of another crisis before long. And if the US and Iran fail to arrive at a stable deal, then Washington is likely to look to ratchet up sanctions even further.[53] That could risk war.

International Cost of Overuse of Sanctions

Iran is a cautionary tale about the diminishing returns of sanctions. Overreliance on sanctions runs the risk of depleting entities that can be sanctioned. As more sanctions are levied, and an economy is increasingly isolated from the world, there will be fewer meaningful targets left to sanction. That in turn will make additional sanctions largely symbolic and toothless, and as a result ineffective. This is especially a concern if there emerge new areas of conflict that demand American reaction. The United States imposed maximum pressure on Iran to force it to negotiate over its nuclear program. In the process Iran's trade, oil exports, and access to global financial institutions were severely curtailed. Iran's principal leaders, and main state institutions including the Revolutionary Guard and the Central Bank, were sanctioned. That left the United States with few, if any, valuable targets for additional sanctions to either increase pressure on Iran on the nuclear issue or respond to Iran's regional policies or violations of human rights. When Iran erupted in protests over Mahsa Amini's death, and soon after Iran supplied Russia with sophisticated drones that were used to devastating effect in Ukraine, the United States, and then Europe, added a bevy of new sanctions on Iran. These new sanctions largely stood to represent Western outrage; none of them had the prospect of materially impacting Iran's economy or policymaking.

Overuse of sanctions also runs the danger of immunizing the world to their effectiveness. The Iranian case raised alarm around the world about unchecked American use of sanctions and the threats that it poses to the interests of all international actors.[54] Now, other nations could find themselves caught in its dragnet as either targets of sanctions or so-called "secondary actors" forced to comply with unilateral US sanctions. American decisions now have the potential to disrupt trade more broadly and force countries to suspend economic ties that run counter to their interests.

India serves as a good example. India had been buying Iranian oil and developed ties with Iran, in line with their shared geostrategic objective of limiting Pakistan's ability to deepen its influence in Afghanistan. In the 1990s, Iran and India had joined hands with Russia to support the Northern Alliance's resistance to the Taliban's drive to take over Afghanistan. Both Iran and India were wary of Pakistan's support of Sunni extremism in Afghanistan: Iran saw Pakistan serving as a pawn of its regional rival Saudi Arabia, and India believed Pakistan was supporting Sunni extremism to establish a base of support from which to launch jihadi operations in India. Furthermore, Iran and India worried that Pakistan sought to control Central Asia's access to the Arabian Sea through Afghanistan.

To circumvent Pakistan as the only trade corridor for Central Asia, India signed an agreement in 2016 with Iran to invest $8 billion in developing the port of Chabahar on the shores of the Gulf of Oman. Chabahar is a short distance from the port of Gwadar that China was developing on Pakistan's Makran coast on the Arabian Sea. The project was intended to connect Chabahar by road and railway links to western Afghanistan and from there to Central Asia. The project was of geostrategic importance to India, allowing it to maintain trade routes with Afghanistan and Central Asia independent of Pakistan. It would also reduce Afghanistan's reliance on the Pakistani corridor for trade with the outside world. Once China and Pakistan forged a strategic partnership that brought China to Gwadar, Chabahar also became important to India's rivalry with China—and by extension to the US desire to bolster India as an Asian counterweight to China.

However, secondary sanctions—as mandated by the Trump administration's maximum pressure—demanded that India suspend its investments in Chabahar. India had to forgo financial investments it had made to date, and, furthermore, cede all access to Afghanistan and Central Asia, allowing Pakistan and China to control that trade corridor. Iran reacted to India's forced exit from Chabahar by suggesting that the development initiative could become a Chinese project instead, which would further strengthen China's position in West Asia.[55] Abiding by US secondary sanctions is clearly at odds with India's vital strategic interests involving its principal regional rivals.

India is not alone. The US ability to force the world to enforce its foreign policy priorities is a predicament for countries large and small.

When economic sanctions were first conceived after World War I, it was assumed that they would not be used.[56] The devastating impact of sanctions would be worse than war, and that would deter countries from engaging in adventurous foreign policy behavior that would disturb the international order. Russia's invasion of Ukraine, coming on the heels of the US sanctions assault on Iran, shows that the deterrence value of sanctions is not what it is made out to be.

If more countries risk sanctions to challenge the international order, then sanctions will become purely punitive. They will no longer deter. Instead, they will simply shrink global economic relations, which would, in turn, make defying sanctions easier.

Currently, countries friendly to the US, as well as those at odds with it, do not have the means to protect themselves against American sanctions. But with the experience of Iran, and then Russia, before them, they have started to invest in mechanisms that would resist or circumvent US pressure.[57]

Rather than deter, sanctions will encourage autarky. Countries that contemplate challenging the US-led international order will delay action long enough to protect themselves against sanctions by building resilience. They will not be successful in doing so fully, but a trend will be set in motion toward the decoupling of global economic relations and self-reliance. Iran sanctions encouraged China, Russia, and other international actors to increase explorations of mechanisms that would allow them to circumvent the dollar, ranging from an alternative to the SWIFT network to greater use of currency swaps and cryptocurrency in trade.[58] The sanctions on Russia after its invasion of Ukraine will only expedite this trend. The larger lesson here for many countries is that globalization and their strategic interests do not align. Removing trade barriers and increasing dependency on the global economy and the US dollar–dominated system renders them vulnerable to sanctions. That would limit their strategic options. To free their foreign policies from that constraint, countries will see benefit in protecting themselves from globalization.

Although these efforts will not immediately dethrone the supremacy of the dollar, they are bringing closer the day when it ceases to be the world's currency. It is not the weakening of the American economy that is the cause, as was the case with the British pound after World War II, but the overreach of US sanctions. The long-term result will be an eroding effect of economic sanctions, as more economies seek to circumvent the global dollar economy. It will also carve the world into economic spheres and reverse the impact of economic globalization: less global prosperity, more poverty, and more conflict and aggression.

America's reliance on sanctions to contain and roll back Iran's nuclear program represents the apogee of the use of economic statecraft in lieu of war. Over the past decade, the United States has shown that it can deploy sanctions expansively and to ruinous effect. It can compel other countries to abide by those sanctions, enhancing their effectiveness. Even so, the power of sanctions has not resulted in their greater effectiveness. Maximum pressure sanctions against Iran were effective and devastated Iran's economy, but they did not force it to abandon its nuclear program. Instead, Iran returned to negotiations only after it had built a *larger* program.

In fact, sanctions have the effect of encouraging those targeted to build leverage to deter sanctions and encourage their lifting. This is only one cost of sanctions. The humanitarian damage they entail, the pressure they put on allies, and the ways in which they open the door to Congress and pressure groups to influence the conduct of American foreign policy—all are costs with which advocates of sanctions must reckon.

CONCLUSION

Permanent Siege

Prolonged and severe sanctions damage societies and economies in ways that cannot be easily reversed when and if sanctions are lifted. It is always the population that is punished for its government's behavior, and it is the population that is tasked to compel the government to change its ways.

Although bombs are not dropped, long-term comprehensive sanctions create an environment of siege, shortage, and intense pressure in sanctioned countries. As this book has shown, the attempted economic suffocation of a nation—with the stated goal of inflicting pain on people to influence the behavior of their government—raises serious moral questions about comprehensive economic sanctions. This moral hazard notwithstanding, this book also shows that the efficacy of sanctions as a foreign policy tool is open to question.

Such broad violence is rarely discussed today. Not so earlier: when economic sanctions were first conceived after World War I, the architects were open about the intent and effect of sanctions. Their goal for sanctions was "to instill fear in civilians."[1] And this was why, in the interwar period, economic sanctions were meant to be employed in order to reduce aggression and avert war. But as the use of sanctions has become prolific, policymakers rarely consider or acknowledge sanctions' impact on societies and individuals. The nomenclature surrounding sanctions today (rather than explicitly "inflicting pain" on a population or "instill-ing fear" in them) conveniently obfuscates *who* the sanctions impact, or talks about that impact as "unintended."

Hundreds of thousands of people have died pursuant to humanitar-ian catastrophes that have followed in the wake of comprehensive sanc-tions in different countries: food shortages,[2] the breakdown of medical systems,[3] and the unavailability of critical medicines have all contributed to the human toll.[4] Comprehensive sanctions regimes also target critical infrastructure and the opportunities available for knowledge producers, professionals, and students, impacting the aspirations of targeted popula-tions. Over time, this leads to compounded crises that span generations: in-terrupted social reproduction, brain drain, declining quality of education.

Yet unlike "just war" theory—in which noncombatants should be pro-tected—in sanctions regimes, the distinction between combatants and noncombatants is purposefully blurred. If the goal of sanctions is to in-flict enough pain on a society to pressure the political elite to change behavior, the target in fact becomes "noncombatants"—ordinary people—violating the very terms of warfare in the current international order. Prolonged comprehensive sanctions regimes distribute pain and death so widely that they function as an invisible war.

Wielding comprehensive economic sanctions as a foreign policy—which we demonstrate in this book has impoverished the Iranian middle class and fostered hardship and poverty among civilian populations—simply is not morally superior to the targeting of civilians in warfare. A central element of US policymaking is to win the hearts and minds of the populations it is targeting with sanctions by questioning the moral stand-ing of their government. However, because this assertion of an American high moral ground is invisible to a population under economic siege, the sanctions themselves ensure that they will not achieve the very thing they are intended to achieve—winning over the population to the extent that they rise up against their government.

The international system currently does not have any clear rules governing the use of sanctions; there are no international guidelines outlining what is ethical or unethical. It is true that the United Nations has critiqued how US comprehensive sanctions against countries such as Iran, Cuba, and Venezuela cause humanitarian suffering and violate human rights. Regardless, these comprehensive sanctions continued, even in the throes of a global pandemic in 2020–21.[5]

Moreover, as we demonstrate in this book, comprehensive economic sanctions have not reduced tensions between Iran and the US, or Iran and US allies in the Middle East. Quite the opposite, in fact. Indeed, as this book has shown, the US has increased the deployment of comprehensive economic sanctions regardless of the result, and with no off-ramps to lift them, it has created a dynamic for permanent conflict with sanctioned nations. Four decades of US sanctions on Iran have only furthered enmity between the two countries, increasing the likelihood of lethal conflict and the prospect of a nuclear Iran, all the while compelling the Iranian population to pay the price.

Sanctions, as we show in this book, are a tool for creating an enemy that only grows more dangerous and aggressive the longer sanctions stay in place. Moreover, with no clear path toward an exit for a comprehensively sanctioned country like Iran, comprehensive economic sanctions contribute to prolonged conflict. Iran has responded to US maximum pressure sanctions by increasing its military posture. On the domestic front, US maximum pressure sanctions have weakened the middle class, enriched the Revolutionary Guard and those loyal to the regime by magnitudes, and led to the further securitization of civil society and militarization of Iran's political culture. Iran's experience with sanctions has also led it to develop policies that inure the country from Western economic pressures, thus pushing the country's trade and relations away from the West and toward Russia and China, an outcome that, in the long term, challenges the United States.

As the US uses the same strategy with even larger economies like Russia and China, it is important to take stock of the lessons of Iran. These sanctions will not produce compliance but instead encourage Russia and China to resist, and then contemplate challenging the US-led international order. They will invest in mechanisms to protect their economies from sanctions, learning the lessons of Iran, and to build social and economic resilience in the process. Although no sanctioned country will be fully successful in deflecting the impact of sanctions, they still can do enough to survive the shocks. The changes that this process will bring to these countries will combine to impact the global economy. As more countries go under sanctions, they will set in motion a trend toward decoupling global economic relations and promoting self-reliance. The Iran sanctions encouraged China, Russia, and other international actors to increase explorations of mechanisms that would allow them to circumvent the dollar, ranging from an alternative to the SWIFT network to greater use of cryptocurrency in trade to investing in transportation networks that would connect Eurasia and circumvent trade routes susceptible to US interdiction.[6] The sanctions on Russia after its invasion of Ukraine have only expedited this trend.

Although these efforts will not immediately dethrone the supremacy of the dollar, they are creating mechanisms with the intent of seriously challenging the dollar as the world's currency. It is not the weakening of the American economy that is the cause, as was the case with the British pound after World War II, but the overreach of US sanctions. This reality will also carve the world into economic spheres and reverse the impact of economic globalization: less global prosperity, more poverty, and more conflict and aggression.

With the United States sanctioning larger economies such as Russia, and threatening more punishing sanctions on a country like China, it behooves us all—as scholars, policymakers, and concerned citizens—to critically examine economic sanctions. Put another way, it is time to understand how sanctions *really* work.

What are the consequences of the economic punishment and siege of a nation—for its people, for its political actors, and for the international system? A century ago, Wilson called sanctions a way to "suffocate" a nation into submission. Now we know better: such suffocation—no matter how painful—only encourages a nation to fight back. The consequences will not be what the United States had expected, but they will be ones which the world will have to contend with long afterward.

NOTES

Introduction

1. Habibe Jafarian, "Something Cataclysmic Every Week," *The Baffler*, no. 53 (September 2020), trans. Salar Abdoh, https://thebaffler.com/outbursts/something -cataclysmic-every-week-jafarian.

2. Quoted in Nicholas Mulder, *The Economic Weapon: The Rise of Sanctions as a Tool of Modern War* (New Haven, CT: Yale University Press, 2022).

3. Madeleine Albright, in an interview on *60 Minutes* with Lesley Stahl, responded to Stahl's question about whether 500,000 Iraqi children dying from sanctions was "worth it": "I think this is a very hard choice. But we think the price is worth it." Olian Catherine, Lesley Stahl, and CBS Video, dirs., *Punishing Saddam*, CBS Video, 1996.

4. For a history of economic sanctions, see Mulder, *The Economic Weapon*. For additional scholarship on the development of the field of studying sanctions and the debates around it, see, among others: David Baldwin, *Economic Statecraft* (Princeton, NJ: Princeton University Press, 2020); Navin A. Bapat, Tobias Heinrich, Yoshiharu Kobayashi, and T. Clifton Morgan, "Determinants of Sanctions Effectiveness: Sensitivity Analysis Using New Data, International Interactions," *International Interactions* 39, no. 1 (2013): 79–98; Risa Brooks, "Sanctions and Regime Types: What Works and When?," *Security Studies* 11, no. 4 (2002): 1–50; David Cortright and George Lopez, "Are Sanctions Just? The Problematic Case of Iraq," *Journal of International Affairs* 52, no. 2 (1999): 735–55; Dan Drezner, "Economic Sanctions in Theory and Practice: How Smart Are They?," in *Coercion: The Power to Hurt in International Politics*, ed. Kelly Greenhill and Peter Krause (New York: Oxford University Press, 2018); Daniel Drezner, *The*

Sanctions Paradox: Economic Statecraft and International Relations (Cambridge: Cambridge University Press, 1999); Bryan Early, *Busted Sanctions: Explaining Why Economic Sanctions Fail* (Stanford, CA: Stanford University Press, 2015); Timothy Frye, "Economic Sanctions and Public Opinion: Survey Experiments from Russia," *Comparative Political Studies* 52, no. 7 (2019): 967–94; Johan Galtung, "On the Effects of International Economic Sanctions, With Examples from the Case of Rhodesia," *World Politics* 19, no. 3 (1967): 378–416; Kerim Can Kavaklı, J. Tyson Chatagnier, and Emre Hatipoğlu, "The Power to Hurt and the Effectiveness of International Sanctions," *Journal of Politics* 82, no. 3 (2020): 879–94; Fiona McGillivray and Alastair Smith, "Trust and Cooperation through Agent-Specific Punishments," *International Organization* 54, no. 4 (2000): 809–24; Dursun Peksen: "When Do Imposed Economic Sanctions Work? A Critical Review of the Sanctions Effectiveness Literature," *Defence and Peace Economics* 30, no. 6 (2019).

5. Mulder, *The Economic Weapon*, 4.

6. For scholarship on the impact of sanctions on targeted populations, see, among others: Nadje Al-Ali, "Reconstructing Gender: Iraqi Women between Dictatorship, War, Sanctions and Occupation," *Third World Quarterly* 26, no. 4/5 (2005): 739–58; Y. Al Jawaheri, *Women in Iraq: The Gender Impact of International Sanctions* (New York: I. B. Tauris, 2007); P. Sean Brotherton, *Revolutionary Medicine: Health and the Body in Post-Soviet Cuba* (Durham, NC: Duke University Press, 2012); Omar Dewachi, *Ungovernable Life: Mandatory Medicine and Statecraft in Iraq* (Stanford, CA: Stanford University Press, 2017); A. Cooper Drury and Dursun Peksen, "Women and Economic Statecraft: The Negative Impact International Economic Sanctions Visit on Women," *European Journal of International Relations* 20, no. 2 (2014): 463–90; T. Dyson and V. Cetorelli, "Changing Views on Child Mortality and Economic Sanctions in Iraq: A History of Lies, Damned Lies and Statistics," *BMJ Global Health* 2, no. 2 (2017); Mohammad Reza Farzanegan et al., "Effect of Oil Revenues on Size and Income of Iranian Middle Class," *Middle East Development Journal* 13, no. 1 (2021): 27–58; Hanna Garth, *Food in Cuba: The Pursuit of a Decent Meal* (Stanford, CA: Stanford University Press, 2020); Joy Gordon, *Invisible War: The United States and the Iraq Sanctions* (Cambridge, MA: Harvard University Press, 2012); Joy Gordon, "A Peaceful, Silent, Deadly Remedy: The Ethics of Economic Sanctions," *Ethics and International Affairs* 13, no. 1 (1999): 123–42; Jerg Gutmann et al., "Sanctioned to Death? The Impact of Economic Sanctions on Life Expectancy and Its Gender Gap," *Journal of Development Studies* 57, no. 1 (2021): 139–62; Mediel Hove, "The Debates and Impact of Sanctions: The Zimbabwean Experience," *International Journal of Business and Social Science* 3, no. 5 (2012); Ehsan Lor Afshar, "Banking the Bazl: Building a Future in a Sanctioned Economy," *Economic Anthropology* 9, no. 1 (2022): 60–71; Yiyeon Kim, "Economic Sanctions and HIV/AIDS in Women," *Journal of Public Health Policy* 40 (2019): 1–16; Matthias Neuenkirch and Florian Neumeier, "The Impact of US Sanctions on Poverty," *Journal of Development Economics* 121 (July 2016): 110–19; Elham Taheri and Fatma Guven

Lisaniler, "Gender Aspect of Economic Sanctions: Case Study of Women's Economic Rights in Iran," *SSRN Electronic Journal* (December 19, 2018); Emrah Yildiz, "Nested (In)securities: Commodity and Currency Circuits in Iran under Sanctions," *Cultural Anthropology* 35, no. 2 (2020): 218–24.

7. US Department of the Treasury, *The Treasury 2021 Sanctions Review*, October 2021, https://home.treasury.gov/system/files/136/Treasury-2021-sanctions -review.pdf.

8. Mulder, *The Economic Weapon*, 8.

9. Two oil booms in recent history, in the 1970s and 2000s, allowed Iranian governments of different political persuasions—one a monarch, the other a populist president—to satisfy with imports the rising aspirations of a large segment of Iranians for a global middle-class lifestyle. The 1979 revolution did not change the political economy of using oil income to boost private consumption at the expense of domestic production and jobs. And as long as oil revenues flowed, governments would not want to voluntarily switch course from a policy of liberal import in favor of an industrial policy that limited dependence on imports to protect key domestic industries from the vagaries of the oil market. The first boom, in the 1970s, ended with the revolution in 1979, and the second with sanctions in 2011.

10. Mulder, *The Economic Weapon*, 4–5.

11. For this research, see the following (all from the Rethinking Iran Initiative, School of Advanced International Studies [SAIS], Johns Hopkins University): Narges Bajoghli, "Iran in Latin America: Striver Cosmopolitans and the Limits of U.S. Sanctions," 2021, https://www.rethinkingiran.com/iranunder sanctions/bajoghli; Esfandyar Batmanghelidj, "Resistance Is Simple, Resilience Is Complex: Sanctions and the Composition of Iranian Trade," 2020, https:// www.rethinkingiran.com/iranundersanctions/batmanghelidj; Orkideh Behrouzan and Tara Sepehri Far, "The Impact of Sanctions on Medical Education in Iran," 2021, https://www.rethinkingiran.com/iranundersanctions/orkideh-beh rouzan-tara-sepehri-far; Shahrokh Fardoust, "Macroeconomic Impacts of U.S. Sanctions (2017–2019) on Iran," 2020, https://www.rethinkingiran.com/iranun dersanctions/fardoust; Kevan Harris, "Iran's Government Expenditure Priorities and Social Policy Burdens during Sanctions," 2021, https://www.rethinking iran.com/iranundersanctions/kevan-harris-irans-government-expenditure-pri orities-and-social-policy-burdens-during-sanctions; Kaveh Madani, "The Unintended Environmental Implications of Iran Sanctions," 2020, https://www.re thinkingiran.com/iranundersanctions/kaveh-madani; Adnan Mazarei, "Inflation Targeting in Time of Sanctions and Pandemic," 2020, https://www.rethink ingiran.com/iranundersanctions/mazarei; Arzoo Osanloo, "Entanglements: Lives Lived under Sanctions," 2021, https://www.rethinkingiran.com/iranunder sanctions/arzoo-osanloo-entanglements-lives-lived-under-sanctions; Hadi Salehi Esfahani, "The Experience of Iran's Manufacturing Sector under International Economic Sanctions," 2020, https://www.rethinkingiran.com/iranunder sanctions/hadi-salehi-esfahani; Djavad Salehi-Isfahani, "Impact of Sanctions on

Household Welfare and Employment," 2020, https://www.rethinkingiran.com/iranundersanctions/salehiisfahani; Nazanin Shahrokni, "Bursting at the Seams: Economic Sanctions and Transformation of the Domestic Sphere in Iran," 2021, https://www.rethinkingiran.com/iranundersanctions/nazanin-shahrokni; Alexander Soderholm, "Sanctions and Illicit Drugs in Iran," 2020, https://www.rethinkingiran.com/iranundersanctions/soderholm; Leili Sreberny-Mohammadi, "Sanctions and the Visual Arts of Iran," 2021, https://www.rethinkingiran.com/iranundersanctions/sreberny-mohammadi; Sara Vakhshouri, "U.S. Sanctions and Iran's Energy Strategy," 2020, https://www.rethinkingiran.com/iranundersanctions/vakhshour.

Chapter One

1. All names have been anonymized.

2. Kevan Harris, *A Social Revolution: Politics and the Welfare State in Iran* (Oakland: University of California Press, 2017).

3. Salehi-Isfahani, "Impact of Sanctions."

4. Richard Nephew, *The Art of Sanctions: A View from the Field* (New York: Columbia University Press, 2017), 10–11.

5. Garth, *Food in Cuba*.

6. Dewachi, *Ungovernable Life*.

7. Gordon, *Invisible War*.

8. Amir Vahdat, "UN Envoy: US Sanctions on Iran Worsen Humanitarian Situation," *AP News*, May 18, 2022, https://apnews.com/article/politics-iran-nuclear-global-trade-united-nations-61ce077f975af481319307ee35dc229d.

9. Osanloo, "Entanglements."

10. Yarimar Bonilla, "The Swarm of Disaster," *Political Geography* 78 (2020).

11. Bonilla, "Swarm of Disaster," 2.

12. It is important to note that after the outbreak of COVID-19 in Wuhan, China, Iran was the next country hit with massive waves of the virus. Coverage in Western media about Iran's handling of COVID-19, with frequent references to mass graves and a state unwilling or unable to quell the transmission of the virus, was meant to vilify the country. It was only after Italy and then New York City became the next hot-spots that coverage in Western media shifted drastically from how poorly Iran and China dealt with the virus to COVID-19 being a phenomena that overwhelmed existing public health infrastructures in wealthy and democratic states as well.

13. Dewachi, *Ungovernable Life*.

14. Zach Dorfman, "Frustrated with CIA, Trump Administration Turned to Pentagon for Shadow War with Iran," *Yahoo!News*, November 23, 2021, https://news.yahoo.com/frustrated-with-cia-trump-administration-turned-to-pentagon-for-shadow-war-with-iran-205152958.html?guccounter=1.

15. Dorfman, "Frustrated with CIA."

16. Donya Alinejad and Ali Honari, "Online Performance of Civic Participation: What Bot-like Activity in the Persian Language Twittersphere Reveals

about Political Manipulation Mechanisms," *Television and New Media* 23, no. 11 (November 2021).

17. Alex Marquardt, "State Department Suspends Funding of Anti-Iran Group Which Targeted Journalists and Activists," *CNN*, June 5, 2019, https://www.cnn .com/2019/06/05/politics/us-suspends-funding-anti-iran-group.

18. See Alinejad and Honari, "Online Performance of Civic Participation"; Murtaza Hussain, "An Iranian Activist Wrote Dozens of Articles for Right-Wing Outlets: But Is He a Real Person?," *The Intercept*, June 9, 2019, https://theintercept .com/2019/06/09/heshmat-alavi-fake-iran-mek/.

19. See Osanloo, "Entanglements."

20. Nephew, *The Art of Sanctions*.

21. Edward Said, *Covering Islam: How the Media and the Experts Determine How We See the Rest of the World* (New York: Vintage Books, 1997).

22. See Ebby Abramson, "Another Iranian Student Deported from Boston Despite Court Order," Endangered Scholars Worldwide, January 23, 2020, https:// www.endangeredscholarsworldwide.net/post/another-iranian-student-de ported-from-boston-despite-court-order.

23. For more on the PEN America legal case, see "PEN, Co-Plaintiffs Settle OFAC Lawsuit," PEN America, October 1, 2007, https://pen.org/press-release/ pen-co-plaintiffs-settle-ofac-lawsuit/ (accessed October 1, 2021).

24. Narges Bajoghli, "The Researcher as a National Security Threat: Interrogative Surveillance, Agency, and Entanglement in Iran and the United States," *Comparative Studies of South Asia, Africa and the Middle East* 39, no. 3 (December 2019): 451–61; Bajoghli, "Iran in Latin America."

25. Hadi Kahalzadeh's forthcoming research focuses on the impact of sanctions on women and poverty. For more on the impact of sanctions on middle-class women, see Shahrokni, "Bursting at the Seams."

26. Salehi-Esfahani, "Impact of Sanctions."

Chapter Two

1. Charles Kurzman, *The Unthinkable Revolution in Iran* (Cambridge, MA: Harvard University Press, 2005).

2. See *U.S. Joint Forces Command Millennium Challenge 2002: Experiment Report*, United States Joint Forces Command, https://www.esd.whs.mil/Portals/ 54/Documents/FOID/Reading%20Room/Joint_Staff/12-F-0344-Millennium -Challenge-2002-Experiment-Report.pdf, accessed September 15, 2022.

3. The four candidates of the 2009 presidential elections in Iran were incumbent president Mahmoud Ahmadinejad; former prime minister (1980s) Mir-Hossein Mousavi; former chairman of the parliament Mehdi Karrubi; and former chief commander of the Revolutionary Guard Mohsen Rezaei. In the aftermath of the June 12, 2009 presidential elections, hundreds of thousands, some claim millions, poured onto the streets of Tehran and other main cities of the country to protest the announcement of Ahmadinejad's victory with 65 percent of the vote. After one week of nonviolent protests, the state deployed anti-riot

police and *Basij* militia to attack protestors. Throughout the summer of 2009, scores of protestors, student leaders, reformist politicians, women's rights activists, journalists, and artists were rounded up and imprisoned. Although estimates vary on the exact number of those imprisoned for taking part in the Green Movement, the BBC reported that 170 people were arrested after the first two days of protests in June. Another 200 students were arrested in the raid on the University of Tehran dormitories on June 15, and 100 students were arrested on June 16 at Shiraz University. During June 2009 alone, *The Guardian* estimated that 500 people were arrested. The Green Movement catalyzed the largest demonstrations in the history of the Islamic Republic, and the state responded by imprisoning former ministers and vice presidents, in addition to activists and lay people participating in the demonstrations. According to opposition accounts, 107 individuals were killed in the period following the June 2009 election to March 2010. These deaths include those killed in the streets during the protests, as well as those in prisons and in the hospital. This number is significantly lower than the number of dead in the Egyptian uprising of 2011, but as news of the torture and killings in the prisons and streets began to leak out, the anger grew, but heavy-handed suppression eventually quelled the Green Movement for the moment.

4. For more on digital media and the Green Movement, see Negar Mottahedeh, *#iranelection: Hashtag Solidarity and the Transformation of Online Life* (Stanford, CA: Stanford University Press, 2015).

5. This six-hour interview was leaked in the lead-up to the June 2021 presidential election. Political commentators believed it was leaked to ensure that Zarif would not be able to run for president given the critical remarks in the interview about Soleimani, who was being immortalized as a national hero.

6. After the return of Ayatollah Khomeini to Iran in February 1979, the ensuing years witnessed battles among differing revolutionary groups for political power. The country saw armed uprisings and nascent civil war in the Turkoman and Kurdish regions of the country; the Mujahedin-e Khaleq organization (MKO or MEK in English), in particular, undertook armed resistance, including assassinations of top-ranking clerics and allies of Khomeini and officials of the new revolutionary state.

7. Seyed Ali Khamenei, "The 'Second Phase of the Revolution' Statement Addressed to the Iranian Nation," February 11, 2019, https://english.khamenei.ir/news/6415/The-Second-Phase-of-the-Revolution-Statement-addressed-to-the.

Chapter Three

1. Nephew, *The Art of Sanctions*.

2. Nephew, *The Art of Sanctions*, 16, 44.

3. Nephew, *The Art of Sanctions*, 45.

4. Nephew, *The Art of Sanctions, 45*.

5. Nephew, *The Art of Sanctions*, 46.

6. 50 U.S.C. Section 1701(a).

7. Christopher Bidwell, "US Courts Say Iran Owes Terrorism Victims Billions: That's an Obstacle to a New Iran Nuclear Deal," *Bulletin of the Atomic Scientists*, August 3, 2021.

8. Yeganeh Torbati, "Deal or Not, Many U.S. States Will Keep Sanctions Grip on Iran," *Reuters*, April 13, 2015.

9. Tom Ruys and Cedric Ryngaert, "Secondary Sanctions: A Weapon Out of Control? The International Legality of, and European Responses to, US Secondary Sanctions," *British Yearbook of International Law*, September 22, 2020.

10. Proclamation 4702, Imports of Petroleum and Petroleum Products from Iran, November 12, 1979.

11. Executive Order 12170, Blocking Iranian Government Property, November 14, 1979. Unlike an act of Congress, an executive order can be unilaterally repealed by the president.

12. Executive Order 12205, Prohibiting Certain Transactions with Iran, April 7, 1980. Food, medicine and humanitarian aid were exempted.

13. Executive Order 12211, Further Prohibitions on Transactions with Iran, April 17, 1980. The Treasury's Office of Foreign Assets Control (OFAC) is in charge of administering and enforcing US sanctions.

14. See Section 6(j) of the Export Administration Act of 1979.

15. Kenneth Katzman, *Iran Sanctions*, Congressional Research Service, February 2, 2022, 2, https://sgp.fas.org/crs/mideast/RS20871.pdf.

16. But arbitrage tended to appear as sanctions in disguise. Indeed, these agreements precluded compensation for the US diplomats held hostage by the young Islamic Republic until January 1981, but the FY2016 Consolidated Appropriation set up a mechanism for paying damages to the US embassy hostages using settlements paid by various banks for concealing Iran-related transactions and proceeds from other Iranian frozen assets, including those assets discussed earlier.

17. Executive Order 12282, Revocation of Prohibitions against Transactions Involving Iran, January 23, 1981. Removal of "all sanctions" was one of the conditions of the Algiers Accords, signed between Iran and the US on January 19, 1981. Both countries agreed to end litigation between their respective governments and citizens, referring the cases to international arbitration at the Iran–United States Claims Tribunal, which continues its work in The Hague.

18. The designation entails a ban on direct US financial assistance and requires US representatives in multilateral organizations to vote against any lending; it also bans exports of arms and dual-use items. These triggers are contained in separate laws, namely the Export Administration Act, the Arms Export Control Act, and the Anti-Terrorism and Effective Death Penalty Act, which apply the provisions to any country on the terrorism list. For a detailed account of the 1983 Beirut bombing, see David Crist, *The Twilight War: The Secret History of America's Thirty-Year Conflict with Iran* (New York: Penguin, 2012), 139–59.

19. The ramifications of such constraints were legion: restrictions on sales of US dual-use items, bans on direct US financial assistance and arms sales to Iran,

requirements to oppose multilateral lending, withholding of US foreign assistance to countries that assist or sell arms to terrorism-list countries, and withholding of US aid to organizations that assist Iran. The president's authority to remove a country from the terrorism list is subject to congressional approval after a forty-five-day notification period. Rescission of the designation would require the president to certify to Congress that Iran has not provided support for acts of terrorism within the preceding six months and has provided assurances that it will not support acts of international terrorism in the future. Congress can block the removal by enacting a joint resolution of opposition, subject to presidential veto, itself subject to override by a two-thirds supermajority. Section 307 of the FAA (added in 1985) names Iran as unable to benefit from US contributions to international organizations, and requires proportionate cuts if these institutions work in Iran.

20. A few months later, the administration violated the embargo by secretly facilitating the sale of arms to Iran in exchange for the release of US hostages held in Lebanon. For more information on the so-called Iran-Contra Affair, see Lawrence E. Walsh, "Final Report of the Independent Counsel for Iran/Contra Matters," United States Court of Appeals for the District of Columbia Circuit, August 4, 1993.

21. Executive Order 12613, Prohibiting Imports from Iran, October 29, 1987.

22. See Section 586G(a) of Public Law No. 101–513.

23. Iran-Iraq Arms Nonproliferation Act, Title XVI of the National Defense Authorization Act for Fiscal Year 1993, Public Law No. 102–484, October 23, 1992. The act imposed sanctions on foreign entities that supply Iran with "destabilizing numbers and types" of conventional weapons or weapons of mass destruction (WMDs).

24. Katzman, *Iran Sanctions*, 50.

25. "Iran, Russia Agree on $800 Million Nuclear Plant Deal," *Washington Post*, January 9, 1995. In 1990, Iran signed a $800 million contract to construct four VVER-1000 reactors and four other VVER-440 reactors, with Russia sending a thousand experts to Iran. See Vladimir V. Evseev, "Russie-Iran: Un partenariat prudent," *Outre-Terre*, February 2011.

26. See Executive Order 12938, Proliferation of Weapons of Mass Destruction, November 14, 1994.

27. Announcing that "the actions of the government of Iran pose an unusual and extraordinary threat to the national security, foreign policy, and economy of the United States," President Clinton declared a state of emergency between the two nations on March 15, 1995. See Paul Richter and Robin Wright, "Clinton Kills Pending Iran-Conoco Oil Deal," *Los Angeles Times*, March 15, 1995.

28. Executive Order 12957, Prohibiting Certain Transactions with Respect to the Development of Iranian Petroleum Resources, March 15, 1995.

29. Executive Order 12957, Prohibiting Certain Transactions with Respect to the Development of Iranian Petroleum Resources, March 15, 1995.

30. Executive Order 12959, Prohibiting Certain Transactions with Respect to Iran, May 6, 1995.

31. Executive Order 13059, Prohibiting Certain Transactions with Respect to Iran, August 19, 1997.

32. Iran Sanctions Act, Public Law No. 104–172, August 6, 1996. The bill passed in the House of Representatives without an opposing vote and received the unanimous consent of the Senate. Over the years, legislation expanded the triggers and sanctions under ISA while circumscribing presidential waiver authority. Whereas the original trigger was established at a $20 million investment in Iran's oil sector, the current list of triggers ranges from selling gasoline to Iran, to investing in Iran's petrochemical sector and providing insurance for Iranian oil tankers. See Katzman, *Iran Sanctions*.

33. For a review of the "critical dialogue" between Iran and Europe, see Bernd Kaussler, "From Engagement to Containment: EU-Iran Relations and the Nuclear Programme, 1992–2011," *Journal of Balkan and Near Eastern Studies* 14, no. 1 (March 2012): 53–76; Council Regulation (EC), no. 2271/96, Protecting against the Effects of the Extra-territorial Application of Legislation Adopted by a Third Country, and Actions Based Thereon or Resulting Therefrom, November 22, 1996.

34. Katzman, *Iran Sanctions*, 7.

35. Special waivers were built in to allow continued cooperation between the National Aeronautics and Space Administration (NASA) and the Russian space agency. See Iran Nonproliferation Act of 2000, Public Law No. 106–178, March 14, 2000.

36. Executive Order 13224, Blocking Property and Prohibiting Transactions with Persons Who Commit, Threaten to Commit, or Support Terrorism, September 23, 2001.

37. Katzman, *Iran Sanctions*, 81.

38. In October 2003, Iran reached agreement with France, Germany, and the UK, pursuant to which it committed to: "engage in full co-operation with the IAEA to address and resolve through full transparency all requirements and outstanding issues of the Agency and clarify and correct any possible failures and deficiencies within the IAEA"; "sign the IAEA Additional Protocol and commence ratification procedures"; "continue to cooperate with the Agency in accordance with the Protocol in advance of its ratification"; and "voluntarily . . . suspend all uranium enrichment and reprocessing activities as defined by the IAEA." In return, the EU-3 stated that "this will open the way to a dialogue on a basis for longer-term cooperation. In particular, once international concerns . . . are fully resolved Iran could expect easier access to modern technology and supplies in a range of areas."

39. On December 18, 2003, Iran signed the Additional Protocols. Mohamed ElBaradei, the IAEA director general, remarked: "If you look at the big picture, we are clearly moving in the right direction. If you compare where we were a year ago and where we are today, that's a sea change."

40. Crisis Group interviews with German and French officials, Tehran, Paris, and Washington, February–March 2004. See Crisis Group Report, *Iran : Where Next on Nuclear Impasse?*, November 24, 2004.

41. Executive Order 13382, Blocking Property of Weapons of Mass Destruction Proliferators and Their Supporters (June 28, 2005), allows the president to block the assets of proliferators of weapons of mass destruction (WMD) and their supporters under the authority granted by the International Emergency Economic Powers Act (IEEPA; 50 U.S.C. 1701 et seq.), the National Emergencies Act (50 U.S.C. 1601 et seq.), and Section 301 of Title 3, U.S.C. The numerous Iranian or Iran-related entities sanctioned under the order are listed in the tables at the end of this report. Entities delisted during US implementation of JCPOA are in italics. See Katzman, *Iran Sanctions*.

42. Crisis Group Middle East Report No. 51, *Iran: Is There a Way Out of the Nuclear Impasse?*, February 23, 2006.

43. The Iran Freedom Support Act, Public Law No. 109–293, September 30, 2006. IFSA prohibits the sale of WMD technology or destabilizing numbers and types of advanced conventional weapons to Iran. The act allocates "sums as may be necessary" to assist Iranians who officially oppose the use of violence and terrorism; advocate for Iran's adherence to the nonproliferation regime; are dedicated to democratic values and respect for human rights; support fundamental freedoms; work to establish equality of opportunity; and support adoption of a democratic form of government.

44. Section 311 of the Patriot Act, enacted in the wake of the September 11, 2001 terrorist attacks on the US, authorizes the Treasury Department to deny access to the US financial system to any entities exposed to or involved in money laundering or terror financing. In September 2005, the Treasury Department designated Banco Delta Asia (BDA), a small Macanese bank holding North Korean assets, as an institution of money laundering concern. In January 2006, Stuart Levey, undersecretary for terrorism and financial intelligence at the Treasury Department, replicated the policy against Iran and spearheaded a global effort to press the private sector to curb business with Tehran. A former Iranian finance minister, Davoud Danesh-Jaffari, characterized Levey's undertaking as "a serious and breath-taking game of chess." A US official said, "It's the most direct and aggressive stuff we've got going. It delivers." See Robin Wright, "Stuart Levey's War," *New York Times*, October 31, 2008.

45. Several international organizations, such as the Financial Action Task Force (FATF, the financial watchdog for the thirty-four largest economies) and the Organization for Economic Cooperation and Development (OECD, which includes thirty of the world's richest nations), warned against dealing with Iranian financial institutions. See Louis Charbonneau, "Iran Bank Hit Hard by U.N. Sanctions: Diplomats," *Reuters*, July 30, 2007.

46. According to a GAO report of February 2013, the Treasury Department convinced at least eighty of them to cease handling financial transactions with Iranian banks.

47. In the wake of his reelection, US president Barack Obama made a direct linkage:

We've imposed the toughest sanctions in history. It is having an impact on Iran's economy. There should be a way in which they can enjoy peaceful nuclear power while still meeting their international obligations and providing clear assurances to the international community that they're not pursuing a nuclear weapon. I very much want to see a diplomatic resolution to the problem. I was very clear before the campaign, I was clear during the campaign, and I'm now clear after the campaign—we're not going to let Iran get a nuclear weapon. But I think there is still a window of time for us to resolve this diplomatically. . . . I think it's fair to say we want to get this resolved, and we're not going to be constrained by diplomatic niceties or protocols. If Iran is serious about wanting to resolve this, they'll be in a position to resolve it. ("Remarks by the President in a News Conference," White House, November 14, 2012)

48. For text of the OFAC ruling barring U-turn transactions, see the document fr73_66541.

49. Crisis Group interview, US officials, Washington, December 2012. Prior to 2008, US banks could clear indirect dollar transactions for Iranian financial institutions, an authorization known as the "U-turn" exception. In 2006, the Treasury Department accused one of Iran's largest banks, Bank Saderat, of facilitating fund transfers to Hezbollah and barred it from using the US banking system. Two years later, the ban was extended to all other Iranian banks. This primarily affected Iran's oil receipts, as the dollar is the international currency for oil markets, and most of Iran's oil income was channeled through the US financial system. See "Revoking an Authorization Previously Granted to U.S. Depository Institutions to Process U-Turn Transfers," US Treasury Department, November 6, 2008.

50. On US-Iranian relations during President Obama's first term and the nuclear fuel swap initiative, see Trita Parsi, *A Single Roll of the Dice: Obama's Diplomacy with Iran* (New Haven, CT: Yale University Press, 2012).

51. Comprehensive Iran Sanctions, Accountability, and Divestment Act of 2010 (CISADA), Public Law No. 111–195, July 1, 2010. CISADA banned the sale of gasoline, related aviation fuel, and other fuels to Iran and barred foreign banks from conducting transactions with Iranian institutions that were blacklisted from accessing the US market. It also imposed travel bans and asset freezes on Iranians who were determined to have violated human rights and proscribed the sale of technology liable to be used to monitor or control the internet.

52. See Section 105 of CISADA; Executive Order 13553, Blocking Property of Certain Persons with Respect to Serious Human Rights Abuses by the Government of Iran and Taking Certain Other Actions, September 29, 2010. On March 2010, a General License was provided for the provision to Iranians of free mass-market software. The regulations change required a waiver of the provision of the Iran-Iraq Arms Nonproliferation Act (Section 1606 waiver provision) discussed earlier.

53. Executive Order 13553—Blocking Property of Certain Persons with Respect to Serious Human Rights Abuses by the Government of Iran and Taking Certain Other Actions, September 29, 2010. The order impounded the US-based assets of eight Iranian officials and banned their entry into the country. The list included Mohammad Ali Jafari, commander of the IRGC; Heydar Moslehi, intelligence minister; and Saeed Mortazavi, former prosecutor-general. See Saeed Kamali Dehghan, "Iranian Officials Put on Travel Blacklist by UK, US and Canada," *The Guardian*, July 8, 2011.

54. "Implementation of the NPT Safeguards Agreement and Relevant Provisions of Security Council Resolutions in the Islamic Republic of Iran," IAEA, GOV/2011/65, November 8, 2011.

55. Executive Order 13577, Concerning Further Sanctions on Iran, May 23, 2011, authorized the implementation of financial sanctions outlined in ISA, while Executive Order 13590, Iran Sanctions, November 21, 2011, extended the list of sanctioned individuals to those knowingly engaged in the country's energy and petrochemical sectors.

56. The action was taken under Section 311 of the USA Patriot Act. The designation was a stark warning about the risks of dealing with Iran's financial institutions—including the Central Bank of Iran. See "Fact Sheet: New Sanctions on Iran," US Treasury Department, November 21, 2011. US officials contended that the designations were justified because the Central Bank was helping other Iranian banks circumvent sanctions. Crisis Group interview, Washington, DC, December 2012.

57. The measures were attached to the defense appropriation bill. David Cohen, undersecretary for terrorism and financial intelligence, testified to the Senate on December 1, 2011, that "[it] is imperative that we act in a way that does not threaten to fracture the international coalition of nations committed to the dual-track approach, does not inadvertently redound to Iran's economic benefit, and brings real and meaningful pressure to bear on Iran." See Section 1245 of the FY2012 National Defense Authorization Act (NDAA, Public Law No. 112–81, December 31, 2011).

58. Executive Order 13599, Blocking Property of the Government of Iran and Iranian Financial Institutions, February 5, 2012.

59. Executive Order 13622, Authorizing Additional Sanctions with Respect to Iran, July 30, 2012. The order essentially sanctions any new customer of Iranian energy products, as NDAA exemptions apply solely to existing ones.

60. See Iran Threat Reduction and Syria Human Rights Act of 2012, H.R. 1905—Public Law No. 112–158, August 10, 2010.

61. Iran Freedom and Counter-Proliferation Act of 2012, Subtitle 1241 of the National Defense Authorization Act of 2013. Repealing or amending NDAA 2013 requires congressional action, but the president enjoys various waiver authorities. See Josh Rogin, "White House Opposed New Iran Sanctions," *Foreign Policy* (online), November 30, 2012, https://foreignpolicy.com/2012/11/30/white-house -opposed-new-iran-sanctions/. The administration obtained exemptions, nota-

bly the right to waive sanctions on Iran's crude oil customers if "exceptional circumstances prevented the country from being able to reduce significantly its purchases of petroleum and petroleum products from Iran."

62. See Executive Order 13608, Prohibiting Certain Transactions with and Suspending Entry into the United States of Foreign Sanctions Evaders with Respect to Iran and Syria, May 1, 2012.

63. See Revocation of Executive Orders 13574, 13590, 13622, and 13645 with Respect to Iran, Amendment of Executive Order 13628 with Respect to Iran, and Provision of Implementation Authorities for Aspects of Certain Statutory Sanctions, White House, January 16, 2016.

64. See Crisis Group Middle East Reports Nos. 18, *Dealing with Iran's Nuclear Program*, October 27, 2003; 51, *Iran: Is There a Way Out of the Nuclear Impasse?*, February 23, 2006; 116, *In Heavy Waters: Iran's Nuclear Program, the Risk of War and Lessons from Turkey*, February 23, 2012; 152, *Iran and the P5+1: Solving the Nuclear Rubik's Cube*, May 9, 2014; and Briefings Nos. 34, *The P5+1, Iran and the Perils of Nuclear Brinkmanship*, June 15, 2012; 40, *Iran and the P5+1: Getting to "Yes"*, August 27, 2014; and 43, *Iran Nuclear Talks: The Fog Recedes*, December 10, 2014.

65. UN Security Council Resolution 2231, July 20, 2015.

66. The almost three-month time span between Adoption and Implementation Days was significantly less than the P5+1's six-to-nine-month estimates. Crisis Group interviews, US and European officials, New York, September 2015. A letter to Rouhani by parliamentarians charging that the pace of centrifuge deactivation exceeded the supreme leader's directive (which conditioned implementation on the IAEA settling allegations on Iran's past nuclear activities) caused the government to temporarily stop the process. "Iran Stops Dismantling Nuclear Centrifuges under Pressure from Hardliners," *Reuters*, November 10, 2015. The government justified the rush, implicitly confirming the accusation, by reiterating the $100 million daily cost of sanctions' continuation for Iran. "Zarar-e takhir-e ejrāe-e barjām" [Damage of JCPOA's delayed implementation], ISNA.ir, September 21, 2015. The February 2016 parliamentary election was also part of the calculus. Crisis Group Middle East Report No. 166, *Iran after the Nuclear Deal*, December 15, 2015.

67. See "Final Assessment on Past and Present Outstanding Issues Regarding Iran's Nuclear Program," IAEA, GOV/2015/68, December 5, 2015, and the related Board of Governors resolution, GOV/2015/ 72, December 15, 2015. Leaks about the Joint Commission's confidential decisions gave credence to these suspicions. David Albright and Andrea Stricker, "JCPOA Exemptions Revealed," Institute for Science and International Security, September 1, 2016. The decisions exempted liquid, solid, and sludge wastes, particularly those in pipes of Isfahan's Enriched UO_2 Powder Plant (EU-PP), and irradiated uranium enriched to below 3.67 percent, from the 300 kg threshold set by JCPOA; near–20 percent enriched uranium in unrecoverable "lab contaminant"; and nineteen "hot cells" (radiation containment chambers for handling radioactive material) that are larger than

the deal permitted. "Decision of the Joint Commission," EU External Action Service, January 6 and 16, December 18, 2016.

68. For instance, plutonium produced in hot cells is neither sufficient nor usable for nuclear weapons without a reprocessing facility, which Iran lacks and is banned from constructing. The same applies to weaponizing waste contaminated with low enriched uranium needing further processing to highly enriched uranium prohibited under JCPOA. Julian Borger, "Obama Administration Denies Secret Loopholes in Iran Nuclear Agreement," *The Guardian*, September 1, 2016.

69. Annex II, JCPOA; US Executive Order 13716, January 16, 2016; Council Decision (CFSP) 2015/ 1863, October 18, 2015; Council Regulation (EU) 2015/1861, October 18, 2015; and UNSC Resolution 2231, "Iran Oil Exports Hit Pre-sanctions High on Run-up in Condensate Shipments," *Reuters*, October 3, 2016; "mizān-e sarmāyeh gozāry-e khārejy e'lām shod" [Amount of foreign investment was announced], ISNA.ir, December 3, 2016; "Inflation Rate Drops to 7.2% in Iran," *Tehran Times*, December 23, 2016; Crisis Group interviews, Iranian entrepreneurs, Frankfurt, November 16, 2017; "Regional Economic Outlook: Middle East and Central Asia," IMF, October 2016.

70. "Europe's Banks Begin Tentative Return to Iran," *Financial Times*, April 3, 2016.

71. "A Conversation with Javad Zarif," event at Council on Foreign Relations, New York, September 23, 2016.

72. "Kerry: Businesses Using US Sanctions as Excuse to Avoid Iran," *Associated Press*, May 10, 2016. For a critical take on Kerry's initiative, see Stuart Levy, "Kerry's Peculiar Message about Iran for European Banks," *Wall Street Journal*, May 12, 2016.

73. For more background, see Crisis Group Middle East Report No. 138, *Spider Web: The Making and Unmaking of Iran Sanctions*, February 25, 2013. One of the most arduous elements of US primary sanctions has proven to be their requirement that multinational companies wall off their US staff and board members from business with Iran. "BP Ring-Fences CEO Dudley from Iran Decision-Making," *Reuters*, November 21, 2016.

74. These have not been affected by JCPOA, since as an executive agreement—unlike a ratified treaty—it is not binding for US states. Eli Lake, "Obama Administration Urges States to Lift Sanctions on Iran," *Bloomberg*, April 18, 2016.

75. Businesses often find OFAC guidelines legalistic and vague. In October 2016, OFAC issued a guideline noting that business dealings with an entity not blacklisted but "minority owned, or controlled in whole or in part" by a blacklisted Iranian "is not necessarily sanctionable for a non-U.S. person." See M.10 in "Frequently Asked Questions Relating to the Lifting of Certain U.S. Sanctions under the JCPOA," US Treasury Department, October 12, 2016. John Smith, OFAC's acting director, said, "We will not be playing 'gotcha' for companies that conducted the appropriate due diligence, collected the documentation, but unwittingly found themselves dealing with a Revolutionary Guards front company"; Atlantic Council, Washington, DC, June 16, 2016.

76. Boeing and Airbus agreements were financed by a consortium of large financial institutions and denominated in euros. "Boeing-Iran Deal for $16.6 Billion of Jets Is First since 1979," *Bloomberg*, December 11, 2016; "Total to Finance Iran Project with Euros to Avoid U.S. Sanctions," *Wall Street Journal*, November 8, 2016. Republican opposition prevented the Obama administration from easing this restriction during and after the negotiations. "Rubio, Kirk Introduce Bill to Block Iran's Access to US Money," *The Hill*, April 6, 2016. In October, OFAC explained that non-US financial institutions may process dollar transactions provided they "do not involve, directly or indirectly, the U.S. financial system." This implies banks can only use dollars at hand, ruling out financing for large development and infrastructure projects.

77. Congress tried repeatedly, for example, to block the sale of civilian aircraft to Iran contrary to Paragraph 5.1.1 of JCPOA's Annex II. "U.S. House Votes to Stop Sales of Boeing Jetliners to Iran," *Bloomberg*, November 17, 2016. More recently, the February 7, 2022 letter from Republican senator Ted Cruz to President Biden embodies such a political limitation from the US internal political system toward sanctions policy—sanctions imposed on Iran being a major source of political divisions among Congress members. He wrote: "The submission of [the Iran Deal Review Act] triggers a statutorily-defined review process, and includes the possibility of Congress blocking implementation of the agreement."

78. This, as another senior Iranian official put it, is not a material breach of the deal, but "at best procrastination, at worst deliberate harassment," and has deepened mistrust. He added: "The JCPOA is moderately healthy, but Iranian confidence in dealing with the U.S. has been bruised and is ailing and failing." Crisis Group interview, New York, September 2016. "Iran's Supreme Leader Says U.S. Lifted Sanctions Only on Paper," *Reuters*, April 27, 2016; "Iran's President Rouhani Slams US 'Lack of Compliance' with Nuclear Deal," *CNN*, September 22, 2016.

79. On August 2, 2017, Trump signed the Countering America's Adversaries Through Sanctions Act (CAATSA) into law. See Public Law No. 115–44.

80. The Treasury Department issued nine tranches of sanctions, designating ninety-five targets in China, Iran, Lebanon, the United Arab Emirates, and Ukraine in connection with the IRGC and Iran's ballistic-missile program, support for terrorism, and human rights violations. For its part, the State Department sanctioned eighteen individuals and entities.

81. The Treasury Department designated the entirety of the IRGC, whose affiliated bodies and leaders were already subject to several other US sanctions, as a Specially Designated Global Terrorist (SDGT) under Executive Order 13224 and Section 105 of CAATSA because of its support for its expeditionary Quds Force, which itself was designated an SDGT in 2007. John Hudson and Borzou Daragahi, "Trump's Boldest Foreign Policy Move Today Wasn't Decertifying the Iran Deal," *BuzzFeed*, October 13, 2017.

82. See "President Donald J. Trump Is Ending United States Participation in an Unacceptable Iran Deal," White House, May 8, 2018.

83. The August sanctions covered "the purchase or acquisition of U.S. bank notes by the Government of Iran; Iran's trade in gold and other precious metals; graphite, aluminum, steel, coal and software used in industrial processes; transactions relating to the Iranian rial; activities relating to Iran's issuance of sovereign debt; and Iran's automotive sector." The November sanctions targeted Iran's energy, shipping, insurance, and financial sectors, and revoked exemptions in US primary sanctions, including those that allowed certain US subsidiaries to conduct business with Iran. "President Donald J. Trump Is Reimposing Sanctions Lifted under the Horrible Iran Deal," White House, August 6, 2018; "Statement by the President Regarding the Re-imposition of Nuclear-Related Sanctions on Iran," White House, November 2, 2018; "U.S. Government Fully Reimposes Sanctions on the Iranian Regime as Part of Unprecedented U.S. Economic Pressure Campaign," US Treasury Department, November 5, 2018. The November designations included "over 300 . . . new targets," putting the total number of designations under the Trump administration at over 900. "Press Availability with Secretary of Treasury Steven T. Mnuchin," US State Department, November 5, 2018.

84. Iran's exports declined from 2.7 million barrels per day (mb/d) in June to 1.9 mb/d in September. "Iran Has Produced and Exported Less Crude Oil since Sanctions Announcement," US Energy Information Administration, October 23, 2018. Precise figures for Iran's total post-sanctions oil exports (i.e., November and December) are nebulous, as is the exact volume of import reductions by the eight countries that were granted waivers.

85. Section 504 of Iran Threat Reduction and Syria Human Rights Act of 2012 makes repatriating Iran's oil export earnings a sanctionable act, thus forcing Tehran to barter with its remaining oil clients. See H.R. 1905—Public Law No. 112–158, August 10, 2012. Iran's fiscal reliance on oil revenues has decreased from 50.5 percent in the 2012 budget to 35 percent in the 2019 proposed budget. Nearly two-thirds of oil revenues will be earmarked for the government budget, with the remainder split between the National Development Fund and National Iranian Oil Company. Donya-ye Eqtesad, December 27, 2018. As a US official explained: "Any time Iran sells oil, that money goes into an escrow account in the importing nation's bank . . . the U.S. will be monitoring these escrow accounts very closely." "Briefing with Special Representative for Iran Brian Hook," US State Department, November 2, 2018.

86. At the time, Secretary of State Mike Pompeo asserted that "more than twenty importing nations have zeroed out their imports of crude already, taking more than one million barrels of [Iranian] crude per day off the market." The eight recipients of these Significant Reduction Exceptions were China, India, South Korea, Japan, Taiwan, Italy, Greece, and Turkey. "Press Availability with Secretary of Treasury Steven T. Mnuchin," US State Department, November 5, 2018.

87. President Rouhani, for example, maintained on May 1 that "we will overcome all problems and sell our own oil and satisfy our own needs." President.ir, May 1, 2019. The Iranian government does not provide details of current crude

oil exports, which industry media estimate are in the region of a few hundred thousand barrels per day. "Iran's Oil Exports Face New Security Threat," *S&P Global*, October 11, 2019. Despite constituting 17.6 percent (nominal) of GDP in 2018–19, the revenue from oil sales made up 26 percent of Iran's government budget that year and around 30 percent in 2019–20. The US Energy Information Administration has estimated that Iran's net oil export revenues for the first seven months of the year were $20 billion (nominal), without factoring in discounts. In 2018, revenue was $67 billion. See "OPEC Revenues Fact Sheet," US Energy Information Administration, August 20, 2019.

88. "Secretary of State Michael Pompeo Remarks to Press," US State Department, June 23, 2019. See also "ZAG IP, LLC Settles Potential Civil Liability for Apparent Violations of the Iranian Transactions and Sanctions Regulations," US Treasury Department, February 21, 2019; "Standard Chartered Bank Admits to Illegally Processing Transactions in Violation of Iranian Sanctions and Agrees to Pay More than $1B," US Justice Department, April 9, 2019; "Italy's UniCredit to Pay $1.3 Billion to Settle U.S. Sanctions Probe," *Reuters*, April 15, 2019; Jacob Rund, "PACCAR to Pay $1.7 Million for Possible Iran Sanctions Evasion," *Bloomberg Law*, August 6, 2019; "Defense Contractor Agrees to Pay $45 Million to Resolve Criminal Obstruction Charges and Civil False Claims Act Allegations," US Justice Department, December 4, 2019.

89. On the IRGC: "Statement from the President on the Designation of the Islamic Revolutionary Guards Corps as a Foreign Terrorist Organization," White House, April 8, 2019; on industries: "Imposing Sanctions with Respect to the Iron, Steel, Aluminum and Copper Sectors of Iran," White House, May 8, 2019; "Treasury Sanctions Iran's Largest Petrochemical Holding Group and Vast Network of Subsidiaries and Sales Agents," US Treasury Department, June 7, 2019. On Khamenei and Zarif: "President Donald Trump Is Imposing Sanctions on the Supreme Leader of Iran and the Worst Elements of the Iranian Regime," White House, June 24, 2019; "Treasury Designates Iran's Foreign Minister Javad Zarif for Acting for the Supreme Leader of Iran," US Treasury Department, July 31, 2019. Iran's information minister, Mohammad-Javad Azari Jahromi, was designated following the internet blackout imposed during the November 2019 protests. "Treasury Designates Iran's Minister of Information and Communications Technology in View of the Regime's Repressive Internet Censorship," US Treasury Department, November 22, 2019. See also "Treasury Sanctions Iran's Central Bank and National Development Fund," US Treasury Department, September 20, 2019; "Secretary Michael Pompeo Remarks to the Press," US State Department, December 11, 2019. On the exclusion of banks in October 2018, see "Treasury Designates IRGC-QF Weapon Smuggling Network and Mahan Air General Sales Agents," US Treasury Department, December 11, 2019.

90. "Intensified Sanctions on Iran," US State Department, January 10, 2020.

91. Executive Order 13902, Imposing Sanctions With Respect to Additional Sectors of Iran, January 10, 2020; "Treasury Sanctions Eighteen Major Iranian Banks," US Treasury Department, October 8, 2020.

92. See John O'Donnell and Jonathan Saul, "Exclusive: European Allies Pushed Back When Trump Sanctioned Iran's Banks," *Reuters*, December 1, 2020.

93. "Treasury Targets Vast Supreme Leader Patronage Network and Iran's Minister of Intelligence," US Treasury Department, November 18, 2020.

94. See, for example, "The United States Imposes Further Sanctions on Iran's Petrochemical Industry," US State Department, January 23, 2020; "Treasury Targets Major Iranian Metals Companies and Foreign Subsidiaries and Sales Agents," US Treasury Department, June 25, 2020; "United States Designates Key Iranian Shipping Entities under Proliferation Authority as Tehran Continues to Expand Proliferation Sensitive Activities," US State Department, June 8, 2020.

95. "Designation of the Atomic Energy Organization of Iran, Its Head Ali Akbar Salehi and Renewing Nuclear Restrictions," US State Department, January 31, 2020; "Expansion of the Scope of Iran Metals Sanctions Targeting Iran's Nuclear, Military and Ballistic Missile Programs and the IRGC," US State Department, July 30, 2020; "Treasury Sanctions Procurement Network Supplying Iranian Military Firm," US Treasury Department, November 10, 2020; "Treasury Designates Entity Subordinate to Iran's Military Firm," US Treasury Department, December 3, 2020.

96. "Iran Nuclear Deal: US Unveils New Sanctions Targeting Arms Sales," *BBC*, September 22, 2020.

97. Treasury Issues General License No. 8 Regarding Certain Permitted Humanitarian Trade Transactions Involving the Central Bank of Iran, JDSupra, March 12, 2020.

98. Tweet by Mike Pompeo, @SecPompeo, US Secretary of State, 10:00 a.m., January 12, 2021.

99. On December 4, Secretary of State Mike Pompeo estimated that the administration had levied "77 rounds of sanctions targeting close to 1,500 individuals and entities." Quoted in "Michael R. Pompeo at the IISS Manama Dialogue," US State Department, December 4, 2020. See also Barak Ravid, "Trump Administration Plans 'Flood' of Sanctions on Iran by Jan. 20," *Axios*, November 8, 2020.

100. See, for example, Ian Talley, "Trump Administration Hopes to Make Iran Pressure Campaign Harder to Reverse," *Wall Street Journal*, October 23, 2020.

101. Joe Biden, "There's a Smarter Way to Be Tough on Iran," *CNN*, September 13, 2020. A senior Iranian official asked: "Is this how Biden wants to rectify his predecessor's mistakes? By being tougher?" Crisis Group interview, Tehran, November 2020.

102. Crisis Group Report, *The Iran Nuclear Deal at Six: Now or Never,* January 17, 2022.

103. "Designation of Iranian Officials Due to Involvement in Gross Violations of Human Rights," US State Department, March 9, 2021.

104. "Targeting Repression and Supporting Democracy," US State Department, December 7, 2021. Iran's judiciary responded by issuing human rights–related sanctions of its own on twenty US individuals and companies. "Iran Imposes Sanctions on 20 American Individuals, Entities," *Mehr News*, December

13, 2021. Tehran had previously sanctioned many of the Trump administration's senior officials as they left office. "Iran Blacklists Trump, U.S. Officials as His Term Nears End," *Reuters*, January 19, 2021.

105. "Iran: Council Concludes Annual Review of the EU's Iran Human Rights Sanctions Regime," Council of the EU, April 12, 2021. Iran's foreign ministry replied that it would "suspend comprehensive talks with [the] EU including human rights talks and all cooperation resulting from these talks, especially in the areas of terrorism, drugs and refugees." "Iran to Suspend Comprehensive Talks with EU: FM Spox," *Mehr News*, April 13, 2021.

106. "Treasury Sanctions Iranian Intelligence Network Targeting Iranian-American Activist in the United States," US Treasury Department, September 3, 2021; "Treasury Sanctions Iran Cyber Actors for Attempting to Influence the 2020 U.S. Presidential Election," US Treasury Department, November 18, 2021.

107. "Treasury Sanctions Network Financing Houthi Aggression and Instability in Yemen," US Treasury Department, June 10, 2021; "Treasury Targets Oil Broker Network Supporting Qods Force," US Treasury Department, August 13, 2021; "Treasury Sanctions International Financial Networks Supporting Terrorism," US Treasury Department, September 17, 2021; "Treasury Sanctions Network and Individuals in Connection with Iran's Unmanned Aerial Vehicle Program," US Treasury Department, October 29, 2021.

108. "United States Seizes Websites Used by the Iranian Islamic Radio and Television Union and Kata'ib Hizballah," US Justice Department, June 22, 2021; "Commerce Department Adds 34 Entities to the Entity List to Target Enablers of China's Human Rights Abuses and Military Modernization, and Unauthorized Iranian and Russian Procurement," US Commerce Department, July 9, 2021; "Commerce Acts to Deter Misuse of Biotechnology, Other U.S. Technologies by the People's Republic of China to Support Surveillance and Military Modernization That Threaten National Security," US Commerce Department, December 16, 2021.

109. The State Department asserted that the June action was "a practice consistent with good sanctions hygiene and administrative process" and came after a delisting petition by sanctioned entities, while the Treasury Department underscored that the July and October decisions were "unrelated to nuclear negotiations." State Department spokesman, quoted in "Department Press Briefing," US State Department, June 10, 2021; Daphne Psaledakis and Arshad Mohammed, "U.S. Drops Sanctions on Three Iranians, Says Move Unrelated to Nuclear Talks," *Reuters*, July 2, 2021; Laura Kelly, "Biden Lifts Sanctions on Two Iranian Missile Producers," *The Hill*, October 8, 2021.

110. These waivers, issued for periods ranging from 30 to 120 days, were last approved by the Trump administration in January 2021 and then renewed three times by the Biden administration. "U.S. Grants 120-Day Waiver for Iraq to Pay for Electricity from Iran," *Reuters*, March 31, 2021; "U.S. Gives Iraq Another 120-Day Waiver to Import Iranian Power Supplies," *S&P Global Platts*, August 5, 2021; Adam Kredo, "Biden Admin Waives Sanctions on Iran as Nuclear Talks Restart,"

Washington Free Beacon, December 3, 2021. In December, Iraq's Central Bank governor estimated Baghdad's arrears for Iranian electricity purchases at $5 billion, indicating that the Iraqi government had earmarked around $250 million for Iranian purchases of COVID-19 vaccines and an unspecified sum for wheat imports (since US sanctions preclude repayment in money). John Davison and Ahmed Rasheed, "Iraq Foreign Reserves Rise on Currency Devaluation, Oil Prices—Bank Governor," *Reuters*, December 14, 2021.

111. "Treasury Sanctions Key Actors in Iran's Ballistic Missile Program," US Treasury Department, March 30, 2022; Anthony J. Blinken, "United States Imposed Sanctions on Iran's Ballistic Missile-Related Activities," US State Department, March 30, 2022.

112. "Treasury Targets Oil Smuggling Network Generating Hundreds of Millions of Dollars for Qods Force and Hizballah," US Treasury Department, May 25, 2022.

113. Anthony J. Blinken, "Issuance of Executive Order on Bolstering Ongoing Efforts to Bring Hostages and Wrongfully Detained U.S. Nationals Home," US State Department, July 19, 2022.

114. "The Statement of the Ministry of Foreign Affairs of the Islamic Republic of Iran on Updating Designations Regarding American Officials and Individuals Supporting the Monafeghin Terrorist Group," Islamic Republic of Iran Ministry of Foreign Affairs, July 16, 2022.

115. "Tehran Feeding Gas into New Centrifuges as Countermeasures to Fresh US Sanctions: Iranian FM," *PressTV*, August 2, 2022.

116. "Treasury Sanctions Iran's Morality Police and Senior Security Officials for Violence against Protesters and the Death of Mahsa Amini," US Treasury Department, September 22, 2022.

117. "Deputy Secretary Sherman's Meeting with Technology Companies on Supporting Internet Freedom for the Iranian People," US State Department, October 12, 2022.

118. "UK Sanctions Iranian 'Morality Police' and Senior Security Officials," Government of the United Kingdom, October 10, 2022.

119. "Iran: EU Sanctions Perpetrators of Serious Human Rights Violation," European Council, October 17, 2022.

120. "Imposing Sanctions on Entities and Individuals in Response to Iran's Transfer of Military UAVs to Russia," US State Department, November 15, 2022; "Treasury Targets Actors Involved in Production and Transfer of Iranian Unmanned Aerial Vehicle to Russia for Use in Ukraine," US Treasury Department, November 15, 2022.

121. "Iran: EU Adopts Additional Sanctions against Perpetrators of Serious Human Rights Violations," European Council, November 14, 2022; "UK and International Partners Announce Further Sanctions against Iranian Officials," Government of the United Kingdom, November 14, 2022.

122. "Treasury Sanctions Suppliers of Iranian UAVs Used to Target Ukraine's Civilian Infrastructure," US Treasury Department, January 6, 2023.

Chapter Four

1. https://twitter.com/realDonaldTrump/status/1072836035514634240.

2. Ellen Ioanes, "Iran's Months-Long Protest Movement, Explained," *Vox*, updated January 21, 2023, https://www.vox.com/2022/12/10/23499535/iran-protest-movement-explained.

3. Djavad Salehi-Isfahani, "Protests, Drones Sends Iran's Economic Recovery in Spiral," *Responsible Statecraft*, December 30, 2022, https://responsiblestate craft.org/2022/12/30/protests-drones-send-irans-economic-recovery-in-spiral/.

4. "Iranian Public Opinion under Maximum Pressure," CISSM, October 16, 2019, https://cissm.umd.edu/research-impact/publications/iranian-public-opin ion-under-maximum-pressure.

5. Figure 1 uses data from Penn World Table (PWT), which is the workhorse of empirical studies of economic growth. Robert C. Feenstra, Robert Inklaar, and Marcel P. Timmer, "The Next Generation of the Penn World Table," *American Economic Review* 105, no. 10 (2015): 3150–82. GDP calculations rely on Purchasing Power Parity (PPP), which measures more accurately quantities produced in different countries because they correct for differences in prices across countries. This is particularly important for Iran, where energy prices have been and are a fraction of their global values and are therefore undervalued in Iran's own national accounts. When evaluated with US prices, which PPP does, they offer a more accurate reflection of the size of the economy. Growth rates in PWT differ from Iranian sources, which use local prices, and therefore undervalue energy used domestically, but they all show that growth ended in 2011.

6. PWT data uses output-side real GDP at chained PPPs (in 2017 US$). Iranian sources that do not use PPP show slower growth during 1990–2010 and a smaller decline after 2010. Much of the difference is in how different sources value production of energy and construction services that grew rapidly during this period.

7. All figures are from the IEA report. Besides crude oil, Iran exports related products, such as condensates, which are liquids that are produced when natural gas is extracted. Exports of these and other closely related products add another 0.5 mbd. See Sara Vakhshouri, "U.S. Sanctions and Iran's Energy Strategy," SAIS Rethinking Iran, Johns Hopkins University, 2020, https://www.rethinking iran.com/iranundersanctions.vakhshour.

8. Alberto Abadie, Alexis Diamond, and Jens Hainmueller, "Synthetic Control Methods for Comparative Case Studies: Estimating the Effect of California's Tobacco Control Program," *Journal of the American Statistical Association* 105, no. 490 (2010): 493–505.

9. Orkideh Gharehgozli, "An Estimation of the Economic Cost of Recent Sanctions on Iran Using the Synthetic Control Method," *Economics Letters* 157 (2017): 141–44; Morteza Ghomi, "Who Is Afraid of Sanctions? The Macroeconomic and Distributional Effects of the Sanctions against Iran," *Economics & Politics* 34, no. 3 (2022): 395–428.

10. Peter A. G. van Bergeijk, "Failure and Success of Economic Sanctions,"

VoxEU, March 27, 2012, https://voxeu.org/article/do-economic-sanctions-make
-sense.

11. Dario Laudati and M. Hashem Pesaran, "Identifying the Effects of Sanctions on the Iranian Economy Using Newspaper Coverage," *Journal of Applied
Econometrics* 38, no. 3 (2023): 271–94.

12. Shahrokh Fardoust, "Macroeconomic Impacts of U.S. Sanctions (2017–
2019) on Iran," SAIS Rethinking Iran, Johns Hopkins University, 2020, https://
www.rethinking iran.com/iranundersanctions/fardoust.

13. Fardoust, "Macroeconomic Impacts."

14. Fardoust, "Macroeconomic Impacts."

15. Fardoust, "Macroeconomic Impacts."

16. Djavad Salehi-Isfahani, "Human Resources in Iran: Potentials and Challenges," *Iranian Studies* 38, no. 1 (2005): 117–47.

17. Adnan Mazarei, "Iran Has a Slow-Motion Banking Crisis," Policy Brief
19-8, 2019, Peterson Institute for International Economics, Washington, DC.

18. Steven H. Hanke, "Hyperinflation Has Arrived in Iran," Cato Institute,
October 3, 2012, https://www.cato.org/blog/hyperinflation-has-arrived-iran.

19. Human Rights Watch, "'Maximum Pressure': US Economic Sanctions
Harm Iranians' Right to Health," October 29, 2019, https://www.hrw.org/report/
2019/10/29/maximum-pressure/us-economic-sanctions-harm-iranians-right
-health.

20. Jalal Hejazi and Sara Emamgholipour, "The Effects of the Re-imposition
of US Sanctions on Food Security in Iran," *International Journal of Health Policy
and Management* 11, no. 5 (2022): 651–57.

21. Lant Pritchett and Marla Spivack, *Estimating Income/Expenditure Differences across Populations: New Fun with Old Engel's Law*, Working Paper 339,
August 2013, Center for Global Development, Washington, DC, https://ciaotest.
cc.columbia.edu/wps/cgd/0028974/f_0028974_23522.pdf.

22. Lisa C. Smith and Ali Winoto Subandoro, *Measuring Food Security Using
Household Expenditure Surveys*, International Food Policy Research Institute,
2007, p. 147, http://cdm15738.contentdm.oclc.org/utils/getfile/collection/
p15738coll2/id/125275/filename/125276.pdf.

23. The estimates of calories and protein are based on food expenditures and
not the intakes of these nutrients based on food actually consumed.

24. Averages are per adult rather than adult equivalent, which weighs children less and therefore would show a higher average.

25. OECD/FAO study, https://www.oecd-ilibrary.org/sites/cf68bf79-en/index
.html?itemId=/content/component/cf68bf79-en.

26. Kevan Harris, "Iran's Government Expenditure Priorities and Social Policy
Burdens during Sanctions," SAIS Rethinking Iran, Johns Hopkins University,
2020, https://www.rethinkingiran.com/iranundersanctions/kevan-harris-irans
-government-expenditure-priorities-and-social-policy-burdens-during-sanctions.

27. Heng Chen and Wing Suen, "Aspiring for Change: A Theory of Middle
Class Activism," *Economic Journal* 127 (2017): 1318–47.

28. Djavad Salehi-Isfahani, "The Reform of Energy Subsidies in Iran: From Promise to Disappointment," Economic Research Forum, Policy Perspective, no. 13, June 2014, https://erf.org.eg/publications/irans-subsidy-reform-from-promise -to-disappointment/.

29. Farnaz Fassihi and Rick Gladstone, "Iran Abruptly Raises Fuel Prices, and Protests Erupt," *New York Times*, November 15, 2019, https://www.nytimes.com /2019/11/15/world/middleeast/iran-gasoline-prices-rations.html.

30. Harris, "Iran's Government Expenditure Priorities."

31. Salehi-Isfahani, "Reform of Energy Subsidies in Iran."

32. Hassan Khajooyi, "Taam talkh baraye ghand-e Neishabour" [Bitter taste for Neishabour sugar], *Khayyam Nameh* 6, no. 133 (August 1, 2009).

33. Fuad Ajami, "The Poisoned Well," *New York Times*, October 17, 2003, https://www.nytimes.com/2003/10/17/opinion/the-poisoned-well.html.

Chapter Five

1. Jacob Lew and Richard Nephew, "The Use and Misuse of Economic State-craft," *Foreign Affairs*, November/December 2018, 139–49; Daniel W. Drezner, "The United States of Sanctions," *Foreign Affairs*, September/October 2021, 142–54.

2. For a list of areas of US sanctions on Iran see Katzman, *Iran Sanctions*.

3. Juan Zarate, *Treasury's War: The Unleashing of a New Era of Financial Warfare* (New York: Public Affairs, 2013); Meghan O'Sullivan, *Shrewd Sanctions: Statecraft and State Sponsors of Terrorism* (Washington, DC: Brookings Institution, 2003).

4. Robin Wright, "Stuart Levey's War," *New York Times Magazine*, October 31, 2008, https://www.nytimes.com/2008/11/02/magazine/02IRAN-t.html.

5. M. P. Doxey, *Economic Sanctions and International Enforcement* (New York: Oxford University Press, 1980), 77–79; James Barber, "Economic Sanctions as a Policy Instrument," *International Affairs* 55, no. 3 (1979): 367–84; Francis J. Gavin, "Economics and U.S. National Security," *War on the Rocks*, June 29, 2021, https:// warontherocks.com/2021/06/economics-and-u-s-national-security/.

6. Bryan R. Early, *Busted Sanctions: Explaining Why Economic Sanctions Fail* (Palo Alto, CA: Stanford University Press, 2015).

7. Robert Pape, "Why Economic Sanctions Do Not Work," *International Security* 22, no. 2 (1997): 90–136; Robert Pape, "Why Economic Sanctions Still Do Not Work," *International Security* 23, no. 1 (1998): 66–78.

8. Personal interviews with President Mohammad Khatami and his chief foreign policy advisor, Ambassador Sadegh Kharrazi, Davos, Switzerland, January 2007.

9. Trita Parsi, *Single Roll of the Dice: Obama's Diplomacy with Iran* (New Haven, CT: Yale University Press, 2012), 2–5.

10. Seyed Hossein Mousavian, *The Iranian Nuclear Crisis: A Memoir* (Washington, DC: Carnegie Endowment for International Peace, 2012).

11. Suzanne Maloney, "Progress of the Obama Administration Policy towards

Iran," Brookings Institution, November 11, 2011, https://www.brookings.edu/testimonies/progress-of-the-obama-administrations-policy-toward-iran/.

12. Trita Parsi, *Losing an Enemy: Obama, Iran, and the Triumph of Diplomacy* (New Haven, CT: Yale University Press, 2017), 103–13; Suzanne Maloney, "Sanctioning Iran: If Only It Were So Simple," *Washington Quarterly* 33, no. 1 (2010): 136–37.

13. Parsi, *Single Roll of the Dice*, 172–93.

14. Nicholas Mulder, *The Economic Weapon: The Rise of Sanctions as a Tool of Modern War* (New Haven, CT: Yale University Press, 2022), 5–6.

15. Mulder, *The Economic Weapon*, 6.

16. Mulder, *The Economic Weapon*, 6.

17. Nephew, *The Art of Sanctioning*.

18. Hadi Kahalzadeh, *Iran after Trump: Can Biden Revive the Nuclear Deal and Does Iran Even Want to?*, *Middle East Brief 145*, Crown Center for Middle East Studies, Brandeis University, January 2022, https://www.brandeis.edu/crown/publications/middle-east-briefs/pdfs/101-200/meb145.pdf.

19. William J. Burns, *The Back Channel: A Memoir of American Diplomacy and the Case for Its Renewal* (New York: Random House, 2019), 337–87; David Ignatius, "The Omani 'Back Channel' to Iran and the Secrecy Surrounding the Nuclear Deal," *Washington Post*, June 7, 2016, https://www.washingtonpost.com/opinions/the-omani-back-channel-to-iran-and-the-secrecy-surrounding-the-nuclear-deal/2016/06/07/0b9e27d4-2ce1-11e6-b5db-e9bc84a2c8e4_story.html.

20. Parsi, *Losing an Enemy*; John Kerry, *Every Day Is Extra* (New York: Simon and Schuster, 2018), 485–523; Wendy R. Sherman, *Not for the Faint of Heart: Lessons in Power, Courage and Persistence* (New York: Public Affairs, 2020); Burns, *The Back Channel*, 337–87.

21. Mohammad Javad Zarif, Ali Akbar Salehi, Seyyed Abbas Araghchi, and Majid Takht Ravanchi, *Raz Sar Be Mohr* (*Sealed Secret*) (Tehran: Entesharat Etelaat, 2021), vol. 2.

22. Conversations with Iran's foreign minister, Mohammad Javad Zarif, Munich, February 2016.

23. Hadi Kahalzadeh, "'Maximum Pressure' Hardened Iran against Compromise," *Foreign Affairs*, March 11, 2021, https://www.foreignaffairs.com/articles/iran/2021-03-11/maximum-pressure-hardened-iran-against-compromise

24. Mulder, *The Economic Weapon*, 6.

25. Michael Barnhart, *Japan Prepares for Total War: the Search for Economic Security, 1919–1941* (Ithaca, NY: Cornell University Press, 1987); Erik Sand and Suzanne Freeman, "The Russian Sanctions Regime and the Risk of Catastrophic Success," *War on the Rocks*, March 8, 2022, https://warontherocks.com/2022/03/the-russian-sanctions-regime-and-the-risk-of-catastrophic-success/.

26. Henry Farrell and Abraham L. Newman, "Weaponized Interdependence: How Global Economic Networks Shape State Coercion," *International Security* 44, no. 1 (2019): 42–79.

27. Daniel Drezner, Henry Farrell, and Abraham L. Newman, *The Uses and*

Abuses of Weaponized Interdependence (Washington, DC: Brookings Institution, 2021).

28. Narrated by a senior European diplomat to Iran's foreign minister, Javad Zarif, from conversations with Zarif at the Munich Security Conference, February 2019.

29. "Iran Sanctions under the Trump Administration," International Crisis Group, January 15, 2020, https://www.crisisgroup.org/middle-east-north-africa/gulf-and-arabian-peninsula/iran/iran-sanctions-under-trump-administration.

30. Mulder, *The Economic Weapon*, 5–6.

Chapter Six

1. Jason Bartlett and Megan Ophel, "Sanctions by Numbers: U.S. Secondary Sanctions," Center for New American Security, August 26, 2021, https://www.cnas.org/publications/reports/sanctions-by-the-numbers-u-s-secondary-sanctions.

2. Tom Ruys and Cedric Ryngaert, "Secondary Sanctions: A Weapon Out of Control? The International Legality of, and European Response to, US Secondary Sanctions," *British Yearbook of International Law* (Oxford: Oxford University Press, 2020), 1–116.

3. Daniel Sargent, *A Superpower Transformed: The Remaking of American Foreign Relations in the 1970s* (New York: Oxford University Press, 2015), 68–99.

4. Charli Carpenter, "Weaponized Interdependence and Human Rights," in *The Uses and Abuses of Weaponized Interdependence*, ed. Daniel W. Drezner, Henry Farrell, and Abraham L. Newman (Washington, DC: Brookings Institution, 2021), 273–89.

5. Mulder, *The Economic Weapon*, 5.

6. Kahalzadeh, "'Maximum Pressure'."

7. Esfandyar Batmanghelidj, "The Inflation Weapon: How American Sanctions Harm Iranian Households," Sanctions and Security Research Project, January 2022, https://sanctionsandsecurity.org/publications/the-inflation-weapon-how-american-sanctions-harm-iranian-households/; Esfandyar Batmangelidj and Erica Moret, "The Hidden Toll of Sanctions," *Foreign Affairs*, January 17, 2022, https://www.foreignaffairs.com/articles/world/2022-01-17/hidden-toll-sanctions.

8. Kahalzadeh, "'Maximum Pressure'."

9. Kahalzadeh, "'Maximum Pressure'."

10. See, for example, Niloofar Adnani, "Irreparable Loss: Sanctions and the Disruptions of Children's Education in Baluchistan, Iran," Bourse and Bazaar Foundation, December 2021, https://www.bourseandbazaar.com/research-1/2021/12/16/irreperable-loss-sanctions-and-childrens-education-in-baluchistan.

11. Hadi Kahalzadeh, "Sanctions Make the Coronavirus More Deadly," *Foreign Affairs*, April 2, 2020, https://www.foreignaffairs.com/articles/iran/2020-04-02/sanctions-make-coronavirus-more-deadly; Miriam Berger, "U.S. Sanc-

tions Could Impede Iran's Access to Coronavirus Vaccines, Experts Say," *Washington Post*, December 7, 2020, https://www.washingtonpost.com/world/middle _east/iran-covax-coronavirus-vaccine-sanctions/2020/12/07/61a721f8-3632 -11eb-9699-00d311f13d2d_story.html.

12. "Farshad Momeni: Tebq Gozaresh-ha Balegh Bar 75% Mardom Bedoun E`aneh Nemitavanand Zendegi Khod Ra Begozaranand" [Farshad Momeni: Based on reports, 75% of people cannot make ends meet without government handouts], *Entekhab*, December 20, 2022, https://www.entekhab.ir/fa/news/ 707623/گزارش-طبق-مومنی-فرشاد%C8%80%2E-نمی-اعانه-بدون-مردم-درصد-۷۵-بر-بالغ-ها توانند-زندگی-خود-را-بگذرانند-پرسش-اصلی-این-است-که-مداراى-نجیبانه-مردمC8%80%2E% تواند-ادامه-داشته-باشد-ایران-دچار-حس-بی-آینده-بودنC8%80%2E%-ایران-با-فقر-تا-کجا-می .شده-مرحله-بعد-از-بی-آینده-بودن-فروپاشی-است.

13. Mahnaz Zahirnejad, "The Economic Effects of Sanctions and the Iranian Middle Class," in *Iran in the International System: Between Great Powers and Great Ideas*, ed. Heintz Gartner and Mitra Shahmoradi (New York: Routledge, 2020), 108–30.

14. Borzou Daragahi, "Middle Class Iranians Sought to Remake Their Nation: Here Is How They Were Betrayed," *Atlantic Council: IranSource*, March 9, 2021, https://www.atlanticcouncil.org/blogs/iransource/middle-class-iranians -sought-to-remake-their-nation-heres-how-they-were-betrayed/; Mohammad Sadeghi Esfahlani and Jamal Abdi, "Sanctions Cripple Iran's Middle Class, Not the Regime," *Foreign Policy*, August 2, 2012, https://foreignpolicy.com/2012/08/02/ sanctions-cripple-irans-middle-class-not-the-regime/; Esfandyar Batmanghelidj, "How Sanctions Hurt Iran's Protesters," *Foreign Affairs*, April 4, 2023, https:// www.foreignaffairs.com/middle-east/iran-sanctions-how-protesters.

15. Kahalzadeh, "'Maximum Pressure'."

16. Joy Gordon, *Invisible War: The United States and the Iraq Sanctions* (Cambridge, MA: Harvard University Press, 2010).

17. Joy Gordon, "The Enduring Impact of Iraq Sanctions," *Middle East Report 294 (Spring 2020)*, https://merip.org/2020/06/the-enduring-lessons-of-the-iraq -sanctions/.

18. Denis J. Halliday, "The Impact of UN Sanctions on the People of Iraq," *Journal of Palestine Studies* 28, no. 2 (Winter 1999): 29–37.

19. Azadeh Moaveni and Sussan Tahmasebi, "The Middle-Class Women of Iran Are Disappearing," *New York Times*, March 28, 2021, SR-10.

20. Hasan Rouhani, *Amniyat-e Melli va Diplomacy-e Haste'i* [*National security and nuclear diplomacy*] (Tehran: Markaz-e Tahqiqat-e Strategic, 2012).

21. Rick Gladstone, "Iran's Top Leader Faults Rouhani for Crisis, Says He Crossed 'Red Lines'," *New York Times*, August 14, 2018, A4.

22. Foreign Minister Zarif said that his European colleagues told him of the US assurance of Iran's imminent surrender; conversations with Zarif, Munich, February 2019.

23. "Mike Pompeo's Speech: What Are the Twelve Demands Given to Iran?"

AlJazeera, May 21, 2018, https://www.aljazeera.com/news/2018/5/21/mike
-pompeo-speech-what-are-the-12-demands-given-to-iran.

24. Noah Annan, "Pompeo Adds Human Right to Twelve Demands to Iran,"
Atlantic Council, October 23, 2018, https://www.atlanticcouncil.org/blogs/iran
source/pompeo-adds-human-rights-to-twelve-demands-for-iran/.

25. "Imam Khamenei: Ettefaqat-e Akhir Jang Tarkibi Boud" [Imam Khamenei:
Recent events were hybrid warfare], *Tasnim*, November 2, 2022; "Hadaf Doshman
Shekastan Iran-e Mottahed Ast" [The enemy's objective is to break Iran's unity],
Khamenei.ir, November 13, 2022, https://farsi.khamenei.ir/others-dialog?id=51314.

26. Bijan Khajepour, "Three Scenarios for Iran's Economic Development,"
Middle East Institute, October 7, 2021, https://www.mei.edu/publications/three
-scenarios-irans-economic-development.

27. See *Bourse & Bazaar,* "China-Iran Trade Report," October 2022, https://
www.bourseandbazaar.com/china-iran-trade-reports/october-2020?rq=China,
and March 2021, https://www.bourseandbazaar.com/china-iran-trade-reports/
march-2021?rq=China.

28. Bijan Khajepour, "China's Emerging Role in Iran's Petroleum Sector," *Al-
Monitor*, January 31, 2019, https://www.al-monitor.com/originals/2019/01/iran
-china-energy-cooperation-nioc-sinopec-sanctions.html.

29. Jacopo Scita, "China-Iran Relations through the Prism of Sanctions,"
Asian Affairs, February 9, 2022, https://doi.org/10.1080/03068374.2022.2029060.

30. Vali Nasr and Ariane Tabatabai, "China Plays the Iran Card," *Project Syn-
dicate*, July 29, 2020, https://www.project-syndicate.org/commentary/china-iran
-deal-implications-for-us-foreign-policy-by-vali-nasr-and-ariane-tabatabai-2020
-07.

31. Benoit Faucon, "Iranian Oil Exports Rise as Tehran Circumvents Sanctions, Finds New Buyers," *Wall Street Journal*, December 15, 2020; https://www
.wsj.com/articles/iranian-oil-exports-rise-as-tehran-circumvents-sanctions
-finds-new-buyers-11608052404.

32. Liz Sly, "Two Saudi Oil Tankers, Norwegian Ship Apparently Attacked
Near the Persian Gulf Amid Rising Iran Tensions," *Washington Post*, May 13,
2019, https://www.washingtonpost.com/world/middle_east/two-saudi-oil-tan
kers-attacked-in-the-persian-gulf-amid-rising-iran-tensions/2019/05/13/c890710
8-755e-11e9-bd25-c989555e7766_story.html.

33. David Axe, "Iran Knocked Out of the Sky a Very Special U.S. Drone (And
Exposed a Key Weakness)," *National Interest*, June 20, 2019, https://nationalinter
est.org/blog/buzz/iran-knocked-out-sky-very-special-us-drone-and-exposed
-key-weakness-63577.

34. John Bolton, *The Room Where It Happened: A White House Memoir* (New
York: Simon and Schuster, 2020); Michael D. Shear, Eric Schmitt, Michael Crowley
and Maggie Haberman, "Strikes on Iran Approved by Trump, Then Abruptly
Pulled Back," *New York Times*, June 10, 2019, https://www.nytimes.com/2019/06/
20/world/middleeast/iran-us-drone.html.

NOTES TO CHAPTER SIX

35. Julian Borger, "How a Drone's Flight Took U.S. and Iran to the Brink of War," *The Guardian*, June 21, 2019, https://www.theguardian.com/world/2019/jun/21/iran-latest-trump-drone-attack-timeline-airstrikes-called-off.

36. Aaron C. Davis, "Contractor Whose Death Trump Cited Was a Naturalized U.S. Citizen Born in Iraq," *Washington Post*, January 7, 2020, https://www.washingtonpost.com/investigations/contractor-whose-death-trump-cites-was-a-naturalized-us-citizen-born-in-iraq/2020/01/07/afa7e774-31ac-11ea-91fd-82d4e04a3fac_story.html.

37. Daniel Lippman, Wesley Morgan, Meredith McGraw, and Nahal Tousi, "How Trump Decided to Kill Iran's Soleimani," *Politico*, January 3, 2020, https://www.politico.com/news/2020/01/03/donald-trump-iran-soleimani-093371.

38. Dexter Filkins, "The Shadow Commander," *New Yorker*, September 23, 2013, https://www.newyorker.com/magazine/2013/09/30/the-shadow-commander; Isaac Chotiner, "The Meaning of Qasem Soleimani's Death in the Middle East," *New Yorker*, January 3, 2020, https://www.newyorker.com/news/q-and-a/the-meaning-of-qassem-suleimanis-death-in-the-middle-east.

39. Maziar Motamedi, "Khamenei Renews Revenge Vow as Soleimani Death Anniversary Nears," *AlJazeera*, December 16, 2020, https://www.aljazeera.com/news/2020/12/16/khamenei-renews-revenge-vow-before-soleimani-killing-anniversary.

40. Louisa Loveluck, "U.S. Commanders at Al-Asad Base Believe Iranian Missile Barrage Was Designed to Kill," *Washington Post*, January 13, 2020, https://www.washingtonpost.com/world/middle_east/al-asad-base-had-minutes-notice-before-the-iranian-rockets-came-crashing-down-in-an-hour-long-barrage/2020/01/13/50fc9dd6-33e2-11ea-971b-43bec3ff9860_story.html; David Martin and Mary Walsh, "Who Would Live and Who Would Die: The Inside Story of the Iranian Attack on Al-Asad Airbase," *CBS News: 60 Minutes*, August 8, 2021, https://www.cbsnews.com/news/iranian-attack-al-asad-air-base-60-minutes-2021-08-08/.

41. "President Trump Minimizes Concussion-Like Injuries in Iraq Attacks as Merely 'Headaches'," *ABC News*, January 22, 2020, https://abcnews.go.com/Politics/president-trump-minimizes-concussion-injuries-iraq-attack-headaches/story?id=68448853.

42. William J. Burns and Jake Sullivan, "Soleimani's Ultimate Revenge," *The Atlantic*, January 6, 2020, https://www.theatlantic.com/ideas/archive/2020/01/soleimanis-ultimate-revenge/604471/.

43. Nicholas Mulder, *The Economic Weapon*.

44. International Crisis Group, "Iran Nuclear Deal at Six: Now or Never," *Middle East Report*, no. 230 (January 17, 2022), 44.

45. International Crisis Group, "Iran Nuclear Deal at Six," 45.

46. International Crisis Group, "Iran Nuclear Deal at Six," 4–5.

47. Ronen Bergman and Farnaz Fassihi, "The Scientist and the A.I.-Assisted, Remote-Control Killing Machine," *New York Times*, September 19, 2021, 1.

48. Ronen Bergman, Rick Gladstone and Farnaz Fassihi, "Blackout Hits Iran

Nuclear Site in What Appears to Be Israeli Sabotage," *New York Times*, April 12, 2021, p.1.

49. David Sanger, Steve Erlanger, Farnaz Fassihi, and Lara Jakes, "As Hopes for Nuclear Deal Fade, Iran Rebuilds and Risks Grow," *New York Times*, November 22, 2021, 1; Francois Murphy, "Iran Adds Machines at Enrichment Plant Struck by Blast—IAEA," *Reuters*, April 21, 2021, https://www.reuters.com/world/middle-east/iran-adds-advanced-machines-underground-enrichment-plant-iaea-report-2021-04-21/.

50. Laurence Norman, "U.S. Sees Iran's Nuclear Program as Too Advanced to Restore Key Goal of 2015 Pact," *Wall Street Journal*, February 3, 2022, https://www.wsj.com/articles/u-s-sees-irans-nuclear-program-as-too-advanced-to-restore-key-goal-of-2015-pact-11643882545?st=ne9ed8ea4mkeiua&reflink=desktopwebshare_twitter.

51. Anonymous interviews with Iranian officials and academics.

52. Norman, "U.S. Sees Iran's Nuclear Program as Too Advanced."

53. Benoit Faucon and Ian Talley, "U.S. Weighs New Sanctions on Iran's Oil Sales to China If Nuclear Talks Fail," *Wall Street Journal*, July 19, 2021, https://www.wsj.com/articles/u-s-weighs-new-sanctions-on-irans-oil-sales-to-china-if-nuclear-talks-fail-11626692402.

54. Agathe Demarais, *Backfire: How Sanctions Reshape the World Against U.S. Interests* (New York: Columbia University, 2022).

55. Nasr and Tabatabai, "China Plays the Iran Card."

56. Mulder, *The Economic Weapon*, 4–5.

57. Stacie E. Goddard, "The Road to Revisionism: How Interdependence Gives Revisionists Weapons for Change," in Drezner, Farrell and Newman, *Uses and Abuses of Weaponized Interdependence*, 84–99.

58. Agathe Demarais, "The End of the Age of Sanctions?," *Foreign Affairs*, December 27, 2022, https://www.foreignaffairs.com/united-states/end-age-sanctions; Henry J. Farrell and Abraham L. Newman, "The Wrong Way to Punish Iran," *New York Times*, November 1, 2018, https://www.nytimes.com/2018/11/01/opinion/swift-iran-sanctions.html.

Conclusion

1. Mulder, *The Economic Weapon*, 5.

2. Hanna Garth, *Food in Cuba: The Pursuit of a Decent Meal* (Stanford, CA: Stanford University Press 2020).

3. Omar Dewachi, *Ungovernable Life: Mandatory Medicine and Statecraft in Iraq* (Stanford, CA: Stanford University Press, 2017).

4. Gordon, *Invisible War*.

5. United Nations Human Rights Office of the High Commissioner, "US Sanctions Violate Human Rights and International Code of Conduct, UN Expert Says," https://www.ohchr.org/EN/NewsEvents/Pages/DisplayNews.aspx?NewsID=24566&LangID=E (accessed October 1, 2021).

6. For more, see Demarais, *Backfire*.

SELECTED BIBLIOGRAPHY

Abadie, Alberto, Alexis Diamond, and Jens Hainmueller. "Synthetic Control Methods for Comparative Case Studies: Estimating the Effect of California's Tobacco Control Program." *Journal of the American Statistical Association* 105, no. 490 (2010): 493–505.

Adnani, Niloofar. "Irreparable Loss: Sanctions and the Disruptions of Children's Education in Baluchistan, Iran." Bourse and Bazaar Foundation, December 2021. https://www.bourseandbazaar.com/research-1/2021/12/16/irreperable-loss-sanctions-and-childrens-education-in-baluchistan.

Al-Ali, Nadje. "Reconstructing Gender: Iraqi Women between Dictatorship, War, Sanctions and Occupation." *Third World Quarterly* 26, no. 4/5 (2005): 739–58.

Alinejad, Donya, and Ali Honari. "Online Performance of Civic Participation: What Bot-like Activity in the Persian Language Twittersphere Reveals about Political Manipulation Mechanisms." *Television and New Media* 23, no. 11 (November 2021).

Al Jawaheri, Y. *Women in Iraq: The Gender Impact of International Sanctions.* New York: I. B. Tauris, 2007.

Baldwin, David. *Economic Statecraft.* Princeton, NJ: Princeton University Press, 2020.

Bajoghli, Narges. "Iran in Latin America: Striver Cosmopolitans and the Limits of U.S. Sanctions." SAIS Rethinking Iran, Johns Hopkins University, 2021. https://www.rethinkingiran.com/iranundersanctions/bajoghli.

Bajoghli, Narges. "The Researcher as a National Security Threat: Interrogative Surveillance, Agency, and Entanglement in Iran and the United States." *Com-*

parative Studies of South Asia, Africa and the Middle East 39, no. 3 (December 2019): 451–61.

Bapat, Navin A., Tobias Heinrich, Yoshiharu Kobayashi, and T. Clifton Morgan. "Determinants of Sanctions Effectiveness: Sensitivity Analysis Using New Data." *International Interactions* 39, no. 1 (2013): 79–98.

Barber, James. "Economic Sanctions as a Policy Instrument." *International Affairs* 55, no. 3 (1979): 367–84.

Barnhart, Michael. *Japan Prepares for Total War: The Search for Economic Security, 1919–1941.* Ithaca, NY: Cornell University Press, 1987.

Batmanghelidj, Esfandyar. "The Inflation Weapon: How American Sanctions Harm Iranian Households." Sanctions and Security Research Project, January 2022. https://sanctionsandsecurity.org/publications/the-inflation-weapon-how-american-sanctions-harm-iranian-households/.

Batmanghelidj, Esfandyar. "Resistance Is Simple, Resilience Is Complex: Sanctions and the Composition of Iranian Trade." SAIS Rethinking Iran, Johns Hopkins University, 2020. https://www.rethinkingiran.com/iranundersanctions/batmanghelidj.

Batmanghelidj, Esfandyar, and Erica Moret. "The Hidden Toll of Sanctions." *Foreign Affairs*, January 17, 2022. https://www.foreignaffairs.com/articles/world/2022-01-17/hidden-toll-sanctions.

Behrouzan, Orkideh, and Tara Sepehri Far. "The Impact of Sanctions on Medical Education in Iran." SAIS Rethinking Iran, Johns Hopkins University, 2021. https://www.rethinkingiran.com/iranundersanctions/orkideh-behrouzan-tara-sepehri-far.

Bolton, John. *The Room Where It Happened: A White House Memoir.* New York: Simon and Schuster, 2020.

Bonilla, Yarimar. "The Swarm of Disaster." *Political Geography* 78 (2020).

Brooks, Risa. "Sanctions and Regime Types: What Works and When?" *Security Studies* 11, no. 4 (2002): 1–50.

Brotherton, P. Sean. *Revolutionary Medicine: Health and the Body in Post-Soviet Cuba.* Durham, NC: Duke University Press, 2012.

Burns, William J. *The Back Channel: A Memoir of American Diplomacy and the Case for Its Renewal.* New York: Random House, 2019.

Carpenter, Charli. "Weaponized Interdependence and Human Rights." In *The Uses and Abuses of Weaponized Interdependence*, edited by Daniel W. Drezner, Henry Farrell and Abraham L. Newman, 273–89. Washington, DC: Brookings Institution, 2021.

Chotiner, Isaac. "The Meaning of Qasem Soleimani's Death in the Middle East." *New Yorker*, January 3, 2020. https://www.newyorker.com/news/q-and-a/the-meaning-of-qassem-suleimanis-death-in-the-middle-east.

Cortright, David, and George Lopez. "Are Sanctions Just? The Problematic Case of Iraq." *Journal of International Affairs* 52, no. 2 (1999): 735–55.

Crist, David. *The Twilight War: The Secret History of America's Thirty-Year Conflict with Iran.* New York: Penguin, 2012.

Dewachi, Omar. *Ungovernable Life: Mandatory Medicine and Statecraft in Iraq.* Stanford, CA: Stanford University Press, 2017.

Doxey, M. P. *Economic Sanctions and International Enforcement.* New York: Oxford University Press, 1980.

Drezner, Daniel. "Economic Sanctions in Theory and Practice: How Smart Are They?" In *Coercion: The Power to Hurt in International Politics*, edited by Kelly Greenhill and Peter Krause. New York: Oxford University Press, 2018.

Drezner, Daniel. *The Sanctions Paradox: Economic Statecraft and International Relations.* Cambridge: Cambridge University Press, 1999.

Drezner, Daniel W. "The United States of Sanctions: The Use and Abuse of Economic Coercion." *Foreign Affairs*, August 24, 2021. https://www.foreignaffairs.com/articles/united-states/2021-08-24/united-states-sanctions.

Drezner, Daniel, Henry Farrell, and Abraham L. Newman. *The Uses and Abuses of Weaponized Interdependence.* Washington, DC: Brookings Institution, 2021.

Drury, A. Cooper, and Dursun Peksen. "Women and Economic Statecraft: The Negative Impact International Economic Sanctions Visit on Women." *European Journal of International Relations* 20, no. 2 (2014): 463–90.

Dyson, T., and V. Cetorelli. "Changing Views on Child Mortality and Economic Sanctions in Iraq: A History of Lies, Damned Lies and Statistics." *BMJ Global Health* 2, no. 2 (2017).

Early, Bryan R. *Busted Sanctions: Explaining Why Economic Sanctions Fail.* Palo Alto, CA: Stanford University Press, 2015.

Fardoust, Shahrokh. "Macroeconomic Impacts of U.S. Sanctions (2017–2019) on Iran." SAIS Rethinking Iran, Johns Hopkins University, 2020. https://www.rethinkingiran.com/iranundersanctions/fardoust.

Farrell, Henry, and Abraham L. Newman. "Weaponized Interdependence: How Global Economic Networks Shape State Coercion." *International Security* 44, no. 1 (2019): 42–79.

Farzanegan, Mohammad Reza, et al. "Effect of Oil Revenues on Size and Income of Iranian Middle Class." *Middle East Development Journal* 13, no. 1 (2021): 27–58.

Feenstra, Robert C., Robert Inklaar, and Marcel P. Timmer. "The Next Generation of the Penn World Table." *American Economic Review* 105, no. 10 (2015): 3150–82.

Filkins, Dexter. "The Shadow Commander." *New Yorker*, September 23, 2013. https://www.newyorker.com/magazine/2013/09/30/the-shadow-commander.

Frye, Timothy. "Economic Sanctions and Public Opinion: Survey Experiments from Russia." *Comparative Political Studies* 52, no. 7 (2019): 967–94.

Galtung, Johan. "On the Effects of International Economic Sanctions, With Examples from the Case of Rhodesia." *World Politics* 19, no. 3 (1967): 378–416.

Garth, Hanna. *Food in Cuba: The Pursuit of a Decent Meal.* Stanford, CA: Stanford University Press, 2020.

Gavin, Francis. "Economics and U.S. National Security." *War on the Rocks*, June

29, 2021. https://warontherocks.com/2021/06/economics-and-u-s-national -security/.

Goddard, Stacie E. "The Road to Revisionism: How Interdependence Gives Revisionists Weapons for Change." In *The Uses and Abuses of Weaponized Interdependence*, edited by Daniel W. Drezner, Henry Farrell and Abraham L. Newman, 84–99. Washington, DC: Brookings Institution, 2021.

Gordon, Joy. *Invisible War: The United States and the Iraq Sanctions*. Cambridge, MA: Harvard University Press, 2012.

Gordon, Joy. "A Peaceful, Silent, Deadly Remedy: The Ethics of Economic Sanctions." *Ethics and International Affairs* 13, no. 1 (1999): 123–42.

Gutmann, Jerg, et al. "Sanctioned to Death? The Impact of Economic Sanctions on Life Expectancy and Its Gender Gap." *Journal of Development Studies* 57, no. 1 (2021): 139–62.

Halliday, Denis. "The Impact of UN Sanctions on the People of Iraq." *Journal of Palestine Studies* 28, no. 2 (Winter 1999): 29–37.

Harris, Kevan. "Iran's Government Expenditure Priorities and Social Policy Burdens during Sanctions." SAIS Rethinking Iran, Johns Hopkins University, 2021. https://www.rethinkingiran.com/iranundersanctions/kevan-harris -irans-government-expenditure-priorities-and-social-policy-burdens-during -sanctions.

Harris, Kevan. *A Social Revolution: Politics and the Welfare State in Iran*. Oakland: University of California Press, 2017.

Hejazi, Jalal, and Sara Emamgholipour. "The Effects of the Re-imposition of US Sanctions on Food Security in Iran." *International Journal of Health Policy and Management 11, no. 5* (2020): 651–57.

Hove, Mediel. "The Debates and Impact of Sanctions: The Zimbabwean Experience." *International Journal of Business and Social Science* 3, no. 5 (2012).

Jafarian, Habibe. "Something Cataclysmic Every Week." *The Baffler*, no. 53 (September 2020). Translated by Salar Abdoh. https://thebaffler.com/outbursts/ something-cataclysmic-every-week-jafarian.

Lew, Jacob, and Richard Nephew. "The Use and Misuse of Economic Statecraft: How Washington Is Abusing Its Financial Might." *Foreign Affairs*, October 15, 2018. https://www.foreignaffairs.com/articles/world/2018-10-15/use-and -misuse-economic-statecraft.

Kahalzadeh, Hadi. *Iran after Trump: Can Biden Revive the Nuclear Deal and Does Iran Even Want To?* Middle East Brief 145, Crown Center for Middle East Studies, Brandeis University, January 2022. https://www.brandeis.edu/crown /publications/middle-east-briefs/pdfs/101-200/meb145.pdf.

Kahalzadeh, Hadi. " 'Maximum Pressure' Hardened Iran against Compromise." *Foreign Affairs*, March 11, 2021. https://www.foreignaffairs.com/articles/ iran/2021-03-11/maximum-pressure-hardened-iran-against-compromise.

Katzman, Kenneth. *Iran Sanctions*. Congressional Research Service, February 2, 2022, 2. https://sgp.fas.org/crs/mideast/RS20871.pdf.

Kaussler, Bernd. "From Engagement to Containment: EU-Iran Relations and the

Nuclear Programme, 1992–2011." *Journal of Balkan and Near Eastern Studies* 14, no. 1 (March 2012): 53–76.

Kavakli, Karim Can, J. T. Chatagnier, and E. Hatipoglu. "The Power to Hurt and the Effectiveness of International Sanctions." *Journal of Politics* 82, no. 3 (2020): 879–94.

Khajepour, Bijan. "Three Scenarios for Iran's Economic Development." *Middle East Institute*, October 7, 2021. https://www.mei.edu/publications/three -scenarios-irans-economic-development.

Khajepour, Bijan. "China's Emerging Role in Iran's Petroleum Sector." *Al-Monitor*, January 31, 2019. https://www.al-monitor.com/originals/2019/01/ iran-china-energy-cooperation-nioc-sinopec-sanctions.html.

Khamenei, Seyed Ali. "The 'Second Phase of the Revolution' Statement Addressed to the Iranian Nation." February 11, 2019. https://english.khamenei.ir /news/6415/The-Second-Phase-of-the-Revolution-Statement-addressed-to -the.

Kim, Yiyeon. "Economic Sanctions and HIV/AIDS in Women." *Journal of Public Health Policy* 40 (2019): 1–16.

Kurzman, Charles. *The Unthinkable Revolution in Iran*. Cambridge, MA: Harvard University Press, 2005.

Lor Afshar, Ehsan. "Banking the Bazl: Building a Future in a Sanctioned Economy." *Economic Anthropology* 9, no. 1 (2022): 60–71.

Madani, Kaveh. "The Unintended Environmental Implications of Iran Sanctions." SAIS Rethinking Iran, Johns Hopkins University, 2020. https://www .rethinkingiran.com/iranundersanctions/kaveh-madani.

Maloney, Suzanne. "Progress of the Obama Administration Policy towards Iran." Brookings Institution, November 15, 2011. https://www.brookings.edu /testimonies/progress-of-the-obama-administrations-policy-toward-iran/.

Maloney, Suzanne. "Sanctioning Iran: If Only It Were So Simple," *Washington Quarterly* 33, no. 1 (2010): 136–37.

Mazarei, Adnan. "Inflation Targeting in Time of Sanctions and Pandemic." SAIS Rethinking Iran, SAIS Johns Hopkins University, 2020. https://www.rethink ingiran.com/iranundersanctions/mazarei.

Mazarei, Adnan. "Iran Has a Slow Motion Banking Crisis." PIIE Policy Brief no. 19–8 (2019).

McGillivray, Fiona, and Alastair Smith. "Trust and Cooperation through Agent-Specific Punishments." *International Organization* 54, no. 4 (2000): 809–24.

Moaveni, Azadeh, and Sussan Tahmasebi. "The Middle-Class Women of Iran Are Disappearing." *New York Times*, March 28, 2021, SR-10.

Mottahedeh, Negar. *#iranelection: Hashtag Solidarity and the Transformation of Online Life*. Stanford, CA: Stanford University Press, 2015.

Mousavian, Seyed Hossein. *The Iranian Nuclear Crisis: A Memoir*. Washington, DC: Carnegie Endowment for International Peace, 2012.

Moyn, Samuel. *Humane: How the United States Abandoned Peace and Reinvented War*. New York: Farrar, Straus, and Giroux, 2021.

Mulder, Nicholas. *The Economic Weapon: The Rise of Sanctions as a Tool of Modern War.* New Haven, CT: Yale University Press, 2022.

Nephew, Richard. *The Art of Sanctions: A View from the Field.* New York: Columbia University Press, 2017.

Neuenkirch, Matthias, and Florian Neumeier. "The Impact of US Sanctions on Poverty." *Journal of Development Economics* 121 (July 2016): 110–19.

O'Sullivan, Meghan. *Shrewd Sanctions: Statecraft and State Sponsors of Terrorism.* Washington, DC: Brookings Institution, 2003.

Olian, Catherine, Lesley Stahl, and CBS Video, dirs. *Punishing Saddam.* CBS Video, 1996.

Osanloo, Arzoo. "Entanglements: Lives Lived under Sanctions." SAIS Rethinking Iran, Johns Hopkins University, 2021. https://www.rethinkingiran.com/iranundersanctions/arzoo-osanloo-entanglements-lives-lived-under-sanctions.

Pape, Robert. "Why Economic Sanctions Do Not Work." *International Security* 22, no. 2 (1997): 90–136.

Pape, Robert. "Why Economic Sanctions Still Do Not Work." *International Security* 23, no. 1 (1998): 66–78.

Parsi, Trita. *Losing an Enemy: Obama, Iran, and the Triumph of Diplomacy.* Yale University Press, 2017.

Parsi, Trita. *A Single Roll of the Dice: Obama's Diplomacy with Iran.* New Haven, CT: Yale University Press, 2012.

Peksen, Dursun. "When Do Imposed Economic Sanctions Work? A Critical Review of the Sanctions Effectiveness Literature." *Defence and Peace Economics* 30, no. 6 (2019): 635–47.

Pritchett, Lant, and Marla Spivack. *Estimating Income/Expenditure Differences across Populations: New Fun with Old Engel's Law.* Center for Global Development Working Paper 339 (2013).

Rouhani, Hasan. *Amniyat-e Melli va Diplomacy-e Haste'i* (*National Security and Nuclear Diplomacy*). Tehran: Markaz-e Tahqiqat-e Strategic, 2012.

Ruys, Tom, and Cedric Ryngaert. "Secondary Sanctions: A Weapon Out of Control? The International Legality of, and European Response to, US Secondary Sanctions." In *British Year Book of International Law*, 1–116. Oxford: Oxford University Press, 2020.

Said, Edward. *Covering Islam: How the Media and the Experts Determine How We See the Rest of the World.* New York: Vintage Books, 1997.

Salehi Esfahani, Hadi. "The Experience of Iran's Manufacturing Sector under International Economic Sanctions." SAIS Rethinking Iran, Johns Hopkins University, 2020. https://www.rethinkingiran.com/iranundersanctions/hadi-salehi-esfahani.

Salehi-Isfahani, Djavad. "Impact of Sanctions on Household Welfare and Employment." SAIS Rethinking Iran, Johns Hopkins University, 2020. https://www.rethinkingiran.com/iranundersanctions/salehiisfahani.

Sand, Erik, and Suzanne Freeman. "The Russian Sanctions Regime and the Risk of Catastrophic Success." *War on the Rocks*, March 8, 2022. https://waronthe

rocks.com/2022/03/the-russian-sanctions-regime-and-the-risk-of-catastro
phic-success/.

Sargent, Daniel. *A Superpower Transformed: The Remaking of American Foreign
Relations in the 1970s.* New York: Oxford University Press, 2015, 68–99.

Scita, Jacopo. "China-Iran Relations through the Prism of Sanctions." *Asian Affairs*, February 9, 2022. https://doi.org/10.1080/03068374.2022.2029060.

Shahrokni, Nazanin. "Bursting at the Seams: Economic Sanctions and Transformation of the Domestic Sphere in Iran." SAIS Rethinking Iran, Johns Hopkin
University, 2021. https://www.rethinkingiran.com/iranundersanctions/naza
nin-shahrokni.

Sherman, Wendy R. *Not for the Faint of Heart: Lessons in Power, Courage and
Persistence.* New York: Public Affairs, 2020.

Soderholm, Alexander. "Sanctions and Illicit Drugs in Iran." SAIS Rethinking
Iran, Johns Hopkins University, 2020. https://www.rethinkingiran.com/iranun
dersanctions/soderholm.

Smith, Lisa C., and Ali Subandoro. *Measuring Food Security Using Household
Expenditure Surveys*, vol. 3. International Food Policy Research Institute,
2007.

Sreberny-Mohammadi, Leili. "Sanctions and the Visual Arts of Iran." SAIS Rethinking Iran, Johns Hopkins University, 2021. https://www.rethinkingiran
.com/iranundersanctions/sreberny-mohammadi.

Taheri, Elham, and Fatma Guven Lisaniler. "Gender Aspect of Economic Sanctions: Case Study of Women's Economic Rights in Iran." *SSRN Electronic Journal* (December 19, 2018).

Vakhshouri, Sara. "U.S. Sanctions and Iran's Energy Strategy." SAIS Rethinking
Iran, Johns Hopkins University, 2020. https://www.rethinkingiran.com/iran
undersanctions/vakhshour.

Walsh, Lawrence E. "Final Report of the Independent Counsel for Iran/Contra
Matters." United States Court of Appeals for the District of Columbia Circuit,
August 4, 1993.

Yildiz, Emrah. "Nested (In)securities: Commodity and Currency Circuits in Iran
under Sanctions." *Cultural Anthropology* 35, no. 2 (2020): 218–24.

Zahirnejad, Mahnaz. "The Economic Effects of Sanctions and the Iranian
Middle Class." In *Iran in the International System: Between Great Powers and
Great Ideas*, edited by Heintz Gartner and Mitra Shahmoradi, 108–30. New
York: Routledge, 2020.

Zarate, Juan. *Treasury's War: The Unleashing of a New Era of Financial Warfare.*
New York: Public Affairs, 2013.

Zarif, Mohammad Javad, Ali Akbar Salehi, Seyyed Abbas Araghchi, and Majid
Takht Ravanchi. *Raz Sar Be Mohr (Sealed Secret)*, vol. 2. Tehran: Entesharat
Etelaat, 2021.

Zetter, Kim. *Countdown to Zero Day: Stuxnet and the Launch of the World's First
Digital Weapon.* New York: Random House, 2014.

Comprehensive Iran Sanctions, Accountability, and Divestment Act of 2010 (CISADA). Public Law No. 111–195, July 1, 2010.

Crisis Group Report. *Iran: Where Next on Nuclear Impasse?* November 24, 2004.

Crisis Group Middle East Report No. 51. *Iran: Is There a Way Out of the Nuclear Impasse?* February 23, 2006.

Crisis Group Middle East Report No. 166. *Iran after the Nuclear Deal*, December 15, 2015.

Department of the Treasury. *The Treasury 2021 Sanctions Review*, October 2021. https://home.treasury.gov/system/files/136/Treasury-2021-sanctions-review.pdf.

Executive Order 12170. Blocking Iranian Government Property, November 14, 1979.

Executive Order 12205. Prohibiting Certain Transactions with Iran, April 7, 1980.

Executive Order 12211. Further Prohibitions on Transactions with Iran, April 17, 1980.

Executive Order 12613. Prohibiting Imports from Iran, October 29, 1987.

Executive Order 12938. Proliferation of Weapons of Mass Destruction, November 14, 1994.

Executive Order 12957. Prohibiting Certain Transactions with Respect to the Development of Iranian Petroleum Resources, March 15, 1995.

Executive Order 12959. Prohibiting Certain Transactions with Respect to Iran, May 6, 1995.

Executive Order 13059. Prohibiting Certain Transactions with Respect to Iran, August 19, 1997.

Executive Order 13224. Blocking Property and Prohibiting Transactions with Persons Who Commit, Threaten to Commit, or Support Terrorism, September 23, 2001.

Executive Order 13382. Blocking Property of Weapons of Mass Destruction Proliferators and Their Supporters, June 28, 2005.

Executive Order 13553. Blocking Property of Certain Persons with Respect to Serious Human Rights Abuses by the Government of Iran and Taking Certain Other Actions, September 29, 2010.

Executive Order 13577. Concerning Further Sanctions on Iran, May 23, 2011.

Executive Order 13599. Blocking Property of the Government of Iran and Iranian Financial Institutions, February 5, 2012.

Executive Order 13622. Authorizing Additional Sanctions with Respect to Iran, July 30, 2012.

Executive Order 13608. Prohibiting Certain Transactions with and Suspending Entry into the United States of Foreign Sanctions Evaders with Respect to Iran and Syria, May 1, 2012.

Revocation of Executive Orders 13574, 13590, 13622, and 13645 with Respect to

Iran, Amendment of Executive Order 13628 with Respect to Iran, and Provision of Implementation Authorities for Aspects of Certain Statutory Sanctions. White House, January 16, 2016.

Executive Order 13902. Imposing Sanctions with Respect to Additional Sectors of Iran, January 10, 2020.

Iran-Iraq Arms Nonproliferation Act, Title XVI of the National Defense Authorization Act for Fiscal Year 1993. Public Law No. 102–484, October 23, 1992.

Iran Freedom Support Act. Public Law No. 109–293, September 30, 2006.

Iran Nonproliferation Act of 2000. Public Law No. 106–178, March 14, 2000.

United Nations Human Rights Office of the High Commissioner. "US Sanctions Violate Human Rights and International Code of Conduct, UN Expert Says." https://www.ohchr.org/EN/NewsEvents/Pages/DisplayNews.aspx?NewsID=24566&LangID=E.

United Nations Security Council Resolution 2231. "On Iran Nuclear Issue," July 20, 2015.

United States Joint Forces Command. *U.S. Joint Forces Command Millennium Challenge 2002: Experiment Report.* https://www.esd.whs.mil/Portals/54/Documents/FOID/Reading%20Room/Joint_Staff/12-F-0344-Millennium-Challenge-2002-Experiment-Report.pdf.

INDEX